Alexander James Beresford Hope

Worship in the Church of England

Alexander James Beresford Hope
Worship in the Church of England
ISBN/EAN: 9783743329690
Manufactured in Europe, USA, Canada, Australia, Japa
Cover: Foto ©Lupo / pixelio.de

Manufactured and distributed by brebook publishing software (www.brebook.com)

Alexander James Beresford Hope

Worship in the Church of England

WORSHIP

IN

THE CHURCH OF ENGLAND.

WORSHIP

IN

THE CHURCH OF ENGLAND.

By A. J. B. BERESFORD HOPE, M.P.,

AUTHOR OF 'THE ENGLISH CATHEDRAL OF THE NINETEENTH CENTURY.'

LONDON:
JOHN MURRAY, ALBEMARLE STREET.
1874.

PREFACE.

THE following Work owes its immediate origin to the incidents of the last Parliamentary Session, but the opinions which it expresses are the results of many years' thought and reading. I have in my first chapter explained the reasons which have induced me, a layman, to take up the question, as well as the point of view from which I regard it, and I need not therefore repeat them in this place.

November, 1874.

CONTENTS.

CHAPTER I.

Importance of worship question — Desirable that it should be treated by a layman — Book, building, and ceremony — Old High Church position — Tracts for the Times — The meaning of "Ritualism" — Improvement during last forty-one years — Archbishop of Canterbury — Condition of churches in reign of George IV. — Own early experience — Oxford influence — Littlemore Chapel — Leeds Church — Ecclesiological Society — Lessons to be drawn from change — Uncontentious advance — Average church of present day, involving ideas unthought of half a century back — Extent of acknowledged gains in buildings and worship — New Lectionary — Shortened Services Act — More recent observances of occasional services, weddings, and funerals — Ely Bissexcentenary — Nave services in Cathedrals — Farewell of Bishop of Ely .. .. Page 1

CHAPTER II.

Critical period reached — Public Worship Regulation Act — Abrupt adoption of ornate ceremonialism — "Liddell v. Westerton" — Surplice riots — Papal aggression and Durham letter — Co-relation of book, building, and rubric — Tests of allowable ceremonies — Continuity of Church of England — Thirtieth Canon — Triple division of Churches — Prayer Book explained by building — Arrangements of nave — Pews and open seats — Chancels as in times past — Ornaments rubric — Vernacular daily services characteristic of English Church — Four English Prayer Books — "Omission not prohibition" examined — "Martin v. Mackonochie" — "Shepherd v. Bennett" — "How is the Church's Prayer Book to be carried on?" — No direction as to manner of singing Psalms, or as to manner of reading Epistle and Gospel — No "Manual Acts" ordered between 1552 and 1662 — Statute and Common Law in Church as well as State — Continuity of English Church, but difference in spirit as well as act between reformed and unreformed services — An important principle apt to be overlooked — Impossibility of reviving literally Sarum rite with present office — Meaning of Ornaments Rubric — "Liddell v. Westerton" — Meaning of "by authority of Parliament" in the second year of Edward VI. — Bishop Cosin and the

Act of Submission — Balance of parties at commencement of Elizabeth's reign — Cosin at the Restoration — Sir J. T. Coleridge — Chancels as in times past — Chancel screen — Bishop Beveridge — Jube, rood-loft — Post-reformational screen — Cross surmounting screen at St. Barnabas legalised by Judicial Committee in 1857 .. .. Page 34

CHAPTER III.

Beveridge calls the Sacrament of the Lord's Supper the highest mystery in our religion — Precise definition of its doctrine not necessary to prove the honour due to its celebration — Distinctive Eucharistic dress — "Address against vestments and eastward position" — Mr. Scott Robertson — Difficult distinction — Surplice obnoxious to Puritans as symbolising sacramental doctrine — Vague assertions of a somewhat rhetorical protest — Voice of formularies speaking for themselves above suspicion — Communion Office speaking for itself on its relative honour compared with other services — Right on its own showing that the celebration should be especially dignified — Burden of proof of contrary on objectors — Inexcusable incaution of ultra-ritualistic language — Use of term Mass — John Evelyn, witness to old High Church view of Sacramental doctrine — Extract from his 'Rational Account of the True Religion' — Old Catholic conference at Bonn — Dr. Howson and Dr. Liddon agree on a statement of Anglican doctrine — Why cannot they agree to differ on the ceremonial showing forth their common doctrine? 73

CHAPTER IV.

The "Distinctive Eucharistic dress," under conditions, a ruled and uncontentious point — The dress ordered by canons accepted in Hebbert *v.* Purchas — All that has to be decided is the conditions — Vestments of first Prayer Book pronounced legal by Liddell *v.* Westerton and Martin *v.* Mackonochie — Does Ornaments Rubric overrule Canons, or do Canons colour Ornaments Rubric? — Canons of 1604 in Latin and English — Canons on copes and surplices in Cathedrals — As High Mass is the highest Roman ceremonial, so Cathedral Communion is the highest English — Cope really ordered in Cathedrals at all Communions — Canons only define who is to be celebrant on principal feast-days — Elizabeth's Advertisements — Difficulty of understanding Canons otherwise — Point proved by wording of Latin Canons — Rubric of 1549 prescribes maximum and Canons the minimum — Descriptions of vestments — Early confusion of vestment and cope — Machyn's Diary — Tunicles — Meaning of "agreeably" — Anyhow the rite on principal feast-days the normal ceremonial — Dilemma from which no escape — Hebbert *v.* Purchas on a maximum and minimum — Blunder of not observing convertibility of alb and surplice — Canon on surplices, for benefit of ratepayers — Bishop Phillpotts's Helstone judgment — Privy

Council argument would make daily service unlawful — Martin v. Mackonochie confesses Liddell v. Westerton — Purchas judgment attempts to escape by distinction between different ornaments rubrics — Meaning of "retain" — Peter Smart and Cosin — Cosin clearly held the rubrics of 1549 to be still valid — Elizabeth's Chapel before and after Advertisements — Her ceremonial Easter, 1593 — Bishop Andrewes' Chapel copied by Laud — Its copes — Archbishop Williams — Parish churches — Wolverhampton — No vestments ordered in Visitation Articles, because not wanted to throw burden on parishioners. Cope practically used in place of tunicle — Advertisements never received Elizabeth's signature — Additional notes to Prayer Book by Andrewes, Overall, and Cosin, published by Nicholls — Cosin on ornaments rubric — Overall on the same — Comparison of Cosin's notes — They show the elastic working of ornaments rubric in those days — Policy of Church leaders after Restoration — Impediments to enforcing ornaments rubric — Its retention proof of animus — They could not see adverse future — Put it on record for futurity — Present revival of distinctive dress proof that their policy was no failure — Cosin at Durham — Circumstances of his diocese and cathedral — His influence at least preserved copes at Durham — Evidence of Thoresby — Not disused till latter half of eighteenth century — Really "Protestant" character of ornaments rubric of 1549 compared with older rites — Pre-reformational dresses — Rock's 'Church of our Fathers' — Changes of 1552 against spirit of Church of England, and a failure — Episcopal dress — Assumption of pastoral staff acceptance of vitality of rubrics of 1549 — Revival of vestments not to be forced on against will of congregations — *Modus vivendi* must be reached — Different rites may be used at different times in same church — Early communions — Churches with several clergymen — Collegiate churches in spirit of canon — Vestments would no longer be burden upon ratepayers — Restriction to copes not satisfactory — Limitation of white vestments suggested — Vestments a link with Universal Church — Vestments in Scandinavia — Forester's description of Norwegian ceremonial — Question complicated by adoption of cope at Magnificat — Indefensibility of practice — Stole or scarf legal — Biretta — Want of tact in dealing with prejudices — Long and short surplices — Episcopal dress — Pastoral staff — Surplice or gown in pulpit — Mutilated Communion service — Prayer for Church militant .. .. Page 90

CHAPTER V.

Position of celebrant — The protest against tolerating this even more unreasonable — Shepherd leading his flock — Sanctioned by Mackonochie judgment — Eight reasons for it — Purchas judgment — Remonstrance of 4761 clergymen — Sir J. T. Coleridge — Lord Cairns in House of Lords 1874 — Present rubrics — Comparison of rubrics touching position in 1552 and 1662 — New rubric of 1662 before Prayer of Consecration — Question not merely of priest's position, but of that of Holy Table — Rubrics of 1549 — " God's

Board" and "Altar" in 1549, "God's Board" and "Lord's Table" in 1552 — Altar and Lord's Table — Omission of "Altar" at foreign dictation — Holy Table and Altar equivalent in Greek liturgies — If Altar is Romanism, then Romanism more ancient than I admit — Βῶμος and Θυσιαστήριον — Communion Table not in rubrics — Bride never taken to the Communion Table — Altar in Canons of 1640 — Liddell v. Westerton on credence — Lord's Table in 1552 put longways — Elizabeth's injunction of 1559 — Clumsy compromise — Consequent varieties of ritual — 82nd Canon — Bishop Andrewes and Laud — The north side became west side — Extraneous circumstances prevented those who secured altarwise place of table from settling celebrant's position — Bishop of Lincoln on celebrant's position — Andrewes' Chapel — Cushion and the cross marked on plan — Positive evidence against Bishop of Lincoln's suggestion — North side became now west side — Cosin and Wren — Wren on trial for his life adopted secondary reason — Laud adopted the same course — Wren and consecration of Dore Abbey Church — Lord Scudamore — Wren's suggested alteration in Prayer Book in 1661 — No contradiction to his previous practice — Wren's share in Scotch Prayer Book of 1637 — His suggestions of 1661 correspond — Wren and Laud's policy explained — Heylin's attempt to justify altarwise position of table by throwing over the priest's position — Hostile evidence of Bayley in 1661 — Present rubric before Prayer of Consecration — Due to Cosin — History of its growth — Condition of things in 1662 — Discovery of Cosin's original draft — Judges in Purchas's case quote Visitation Articles of Cosin which never were published — "Ne pueros coram populo Medea trucidet" — Real meaning of breaking bread before the people — Celebrant looks with, does not turn his back to, his people — Bishop of St. Andrews — Bishop of Lincoln — Basilican usage — Great wrong done if eastward position forbidden .. Page 168

CHAPTER VI.

Furniture of altar — Credence Table — Immovable stone altar prohibited in the St. Sepulchre's case, but solid wooden altar with stone or marble slab legal — St. John's chapel, Westminster Abbey — Frontals varying according to season legalised by judgment in Liddell v. Westerton — Altar crosses legalised by the Liddell v. Westerton judgment as explained by the second judgment in Beal v. Liddell — Crucifixes in Lutheran and "Evangelical" churches abroad — Potsdam and Berlin, Berchtesgaden and Salzburg — Against present English feeling, but not Popish — Lighted candles enjoined by Edward VI. — Candlesticks and candles on the altar in cathedrals and chapels before the revival — Candles forbidden by Dr. Lushington, allowed by Sir R. Phillimore, forbidden by Mackonochie judgment — Disallowed by Ritual Commission — Its unfounded distinction between cathedrals and parish churches — Ambiguous use of phrase "sufficient evidence" — Fuller — Dr. Donne's sermon on Candlemas day — The symbolism of the lights defended from the teaching of that day — Our Lord "a light to lighten the Gentiles" — Cosin's notes — Archbishop Sancroft — Appeal to common sense, do lighted or unlighted candles best typify that Christ is the very true light?— We have got candles and candlesticks, and may light them on dark days, frivolous to impose restrictions on lighting them according to the teaching of the injunction — Only pleading for the two lights according to injunction — No more than two used in old English Church — Constitution of Archbishop Walter — Abroad use even of two candles appears not to have been universal — Perkins' Tournay Pontifical — Numerous candles modern Rome use — Greater beauty of more simple altar with two lights — Altar nosegays lawful — Ceremonial compensation of present age — Mixed chalice — Reasons for valuing the rite — Forbidden by Purchas judgment — Judges mistaken in supposing that private mixture not in Eastern Church — Supported by First Prayer Book, Andrewes, Overall, Laud, Wren, Sir W. Palmer — Impolicy of crushing it out — Question of leavened or unleavened bread stands on a quite different footing — East used leavened, West unleavened bread — Dispute whether Last Supper was Passover or not — Wafers ordered by Elizabeth and Parker — In Elizabeth's and Andrewes' chapels — Defended by Hooker, sanctioned in Andrewes' Notes to Prayer Book — Their revival dissuaded — Incense differs from other rites — Practice of almost every religion true or false — Altar of incense commanded to Moses for all generations — At altar of incense Gabriel appears to Zacharias — Frankincense offered by the wise men — Incense in the Apocalypse — Naturally adopted in Christian Church — Not in Prayer Book, but supported by Andrewes, Herbert, Cosin, Sancroft — Censing of persons and things forbidden by Sir R. Phillimore — Not to be regretted — Custom deteriorated by Roman ceremonialists — Censing of persons and things differs from offering incense to God — If revived, must be so by authority, and as such offering .. .. Page 212

CHAPTER VII.

Ideal of an Anglican communion — Distinctive simplicity — Capacity of highest beauty — "Statuesque" — Growth of complicated unreformed rites — Benedictine order — No distractions, minds concentrated on worship — Our office and mediæval like in main features of Eucharist, for the Church at both dates the same — Literal and uncritical use of Sarum ritual a snare more than a help — Minute changes of posture unmeaning to us — Ceremonious reading of Gospel — Two particulars in which I hope our service may never be altered — Audible reading — Communicants at principal celebration — Retirement of non-communicants not to be compulsory — Classes specially attracted by ritualism — In rich services they find those forms of beauty of which they have glimpses, but cannot otherwise gratify — Souls risked by sweeping away system — Not to be supposed they are specially attracted by illegal peculiarities — General beauty, lightsomeness, and warmth — Attraction of hearty hymnody — Take ultra-ritualism at its worst — Is it worst evil of the times? — Condition of spiritual things about us — Apathy, false doctrine, scepticism, superstition, gross vice — Prelates as peers of Parliament can pass this by, and pronounce harshest censures on those brethren who believe highest Christian truths and devote their lives to the ministry — Do they expect by this to advance Christ's kingdom or strengthen the Establishment? — Conduct of policemen not natural action of spiritual fathers — Ritualistic excess no reason to refuse reasonable claims — Position and distinctive dress — We want peace, but not peace which means worse, war — Treaty must be based on self-respect and principle — Balance of dress and position by giving up Athanasian Creed and Communion service emphatically rejected — Compromise must be within service itself — Dress and position alternative; gown, railsfuls, evening communions permissible .. .. Page 243

WORSHIP
IN
THE CHURCH OF ENGLAND.

CHAPTER I.

Importance of worship question — Desirable that it should be treated by a layman — Book, building, and ceremony — Old High Church position — Tracts for the Times — The meaning of "Ritualism" — Improvement during last forty-one years — Archbishop of Canterbury — Condition of churches in reign of George IV. — Own early experience — Oxford influence — Littlemore Chapel — Leeds Church — Ecclesiological Society — Lessons to be drawn from change — Uncontentious advance — Average church of present day, involving ideas unthought of half a century back — Extent of acknowledged gains in buildings and worship — New Lectionary — Shortened Services Act — More recent observances of occasional services, weddings, and funerals — Ely Bissex-centenary — Nave services in Cathedrals — Farewell of Bishop of Ely.

THE question of worship within the Church of England has occupied so much general attention during the living generation, and its importance has within the few last months been so emphatically declared by the voice of Parliament and of public opinion, that no excuse is needful on the part of a writer, who believes that he can assist the discussion, for contributing his views to the common stock. For my own part, I venture to hope that I may be of some help to my fellow Churchmen, because the topics which I propose to handle have been subjects of interest to me all through my adult life, and especially because I have studied, and am now intending to write about them with the eye and in the spirit of a layman. As a layman, I have strongly felt the pertinacity with which the disputants on one side of the question have reiterated the assertion that the controversy lies between a knot of clergymen and that which is practically the whole body of lay Church people. I take this earliest opportunity of protesting most strongly against such a representation. The contrary is no question of comparative numbers, but of absolute fact. One section may contain more or fewer lay sympathisers; but, as a fact, there is as little fairness in calling one party as the other either clerical or lay. Each has its devoted and learned clerical leaders, and each its devoted and enthusiastic lay followers; and if in many cases the clergyman is either encouraged in adhering to simple and inartistic forms, or prevented from exchanging them for a more ornate worship by the clearly-expressed wishes of his flock, in many others he is encouraged or incited to a richer ceremonial by the voice of his own congregation. The discussion has already been very fully and learnedly elucidated in many tomes of exhaustive lore. Still there seemed to be a want of an examination of the matters under controversy by a friendly layman, whose feelings should be with and for his fellow layfolk, but who did not regard the clergy as a hostile armament. My wish is to offer a plain and simple explanation of English worship to readers who may not have the opportunity of grappling with the more systematic treatises which already exist on the question. The audience whom I desire to address are those whom I may describe as contented members of the Church of England, men and women who accept on the whole the Prayer Book of the Church of England as their rule of holy living, and as the touchstone of doctrine and practice. I am well aware that I should make my argument more complete by proposing to demonstrate the reasonableness of my positions. But I should at the same time make it more bulky, so, as I am, after all, pleading to Churchmen in behalf of the Church, I venture, for the sake of brevity, to take the Prayer Book for granted, of course reserving the rubrics in contrast to the text, as now to a great extent an open question. From those who repudiate the Church of England altogether, as well as from those who are only willing to accept it on the condition of some radical revolution in its system, I can of course claim no sympathy for my views, much as I respect the honesty of their opinions. If any such persons condescend to look at these pages, all that I ask from them is, that, differing as they must do from my premisses, they should test my conclusions in reference to those premisses, not to those which they would for their part have set up. As to the way in which I propose to treat my subject, I shall only in this connection observe that, as all worship requires a form of words, that is a ritual (whether written or extempore), a place in which to use it, and rules more or less definite to guide that use, I shall, in everything which I say, respect this triple connection of book, building, and ceremony; or in other words that I shall handle worship in the Church of England as the carrying out of its Prayer Book in her churches, and according to her rubrics. Moreover, of these three elements of worship I shall always regard the book as the fundamental and most important, for the building can only claim the character of truthfulness so far as its arrangements are accommodated to the requirements of the actions which are to be performed within its walls, and the rubrics owe their very *raison d'être* to their practical use in explaining the procedure of worship. Indeed I find that I have, in explaining my three heads, been led to speak of the third consideration first as "ceremony," that is, as the procedure itself, and then as "rubrics," that is, as the code which regulates that procedure. This may not have been quite accurate, but it shows how much I feel that rubric means action, and that action presupposes some law which has to guide it.

My own reading of the Prayer Book and of its rubrics is that of a High Churchman, of the school which in my younger days would have been called the new one, but which is now decidedly recognised on the one side in commendation, and on others with feelings, which may be very good-natured without being necessarily deferential, as old-fashioned. I mean that for the formation of my views upon Christian antiquity and upon the Church of England I was mainly indebted to that school of writers whose public notoriety dates from the commencement of the Tracts for the Times in 1833, and who again send us back to seek the fullest exposition of the voice of the Reformed Church of the land in a succession of English writers, among the earliest of whom stand Hooker and Andrewes, and among the latest Wilson and Butler. After many trials and vicissitudes, and most deplorable losses to an alien communion, the revived High-Church party of 1833 has lived on to make a mark, great alike by the testimony of friend and of foe, upon the Established Church of England. This mark extends over that Church in every function of its activity; and it is of course as manifest upon its visible worship as upon the character of its doctrinal teaching, or its performance of moral and social obligations. My own conclusions upon the worship question, to which I desire to confine this enquiry, are of considerable standing, and were formed both antecedently to, and independent of, the growth of that modern school of "Ritualism," with the founders of which, generally speaking, I have had very slight acquaintance, and over the development of which I have had absolutely no influence. This is a point upon which I desire to be both clear and emphatic. The views which I shall offer upon ceremonial have not been formed either in accordance with, or in opposition to, "Ritualism," for they existed in their integrity while "Ritualism," as the word is now understood, was not yet devised. I can, therefore, honestly claim to be entering upon my task with the desire of showing genuine impartiality towards "Ritualism," by which I imply the intention of testing it by the conditions of true and not true, rather than by those of popular and unpopular. If I find any practice among those for which the ritualists plead which approves itself to me as consonant with the letter and spirit of the Prayer Book, I shall applaud it accordingly, not because it is a ritualistic, but because it is a Prayer Book ceremonial; but if

I come across an observance in which that letter appears to me to have been transgressed, or that spirit strained, I shall not be debarred from saying so, because it might seem to a superficial examiner to depend upon something else which was harmless or even laudable.

I must take a preliminary objection to the term in its various forms of "Ritualism," "Ritualist," and "Ritualistic," as being both indefinite and incorrect. These expressions are all used in reference to ceremonialism of a specific description, more ornate, that is, than that which is found in the usual run of English churches, and more immediately referable, than we have for a long time been accustomed to think possible, to the pre-reformational Church of England. It is obvious that there is nothing in the words themselves to point to this specific meaning, for a ritual *per se* may be a modern as well as an ancient one, a plain as well as a gorgeous one. So much for the indefiniteness of the expression; but it is also grammatically incorrect. A "ritual" means a book which contains "rites," that is, the forms of words by which certain Church privileges are conveyed, or Church conditions created—the rite of Baptism for instance, or the rite of Confirmation or the rite of Marriage. "Ritualism" accordingly means the science of such rites so recapitulated in a ritual. It deals in short with the words, and not, as in its modern conventional sense, with the way of acting out those words. The phrase which the inventors of "Ritualism" ought to have adopted, if they had intended to be grammatical without caring so much for being definite, was "ceremonialism," and they should have styled themselves "ceremonialists."

Having made this protest in behalf of accurate language, I shall bow to a phraseology for which I am in no way responsible, and shall continue to use "Ritualism" in the conventional sense of the few last years, as I should employ any other of those words, of which "Evangelicalism," "Conservatism," "Liberalism," are conspicuous examples, in which analogy has had to yield to the imperiousness of partisanship, and the practical necessity for an appellation.

During the forty-one years which have elapsed since the first Tract appeared at Oxford, European society has in almost every conceivable respect changed its aspect, but it is, happily, no part of my task to write the history of nineteenth-century civilisation. Of those changes, the only two which are valuable to the present argument are, that educated England, like other countries, has become archæological as it had not formerly the knowledge, and artistic as it had not formerly the taste to be; while, alike in its archæology and in its art, it has studied those Christian ages of its own and of neighbouring nationalities, which older critics, in their narrow admiration of Greek and Roman culture, were wont to despise. Very certainly, too, the Holy Spirit of God has marvellously put it into the hearts of His servants in this land to spend and be spent in His service, both in their material substance and in their personal labours, with a devotion unknown to the phlegmatic generations from whom they are more immediately sprung. The result of all this has been that while the home of man has been made more dainty during those years, the House of God, in its structure, in its appointments, and in the worship which is conducted within its walls, has also within that period put on a decorum and a beauty to which those who are no longer young were strangers in their youth, and that along with this beauty and decorum the fervour and the frequency of worship have alike and generally asserted themselves. As my witness—not so much to the comparatively satisfactory condition of the ceremonial worship of the English Church at present, as to the very different state of things out of which it has grown, thanks very decidedly—who shall dare gainsay it?—to the self-sacrifice of the reinvigorated High Church party—I shall quote an authority whom no one can charge with undue proclivities toward ritualistic excess. The Archbishop of Canterbury, during the speech which he delivered at Canterbury in August

1874, in presiding over the Diocesan Church Building Society, said:

"I do not mean to say that we should take everything as we find it, but that we should be very jealous of changes. The services of the Church, it should be remembered, do not exist for the benefit of the Clergy, but for the benefit of the laity; and we are bound by a free intercourse with those persons to consult their feelings and to prevent any of that sort of suspicion which very often springs up; but, on the other hand, I say the laity are to be on their guard against entertaining these suspicions towards the clergy. They may remember that many things to which they were perhaps accustomed in old times are remains of an age when great apathy prevailed, and must be prepared not only for improvements in the outward appearance of the Church, but also in the services. I suppose there is no one of my age here but looks back with a kind of shame to the sort of sermons which were preached, the sort of clergyman that preached them, the sort of building in which they preached them, and the sort of psalmody with which the service was ushered in, and, remembering these, I am perfectly astonished the whole of the attachment of the people to the Church did not evaporate. But if all improvements had been resisted we should not have been where we are now. I therefore hope that the laity will not look with any amount of suspicion upon the movements of the clergy, but that they will give them their best consideration."

As a lively illustration of the state of things which the Archbishop has so graphically summed up, I may as well attempt to describe the visible form in which the Church of England and its worship were first made palpable to my childish senses in the reign of George IV., and at an opulent and beautiful market town of Surrey, not thirty miles from London, which is now accustomed to very different services. The building was a large, and had been a handsome, Gothic church, but of its interior the general parish saw very little, except the nave and aisles, for the chancel was cut off by a perfectly solid partition, covered with the usual sacred writings and some strange painting, among which Moses and Aaron shone in peculiar uncouthness. The eastern portion of the aisles was utilised for certain family pews or private boxes, raised aloft and approached by private doors and staircases; these belonged to the magnates of the neighbourhood, who were wont to bow their recognitions across the nave. There was also a decrepit western gallery for the band, and the ground-floor was crammed with cranky pews of every shape. The pulpit, of the age of Charles I., stood against a pillar, with the reading desk and clerk's box underneath. I need hardly explain that the portion of the Communion Office, preceding the sermon, was, Sunday after Sunday, read from the desk, separated from the Litany on the one side, and from the sermon on the other, by such a rendering of Tate and Brady as the unruly gang of volunteers, with fiddles and wind instruments, in the gallery, pleased to contribute. The clerk, a wizened old fellow, in a brown Welsh wig, repeated the responses in a nasal twang, and with a substitution of "w" for "v" so consistent as not even to spare the Belief; while the local rendering of "briefs, citations, and excommunications," included announcements by this worthy, after the Nicene Creed, of meetings at the town inn of the "execūtors" of a deceased Duke. Two hopeful cubs of the clerk sprawled behind him in the desk, and the back-handers, occasionally intended to reduce them to order, were apt to resound against the impassive boards. During the sermon this zealous servant of the sanctuary would take up his broom and sweep out the middle alley, in order to save himself the fatigue of a week-day visit. Yet, repulsive and grotesque as were these accessories of worship in this town of three London coaches, it could at least boast, as countless country churches at that period could not, that it was open twice upon every Sunday, that Good Friday was not forgotten, and that on Christmas Day the frequent holly sprigs betokened a faint recognition of Christian seasons. It also possessed one of the earliest National Schools which had been built, so it was really not so very backward a parish. The pictures and the rustic band at length had worked out their term, for a faint awakening of the ceremonial conscience in the townspeople led to the purchase of an organ, for which no better place could be found than a heavy new gallery stretching across the eastern portion of the nave, and still more effectually blocking out the chancel. Had the poor old church weathered some seven or eight more years of degraded existence, it would probably be now standing as a handsome and well-restored structure. It was doomed to be replaced, in the year 1835, by a broad but flimsy galleried apartment, in which, at all events, there was an apparent Lord's Table, flanked by corresponding praying and preaching pulpits. The clerk and his broom followed Moses and Aaron, the fiddle and bassoon, to the land of shadows, and public worship was, for successive years, continued in forms of cold decorum, till in fresh hands this second temple gave place piecemeal to a newer and nobler fane.

I shall not waste time in commenting on the alternative which London offered to me for this repulsive presentment of Prayer-Book worship. It was my weary lot to be carried off each Sunday to a huge modern church, which all the zeal and right feeling of one who was spared as Dean of Chichester, and in his own metropolitan cure, to be more than any man of his generation a fostering father of the new life of revived English worship,* could not make anything but insufferably dull and unmeaning to a childish imagination.

I have dwelt upon these particulars, because I feel how impossible it is for any one accurately to gauge the present condition of the worship question, unless he should have realised the depth into which the religious instinct of the people had sunk. It was not simply that a bad tradition had taken possession of the whole country, but that, with the honourable exception of the churches held by the Evangelical party, of which I then knew nothing, the classes of society which gave the tone to public opinion has grown into considering

---

* George Chandler.

attendance at church as a fragmentary episode, projected into the week's circuit without influence upon, or relevancy to, the other social or moral duties of reasonable beings.

The one redeeming point was that the often derided, but in its subordinate way far from useless, appreciation of what English people recognise as respectability had come to the succour of robuster or more spiritual considerations, and sustained the wholesome feeling, that whether or not a man left his wife and family to go to church without him, it was at least the right thing to have gone with them. At the worst of times, the average Englishman of proper instincts had never lowered himself, like the ruck of Voltairian Frenchmen, into treating Church as the congruous resort of women, priests, and bigots; or, like the Berlinese bourgeois, into simply ignoring the responsibilities of worship altogether; while in the Cathedrals and the College Chapels the standing protest for a daily order of divine service was kept alive.

As to the change which has since taken place, we can only say with genuine thankfulness, " it is the Lord's doing, and it is marvellous in our eyes." While I do not hesitate to class it as an incident of the movement of which the Tracts for the Times were the chief visible symbol, I only ascribe a secondary share in the work to that series. Several of the tracts are concerned with the structure and contents of the Prayer Book, and of the Service books of the unreformed Churches; but not one, as far as I remember, occupies itself with the working of the book, or of the arrangements of the building in which it is to be used. Indeed, the slight appreciation which the Tractarian leaders seem ever to have had of the influence of the eye, or of the senses generally upon human nature, may almost be reckoned as a deficiency, tactically viewed, in their capacity to head a wide movement. At all events, it allowed the regulative voice in such matters to pass from their keeping, as has been pleaded in tones of pathetic moderation within the present year of perplexities, by the one venerable survivor of that famous band who still adheres to the Church of England and the University of Oxford. In spite, however, of this drawback, the natural religious instinct of such men led them, when they had to provide a church, to build it churchlike, and so we may say that the earliest visible specimen of a place of worship which was consciously intended to embody the Prayer-Book spirit, was that chapel-of-ease to St. Mary's, Oxford, raised at the hamlet of Littlemore, in the incumbency and under the guidance of Mr. Newman, while Mr. Newman was all our own. This tiny fane, as first constructed, was simplicity itself, a mere oblong shell of the plainest lancet architecture, and it based its claims to sympathetic admiration rather upon what it did not than what it did comprise. It had no obtrusive selfish pews, but simple and uniform open sittings; it had no tub-like pulpits, obstructive of all sight of the altar, for preaching prayers and sermons, but a light desk modestly placed on one side. It had not a mean small Holy Table, or one crammed up with tasselled cushions, but a plain and solid stone construction. Such as it then was—for it has been enlarged, with advantage to its architectural completeness, but with undeniable loss to its historical interest—Littlemore Chapel, without carving, unrelieved by colour, destitute of chancel, served by single-handed clergymen, using unmusical services, was the undoubted visible germ of the revived worship of the English Church. Shortly after the completion of this interesting building, the institution at Oxford of its still existing Architectural Society invited the attention of those younger members of the University whose minds were open to studies which would bear no fruit in the schools, to a systematic investigation of the style and arrangements of the old parish churches, which was soon, though rather elsewhere than on the Isis, found to throw a light as strong as it was unexpected on the letter of the Prayer Book. At the same time the literature of Church building—now a very bulky collection—burst at one bound into adult vigour in some articles, as cleverly illustrated as they were trenchantly written in that brilliant organ of the Oxford School, 'The British Critic,' which were well known at the time to have been the production of Mr. Thomas Mozley.

These various contributions of Oxford to the movement bring us to 1839—which I believe to be the date at which the lead began to pass from that University. In that year two incidents occurred worthy of our notice. As Littlemore Chapel was the first place of worship at which the new spirit conspicuously asserted itself, so the rebuilt parish church of Leeds, commenced in 1839, may be esteemed the second. All persons, I should suppose, know that it was the first fruit of that noble vicariate, which will ever be identified with the name of Hook, and of which the Church of England in its parochial character will bear the lasting mark. The building was in every respect, except its spirit, the opposite of Littlemore Chapel—as large as that was small, as composite in its features as the other was simple, and as obviously planned for crowded town congregations as Littlemore for the village handful. A large cruciform structure, with aisles blocked by galleries, it stood distinguished from previous new churches, and may still claim discriminative approbation by the dignified breadth of its central area, its ample arrangements for constant choral worship, and the solemn elevation of an altar platform, conspicuous to the wide interior. It was, in short, the proclamation to a generation which had learned to treat churches as halls for sermons, that they were the temples for the worship, in its various forms, of the Almighty. The same year, 1839, likewise witnessed the foundation in Cambridge of a society with the incongruous name of Camden, which, with an energy which sometimes showed more determination than tact, but which was always impelled by a convinced will, devoted itself to the cultivation of church architecture in connection with worship, and of worship in reference to that architecture, under the name of Ecclesiology. A few years saw the association removed to

London, under the longer but more logical name of Ecclesiological Society, and it continued for many years to interest itself in the revival of worship according to the High Church rendering of the Prayer Book, which preceded the Ritualistic movement.

Here, however, I am warned to pause for fear of further entangling my readers in a narrative which could not be pursued with even an approach to completeness, without burdening these pages with an episode of inordinate prolixity. Having claimed on behalf of the renovated High Church party that it was the chief author of that improvement in the method of conducting worship, by which all Church parties of the present day are profiting, I felt bound to substantiate my assertion with some particulars as to the origin of the movement, but to protract the story would be to convert a sketch into a history. I have shown that it began at Oxford, and I have indicated how soon the active promoters of the beneficent change were found in the sister University, and in the large towns. Some one will, I hope, be found in more quiet times to tell how the spirit of church restoration and church building has leapt from county to county, and from parish to parish; how one Cathedral after another has shaken off sleep, and arrayed itself in the glorious apparel of the King's daughter; and how the spiritual works of a Church in vigorous life have followed the outward adorning of the Sanctuary.* The retrospect into the cold darkness of the Georgian age carries with it useful lessons, both to the world in general and to the too impatient pioneers of new developments of higher worship. What it ought to teach the world in general is, that everything which is unfamiliar need not be wrong, aggressive, or Popish. The internal appearance of an old-fashioned church, like the one which I have lately been describing, is not less different

---

* A contribution towards this history, although of course treated from an artistic standing-point, has been made in Mr. Eastlake's 'History of the Revival of Gothic Architecture.'

from that of a new one in our own days, in which those modest decencies are observed, with which no party as a whole, and only a few extreme men of any party, will quarrel, as the latter may possibly differ from one arranged according to the claims of what is termed "advanced ritualism;" while incidents of arrangement and of worship which are now as household words among lay persons who are careful in their Church life, would at the former date have simply been pedantic and suspicious enigmas, even to clergymen of theological reading. This is the lesson which I press upon the world when I contemplate that great change. The lesson which those who are advanced in ritual might, as wise men, draw from it is, that they really do not appreciate or know the advantages which they enjoy as Churchmen of a young generation. They are really not aware at how conspicuous an altitude they would be standing, not only when ranging with those friends at whose moderation they may be chafing, but even were they to be brought down to the ceremonial depth of others against whom they may be actually protesting, in comparison with the depressed level of worship which was thankfully occupied but a few years since by men whose faith and practice are to them as brightly burning beacons. The unimproved worship of be-wardened Churches was the external influence under which Keble braced himself up to write the 'Christian Year.' It was, speaking generally, the system which existed through the lives of Rose, of Archer Butler, of Bishop Jebb, as it had done through those in a former century, of Wilson, Butler, and Horsley. If they would more constantly keep this historical fact before their eyes, they would not so often err in the proportions of incidents. They might not so often confound the desirable with the essential, or imagine that all would be lost if only it were found impossible to add one or two more enrichments to an already ample repertory of well-secured advantages.

In fact, I venture, without fear of contradiction, to lay down that the labours of these forty years have made good within the

Church of England a system of popular congregational worship corresponding with that sacramental teaching of the Prayer Book, of which High Churchmen have been the unswerving upholders, which is, and can be, sustained and used in its main features without fear of repression, and of which many of the leading elements are alike the common property of High Churchmen and of the best and most reverential members of the Low and Broad Church parties. It will naturally be the scope of the following pages to justify this assertion, which I have thus early put forward in a somewhat dogmatical form, in no spirit of defiance, but so as to present my views with the utmost unreserve. In proof of this assertion I will, before entering on any controverted particular, endeavour to collect those incidents of improved worship which are by this time happily purged of all partisan taint.

I shall limit my list of incidents belonging to the construction and arrangement of the buildings to such as, by common consent, every church-building clergyman, patron, congregation, or architect either adopts in the new churches now so frequent, or, if he does not adopt them, omits for reasons which imply no objection on the score of principle. Those which belong to the conduct of Divine service shall be such as if put aside are only so from local circumstances, and not on grounds of fundamental antagonism. This recapitulation of ceremonial universally accepted in the existing English Church will be the fairest possible test of the favour with which that Church regards a formal and ornamental worship, upon the well-known scientific principle that the strength of any material body, chain, bar, beam, or so forth, is its strength at its weakest point. Beyond this class of well-admitted things, as I have hinted, lies that other one, of those over which recent disputes have waged, and about which, as in duty bound, I shall have to speak my opinions. Some of them, I trust, I shall on very sufficient grounds show to be within the category of that which is undoubtedly lawful, although in no respect compulsory. Other matters will be found doubtful, and there will, I fear, be a final class for which the permission, so often and so earnestly claimed, cannot be granted consistently with the letter and spirit of the Prayer Book of the Church of England, of which a grave and simple dignity may well be said to be the leading characteristic, in contrast to the minute forms and gorgeous exuberance of the unreformed rites.

The new church of our own day—not the exceptional one, so frequently planned by some single founder, and carried out at a cost of which his own large heart is the sole arbiter; but that which is the average result of a subscription, and is constructed under the double restraint of specified, without being always realised, means and of varied tastes—is usually a reproduction of the general type of a mediæval English parish church, and most commonly of one of the thirteenth or fourteenth century, when Gothic architecture was in its prime in this island. Far from being the one large room of the old cheap church, such as Mr. Mozley figured in many examples in 'The British Critic,' it is duly distributed into parts, with their various uses. The nave is provided for the general use of the congregation, flanked, when the church is of the larger kind, with aisles, and often supplemented with transepts, so as to present the symbolical ground-plan of the cross; while the same sacred emblem habitually tops the gables. If possible, the building, in accordance with a very old and general tradition, ranges east and west; the roofs are all of a sufficient pitch. Beyond the nave, and usually distinguished from it both on the outside and the inside, a chancel is provided for the more immediate performance of Divine worship. The typal church of forty or fifty years ago was, as I have noted, a disproportioned parallelogram, low ceiled, crammed up with galleries, innocent of chancel. Of the shapely towers and steeples which modern architects have learned to rear I will not speak, because they have only an indirect connection with worship. Inside, the new church is constantly seated with open uniform benches, alike for rich and poor, so as visibly to represent the communion of saints; and in the most unsatisfactory cases, if there is a gradation of comfort in them, or if any jealous right of proprietorship intervenes to dictate the selfish pew-door, at least the great bulk of the sittings uniformly faces the Lord's Table. Hard by the entrance of the church, as "the ancient usual place," is commonly found an ornamental font of stone, in accordance with early usage and with the prescription of the 81st Canon of 1604.

"According to a former constitution, too much neglected in many places, we appoint, that there shall be a font of stone in every church and chapel where baptism is to be ministered; the same to be set in the ancient usual places: in which only font the minister shall baptize publicly."

In the church of the last generation, old or new, the pews were of all or any shape, sometimes square, sometimes curtained, sometimes filled with sofas or tables, or even provided with fireplaces; while the free seats, as those for the poor were mockingly termed, were always uncomfortable, often squalid, and habitually planted in the worst places; and as for the font, it might be before the communion rails or in some corner under a gallery, and its material would be cement or crockery, or if the old stone font had been preserved, a little crockery substitute would certainly stand within its capacious bowl.

In the new church the desk at which the minister says the prayers is habitually placed to the eastward of the congregation and westward of the Lord's Table; sometimes it stands within the chancel, sometimes just outside of it, but it invariably has a sideward position assigned to it so as not to obstruct the view into the chancel, although it is frequently so contrived that the reader looks into the faces of the congregation, and with his back to the Holy Table, instead of more modestly across the church. When the stand at which the lessons are read is not a portion of the reading-desk, the lettern or eagle of brass or wood has often been introduced, and will never now, I believe, excite the most sensitive spirit into theological strife. The separate litany desk is of less frequent occurrence, but its harmless and lawful character is, I should trust, universally acknowledged. The pulpit, like the prayer-desk, is habitually given a sideward place, always of course in the nave, while its design is an admitted opportunity for the resources of sacred sculpture. If the chancel rises on a few steps, the dignity of the arrangement is generally admitted, and the increment of beauty which a well-defined chancel arch usually adds is an uncontroverted canon of taste. For the floor of the chancel ornamental tiles are very frequently provided, while its usual furniture is a row or rows on each side of longitudinal benches or stalls, used by, or adapted for, the choir, and very frequently flanked by the organ, to which a chancel aisle has been allotted. The space in immediate juxtaposition to the Lord's Table is usually elevated by at least a step above the remaining chancel, and parted from it by an ornamental rail running across the entire width of that part of the building. The Lord's Table itself is, with rare exceptions, draped in a rich cloth, usually red, perhaps of velvet, and perhaps having some appropriate monogram. For the use of the clergy officiating there the old *sedilia* so-called or architectural seats in the side wall, are widely replacing the immodest "altar chairs," in which the vicar and the supplementary curate were planted, to stare in pairs all down the church throughout the service. Over the Lord's Table, and upon the east wall, some appropriate colouring, some lining of tiles, or some modest carving, frequently and blamelessly exhibits the emblem of salvation, or at least the sacred monogram, and thus proclaims that the building is the Church of Christ. The use of painted glass to embody sacred story is now so universally admitted, as to render an occasional refusal on the part of some strongly-prejudiced incumbent a subject of public comment; while natural congruity generally prompts the selection of the east window as first to be taken in hand for the representation of the Nativity or Passion, the Resurrection or Ascension.

In giving this inventory of the now habitual apparatus of worship, I have simply scheduled a whole body of ideas which would have lain absolutely beyond the sphere of thought of our predecessors of half a century back. A Lord's Table to any extent mean, to any extent crowded up, would in those days be fenced by a rail, merely to help the communicants to kneel, and perhaps running round it on three sides. The prayers and sermon would be read from any combination of pulpit and reading-desk which took up the least room. The favourite form for this erection in a new church, and one which was far from uncommon in an old one, was a sort of tower, in which the reading-desk surmounted that of the clerk, and the pulpit frowned over them both, like a miniature representation of the mountains which the giants piled wherewith to scale heaven. This combination, irreverently called a three-decker by a later generation, was commonly planted in the direct centre of the building, so as absolutely to conceal the Lord's Table from the entire congregation. Sometimes in an old church the rickety piece of furniture would lean against one of the nave pillars. Another variation was to provide two corresponding pulpits on either side for the preaching of, respectively, the prayers and the sermon; while in a few abnormal instances, particularly in watering-places, the rostra would even overhang the altar or occupy a sort of gallery behind it. Lettern and litany desk were, of course, ideas which had never crossed the mind of any person of the Georgian era. Over the lawfulness of painted glass many an angry controversy raged; while offerings to beautify in any other way the sanctuary were, with very rare exceptions, not so much as dreamed of by the most liberal-hearted Christian.

If we proceed from the building to the worship for which it serves, the extent of acknowledged and uncontroversial gain is not less amazing. In Cathedrals, in College Chapels, and in a few old-fashioned town churches, the good tradition of daily prayers had still survived; elsewhere happy was the parish that was secure of a double Sunday service, and of even so much as a quarterly celebration of the Holy Communion. It would not be easy to find words to describe the dreariness of the habitual parochial service on Sundays. Music, except in the shape of village bands murdering Sternhold and Hopkins, or Tate and Brady, was well-nigh unknown. The single-handed minister plodded through his monotonous office. The song of Zacharias, with its wealth of Christian prophecy, never diversified the shorter and therefore more favourite Hundredth Psalm; the Benedicite, with its minor key, never replaced the jubilant Te Deum even in Lent; that prior portion of the Communion Office which ought, Sunday after Sunday, to have recalled the loss of higher privileges to a dull generation, was frequently delivered from the reading desk. Now, at all events, the full Prayer Book is no longer the badge of party, and although persons in high places, from whom such a suggestion emanates with peculiar and jarring inappropriateness, have proposed to weaken the order (already so thoughtfully indulgent) in which the Church lays down the rule of daily prayer, at least the parish priest who obeys that plain direction is past being pointed at for singularity or backbitten by vague calumnies. Monthly Communions are the least measure of the highest worship in places which put out any claim to share in the general uprising, while the frequency of weekly celebrations is an ever-increasing fact. The vague suspicions which used to gather round a musical rendering of the service have vanished away, and choral worship is generally acknowledged to be a matter which each church may rightfully adopt or dispense with, according to its local circumstances, while the singing, at all events, of the Psalms and of the

Canticles is everywhere accepted as the most congruous way of dealing with those sacred poems. With the recognition of choral worship has naturally come in that of choirs, and the placing of those choirs in the part of the church which common sense points out as most suitable for them, namely, the chancel. With choirs, and with chancels in which to dispose them, the use of the surplice as their appropriate dress has also taken its place among the matters on which parishes or congregations have the right to suit themselves. I remember having, about two years since, read a vigorous defence of surpliced choirs and chancels, from the mouth of a prelate more distinguished for earnest zeal than ritualistic prejudice, Bishop Fraser of Manchester. As to the lessons, the use of the lettern emphatically marks them off from the songs of praise with which they are preceded and followed. In the Communion Service, too, the aid of the "Gospeller" and "Epistler" (to borrow the phrase of Queen Elizabeth's Advertisements) is constantly now invoked by the celebrant, whose predecessors of the former epoch would have thought it much to be helped by one assistant. A choral Nicene Creed no longer provokes remarks. With the revival of the prayer for the Church Militant has come that of the offertory collection, instead of the old-fashioned plate smirkingly held by the churchwarden behind the door at the close of some elegant charity sermon. The holy days and seasons of the Church are observed with very varying strictness, but whether for observance or neglect, for commendation or criticism, they are accepted facts. It was not so in the time of our grandfathers. I was much struck, while sitting a few years ago upon the Ritual Commission, with some particulars brought before us in defence of an argument similar to that which I am now advancing, of the rough usage which Bishop Porteous met with towards the close of the last century, for attempting to revive the lost observance of Good Friday in London, for which he was rewarded by being abused in the leading journal of the period as a Papist. To come down to a much later date, those who have read the Life of Bishop Blomfield by his son will recollect the graphic description of the deep disgust inspired in that good prelate's mind by the spectacle of London fashionables habitually desecrating Easter Day in his early parish of Chesterford, as on that holiest of days they posted down, generally changing horses as people were leaving church, and shouted for fresh packs of cards at the village inn, in hot haste to be at Newmarket for the spring meeting. Now, at least, when Volunteers are most fussy on Easter Day for the morrow's review, they have the grace to muster at a "church parade." In contrast with the blank indifference of Georgian days, I need hardly note the competitive zeal with which clergymen of all complexions allure their congregations to make good use of Lent and Holy Week by multiplied services and frequent sermons, and I will only in passing notice the introduction at that season, not only into minsters but into parish churches, of that peculiarly impressive form of choral service the "Passion Music." The observance of Ascension Day, not long since as thoroughly forgotten an anniversary as Good Friday was to an earlier generation, is steadily gaining ground; while the religious use of Advent, although a season far less emphatically marked out by the Church than Lent, is no longer strange. Harvest Homes and Church anniversaries, and courses of services to keep up the solemnity of a consecration or first opening are quite acclimatised in our ecclesiastical system. When I first entered Parliament the House of Commons ignored the existence both of Ash Wednesday and of Ascension Day. Thanks to the initiative of the late Sir John Simeon, while still a member of our Communion, the Parliament, elected in 1847, agreed, under the Ministry of Lord John Russell, to recognise both these days by appointing a later time for the day sitting on the one occasion, and upon the other by fixing a later hour for the meeting of committees, so as in either case to give opportunity to the members to use the time so generously accorded to them in frequenting church. The good custom so commenced may now, after several vicissitudes, be considered as definitely established.

The only material recognition of the Church's seasons which had at the period at which I have commenced my comparison survived the destructive efforts of Puritanism and indifference, was the quaint custom of the clerk sticking holly boughs over the church at Christmas time. But now who can do justice to the artistic taste and patient labours which deck the fane— whether the utterance which the pulpit is to send forth will be high or low or broad—with the varied devices of mingled leaf and fruit for the great festival of the Nativity, and at the more genial seasons of Easter and Whitsuntide with the gay profusion of woven flowers and carefully compacted nosegays? I lately referred to a hearty defence of surpliced choirs by the Bishop of Manchester, and I must not forget that he has on a later occasion spoken out with equal vigour for the floral decoration of churches. Neither must we forget that the practice of placing nosegays on the Holy Table was the one concession to Mr. Purchas against which his opponents did not appeal.

I resist the temptation of dwelling here upon the influence which the "Choral Unions" which have grown up in various dioceses must have exercised upon the increasing popularity of musical services in our country parishes, for my object at this moment is rather to sum up results than to work out causes, and I am not sure whether these Unions ought rather to be classed as causes or effects. I have reserved this place for pointing to the hardly yet developed elasticity and variety which has been imparted to the services of the Church by two Acts of Parliament passed in 1871 and in 1872, the New Lectionary Act and the Act of Uniformity Amendment Act, in compliance with previous decisions of Convocation—in the former case I must own not quite satisfactorily reached, but, in the latter one, leaving nothing to be desired. No unprejudiced person, after comparing the old and the new Lectionaries, whether or not he regrets any of the omissions made in the latter, can refuse to acknowledge that the recognition of the Christian seasons, and high days of the Church, with their various teachings which the new table of lessons extracts alike from Old and New Testament, is far more full and edifying than that of the older one. But there is likewise in this Act a provision of which the Church, when it has got more familiar with its capabilities, will, I am sure, take frequent and grateful advantage. The Ordinary may now on occasions give a permission, only limited by his own discretion, for special lessons and for proper psalms. This new power in the hands of a sympathetic bishop and zealous parish priests goes far to invest our services with that adaptability for occasional demands, and that variety of colouring in correspondence with the Christian calendar in which, with all its substantial merits, the Prayer Book has hitherto been somewhat wanting. More particularly will it do so if taken in connection with another popular development, of which I might previously have spoken, for it has had a wide effect on the religious life of the people, that of hymnals, comprising sacred songs adapted to the various occasions of the Christian year, liberally drawn from ancient and from modern sources, in substitution for the dreary "old" and "new" versions of our forefathers. To show how this permission may be worked, I have only to note that under it the Bishop of Lincoln has put out a table of proper psalms for various holy days to be used within his diocese. The Act of Uniformity Amendment Act is now commonly known as the Shortened Services Act; and inasmuch as it provides abbreviated forms of daily service, it may very often bridge over a difficulty as to any public worship on the week-days, but it may occasionally also lay a snare, when a clergyman who might well have given a longer form of public prayer to a willing congregation is tempted to serve them with short measure. But the Act, moreover, comprises two general provisions which still further carry out the wholesome principle of regulated elasticity of which the Lectionary Act gave the first example. By this Act the Ordinary may on any Sunday, when the full morning and evening services have been performed, authorise a third service constructed of Prayer Book and scriptural materials, and he may on special occasions allow the use of an extraordinary office similarly constructed. The "Passion Music" to which I have referred was sanctioned by the careful Bishop of London under this Act, and extra Lenten services, partially composed of the latter portion of the Commination Service, have in various churches been profitably introduced. Under these provisions, indeed, if only generous confidence on either side could be secured, a regular place with due regulation might be found in our worship system for additional devotions which have in various places been adopted in a startling and abrupt manner, and upon individual responsibility. For instance, the "Tenebræ" services of Holy Week (unaccompanied by that gradual and symbolical extinction of lights which appears so odd to the average English spectator) is in the main an arrangement of psalms with intervening "antiphons" or "anthems" taken from Scripture. Such services, involving no other ceremonial than that of the habitual Evensong, might be sanctioned for the use of congregations desirous, at seasons of special solemnity, to join in public devotion beyond the measure provided by the almost unvarying length of the regular Morning and Evening Prayer. The second specific gain secured by this Act is that the separate use of the Litany, about which there never was any doubt, if it were accompanied with the antecedent permission of the Ordinary—which had in fact already been plenarily conceded by the whole Bench of Bishops—is by this Act specifically marked with a legislative recognition.

So much for the current use of the Prayer Book in 1874 as compared with 1824 or 1834. A similar change in the national appreciation of the occasional services is an equally patent fact. The total extinction of the lazy practice of baptisms in private houses, which used to be a fashionable folly, is in point. Then confirmations, which were at one time septennial in some dioceses in spite of the canons, and never more than triennial, are now the never-ceasing occupation of the episcopate. But if we desire to follow the broader, brighter, and more really philosophical appreciation of the influence which forms of beauty exercise upon the mind in times of exceptional tension, we must turn to those services which most powerfully awaken human emotions, the joy of wedding and the sorrow of burying. I remember the time when it was the fashion amongst those who could best afford to be bountiful, most strenuously to argue for what they called a quiet wedding as due to their self-formed canons of good taste. Indeed of all ways of using the marriage rite, a hasty recitation of the service duly mutilated to suit that fastidiousness which apes modesty, over a drawing-room table by special licence from the See of Canterbury was deemed the most aristocratic. I do not of course attach any moral value to those modern accompaniments of a wealthier marriage, the troops of bridesmaids, the bowers and nosegays, the wedding march and Keble's hymn. But I do appeal to those enrichments of a rite in which joy should abound, in proof that during the time through which the present generation has been marching towards the end of all things, the spontaneous instinct for the beautiful on occasions when the Author of all beauty and goodness is approached has been ripening in the English mind, and has very naturally displayed itself on an occasion when feelings are the warmest and therefore the least hypocritical. The change which is coming over the ceremonial of our funerals is even more remarkable than that which has modified our marriages. In their case it has been the substitution of graceful and symbolical accompaniments for puritanical dryness. In our funerals it has been a growing disgust to a cumbersome and effete system of cold repulsive ceremonialism, and the substitution of forms more truly speaking of Christian hope to the heart of the mourner.

The antiquarian might, in the hearse with its dusty drapery, in the vested staves and the heavy scarves, trace the degraded forms of what were once the seemly accompaniments of a Christian burial. But they had long since ceased to speak an intelligible language, and had become the mere badges of an undertaker's greed. The cross-embroidered pall, the wreaths, and floral crosses, which loving hands now gently place upon the coffin, speak of that sure and certain hope of the resurrection of the dead with which we join dust to dust. It was with much interest that I lately read of these beautiful symbols of the everlasting life appearing at the funeral of the venerable Bishop Sumner. No right-thinking person, I am sure, would say that their presence conveyed any idea alien to the religion—even in its most marked characteristics—of that good man. But of how great a load of prejudice removed are they the evidence when we recall what used to be the code of ceremonious practice of the school to which the former Bishop of Winchester professedly belonged.

I have on purpose been confining my sketch of an uncontentious ceremonial advance to the services which gather round our parish churches. Instead of attempting any general history of the changes which have passed over our Cathedrals, I shall take one event in one of them as an evidence of how a Cathedral could have been used in 1873, and could not have been so employed in 1833. Twelve hundred years had been told up in 1873, since the pious East Anglian Queen Etheldreda had fallen asleep in the little monastery which she had raised in the lonesome island of Ely, to be both a refuge for herself and a home of gospel light to a still half-pagan land, in the dreary days of the so-called Heptarchy. Through all those centuries the memory of this holy lady had been fresh in the minds of the people of Ely, while a Cathedral hardly second to any in the world for its artistic magnificence had replaced St. Etheldreda's humble dwelling. Of late years, too, a movement set on foot by that distinguished man, Dean Peacock, had gradually carried out in Ely Minster a restoration worthy of the structure.

It struck the present Dean, Dr. Merivale, whose large sympathies have never been claimed by the ritualists that "a course of twelve centuries seems something round and complete in itself, and such a course happens, in fact, to comprehend some of the most remarkable cycles of human history," and he proposed, accordingly, that St. Etheldreda's Bissexcentenary should be worthily kept in her church. The then Bishop and the remaining Chapter warmly assented, and although it became known while the arrangements were still pending, that the generally beloved Diocesan had been called away to the higher throne of Winchester, the news only made the occasion in its second character of his leave-taking more emphatic. The special services commenced on Friday, October 17, St. Etheldreda's day, and continued on the 18th, St. Luke's day, the Sunday, Monday, and Tuesday. I hardly know whether I need explain that the special architectural characteristic of this huge church is the central octagonal lantern in the rich Gothic of the fourteenth century, from which branch the vast Norman nave and transepts, and the long Gothic choir. The uniformity of the general level of the whole church, while in some respects an architectural defect, in others lends itself to great popular services by the facilities which it gives for crowded congregations to see and hear what passes in the stalls and at the altar. At an earlier date Ely, like every other cathedral, was sharply parted into a choir, boxed off for public worship, and indiscriminately filled with clergy and laity, and a nave kept uselessly open and bare for sightseers to ramble over, with the local exception of a Sunday sermon which was of old preached in it. On the morning of St. Etheldreda's day, as had been the case on many previous days since the restoration of the cathedral, though not in such impressive numbers, the octagon and a large part of the nave were thronged with worshippers, while the choir—

visible from the remaining church through its rich open screen of wood and brass, and bounded by its beautiful stalls of the fourteenth century—was filled with lines of surpliced occupants, the Chapter, the strongly reinforced choirmen and boys, and the collected clergy of the neighbouring Isle of Ely. The utmost resources of sacred music were put out to do honour to the day, and at the Holy Communion (where the Diocesan was celebrant), the choir did not, as too often in our cathedrals, walk out and leave the most sacred of all the Church's offices to be carried through in the unimpressive tone of ordinary reading. On St. Luke's day, the mid-day service was again very noble, but not so noble as on that of the foundress, for the Holy Communion had been forestalled in the morning, and there were fewer clergy in the choir. Each afternoon, I ought to add, the Evensong was offered up with all the wealth of sacred music, and every morning an appropriate sermon was preached. But on the Sunday, again, the morning service was complete, and the celebrant was the Archbishop of Canterbury. The evening service was twice repeated, and on the second occasion after nightfall, the pulpit which stands in the octagon, just outside of the choir, was occupied by the Bishop of Peterborough. Of the crowd which the force of his oratory brought together a verbal description can give no vivid idea; whence it came was a puzzle to conjecture, for Ely is but a little country town. There they were, cramming the octagon, stretching into the dim distances of the nave and either transept, peering out from the dark arches of the triforium,— thoroughly, greedily, using one of the oldest and hugest of those cathedrals which, as Dissenters and Freethinkers, and Radical Reformers had so pertinaciously been dinning into our heads for years and years were the useless and obsolete excrescences of a worn-out Establishment. And they had not come merely for the sermon—for the choral service, which was of a simple popular character, interspersed with stirring hymns, had been taken up by hundreds of voices. I have already explained that I am describing this one occasion at Ely as a sample of the aspect of the work at our resuscitated cathedrals, so as to spare my readers the long catalogue of the many symptoms of new life which every English minster, in more or less a degree, now happily exhibits. This treatment enables me better to focus my subject, and I accordingly make a pause at this memorable evening service to claim the so-called "nave services" of our cathedrals as a distinguished component of that varied list of uncontentious ceremonial by which the Church of England is richer during the last forty years, and for which I have no fear of asserting that she is, humanly speaking, more entitled to the High Church movement than to any other tangible cause. The immediate cause of these now widespread nave services is so curious, that it deserves to be rescued from oblivion by a brief narrative.

It is some twenty years since a knot of earnest persons, whose spiritual zeal was greater than their instinct for congruity, conceived the idea of turning the London theatres into Sunday preaching stations. A clergyman, in whose parish one of these theatres was situated, interposed canonical objections to the proceedings, and led other persons to appreciate that it was a question having more than one side. Among the aspects in which it presented itself was that telling sermons to large bodies of listeners in populous places was a religious engine which our Church had been too chary in using; another consideration, which followed quickly upon this one, was that there were other large buildings more convenient and more seemly for spiritual exercises than playhouses, and also that the forms of the Church could be as effectively married to the discourses as any extemporary supplications; and so the popular evening services chorally rendered by the help of thronging volunteers, and their accompanying sermons come into existence in the naves of St. Paul's and Westminster Abbey. London was not long allowed a monopoly of the good idea; and I am unable to say in how many of the other cathedrals they are now in more or less constant use.

The one which I have described at Ely was uniquely picturesque in its accompaniments, but it was one instance of a system which had long been established in many similar churches. I shall not readily forget the throng, and the heartiness of the nave service in York Minster at the close of the Church Congress in that city. This institution alone has effectively and for ever dispelled in the most practical manner the reproaches aimed at the choral services of our cathedrals and other churches, with their anthems and their organs, and their surplices, as the cold, unedifying taskwork of hirelings. Whatever else a cathedral service may be, it can, at all events, be made the most popular of performances.

But I have been straying from Ely. On Monday the services were varied by a public dinner, with the usual speeches. Among the speakers was the Archbishop of Canterbury, who summed up his impressions in these sentences:—

"All honour was due to those who, in past times, had devoted their substance, their time and their abilities to the great work of restoration, which they now saw spreading through the land. It was something to have the privilege of being present in so splendid a building on that occasion; and it was something, also, to have heard the music which pealed under its roof, and to have appreciated the skill and ability with which the ceremonial of Divine Service had been performed; but it was something even better to have seen the vast crowds, of rich and poor alike, gathered together to worship God under the noble roof, and to express their thankfulness to Almighty God for the privileges which they enjoyed. A man must have had a heart of stone who could have been present at the services of the previous day without being moved. Whether they thought of the more popular evening service, or of the eloquent addresses they had heard, morning, afternoon, or evening, all so worthy of the noble building, they had reason to be thankful that they had been privileged to take part in that great celebration. For his own part, he should go back to his labours elsewhere, cheered by the sights and sounds he had witnessed; and no man would convince him that the Church of England did not live in the hearts of the people, after attending such gatherings as they had witnessed there, and which were to be witnessed elsewhere, wherever there were great opportunities for members of the Church of England to gather together."

The value of these words will be best appreciated when the characteristics of the occasion which called them forth are recollected. The commemoration was of no hero or heroine of modern controversy, of no one whose canonisation was ratified by the cheers of Exeter Hall, or the fiat of self-sufficient journalism, but of an Abbess far back in the darkest ages, of a woman who built a convent, and herself crept into it to die there, only thinking of her own and of her neighbours' souls. Then twelve hundred years after Etheldreda was laid in her grave, the Bishop and Chapter of a Cathedral in our Reformed Church of England solemnly gather together men and women, clergy and lay folk, rich and poor, learned and simple, representatives of all parties, and people of distinguished positions, to keep alive her memory, and render thanks for all the blessings of which her gift to God was the undoubted source, in a great triumph of prayer and song, and choral communion. At the head of this goodly gathering was the Primate of All England, who was inspired by the circumstances of this grand anniversary to speak his full heart in words which I have recited. I think it is quite consistent with the deep personal respect which I feel for my Archbishop to say that I like his speech at Ely far better than others which he has since delivered elsewhere.

The last day of the anniversary was, in some respects, the most remarkable as a spectacle. It was devoted to the Choral Festival of the diocese. Morning and afternoon the various choirs, to the number of more than six hundred persons, each parish marked by its distinctive banner, walked in long procession up the nave, through the close-packed multitude, singing the inspiring 'Onward, Christian soldiers,' and appropriately accompanied by a military band, which marched unseen on a parallel line up the triforium. The procession was closed by the Chapter, and finally by the Bishop, with his pastoral staff borne by his Chaplain. The retrocession was similarly arranged, and in the afternoon—the closing scene of the Bissexcentenary—this ceremonial appealed with a peculiar pathos to the congregation, as the solemn farewell to his diocese, of Bishop Harold Browne, who had just given his fatherly blessing in the mid Octagon, with the emblem of his pastoral office grasped in his left hand. There is nothing strange in a Christian Bishop bearing his shepherd's crook; but forty years ago no English Bishop would have thought of such an action.

CHAPTER II.

Critical period reached — Public Worship Regulation Act — Abrupt adoption of ornate ceremonialism — "Liddell v. Westerton" — Surplice riots — Papal aggression and Durham letter — Corelation of book, building, and rubric — Tests of allowable ceremonies — Continuity of Church of England — Thirtieth Canon — Triple division of Churches — Prayer Book explained by building — Arrangements of nave — Pews and open seats — Chancels as in times past — Ornaments Rubric — Vernacular daily services characteristic of English Church — Four English Prayer Books — "Omission not prohibition" examined — "Martin v. Mackonochie" — "Shepherd v. Bennett" — "How is the Church's Prayer Book to be carried on?" — No directions as to manner of singing Psalms, or as to manner of reading Epistle and Gospel — No "Manual Acts" ordered between 1552 and 1662 — Statute and Common Law in Church as well as State — Continuity of English Church, but difference in spirit as well as act between reformed and unreformed services — An important principle apt to be overlooked — Impossibility of reviving literally Sarum rite with present office — Meaning of Ornaments Rubric — "Liddell v. Westerton" — Meaning of "by authority of Parliament" in the second year of Edward VI. — Bishop Cosin and the Act of Submission — Balance of parties at commencement of Elizabeth's reign — Cosin at the Restoration — Sir J. T. Coleridge — Chancels as in times past — Chancel screen — Bishop Beveridge — Jube, rood-loft — Post-reformational screen — Cross surmounting screen at St. Barnabas legalised by Judicial Committee in 1857.

So far I have been navigating the smooth seas of uncontroversial ceremonial, and I believe that the result of my voyage must be to bring home to dispassionate minds the conviction that the Church of England, in its corporate character, has, during a period which now runs back to days before the birth of many persons in places of high trust and honour, been engaged with her whole heart in the pious work of elevating and embellishing her worship alike to the glory of God and to the edification of man. Many temperaments have shared in the task under the widest variety of circumstances, and with little or no central control. If the enterprise had not been of God, it must, under the many environing difficulties, have long since broken down. It might have been popular for a decade or so, but then it would have been no more heard of. It has instead, by a gradual progression, changed the external aspect of worship throughout the land. Accordingly—while they realise that a critical period has at last been reached in which men are asking each other " How far ? " " Where are we being driven ? " " What does it all mean ? "—Churchmen may be surprised that these enquiries have been so long delayed. I have publicly and privately expressed my sorrow at the way in which the promoters of the Public Worship Regulation Act chose to force on that measure; so I shall not, I hope, be now misunderstood in considering it the climax of an agitation which has lasted over several years of ritual suits promoted by the Church Association and of the deliberations of the Ritual Commission; these, on the other hand, having been fostered by the abrupt adoption on the part of the new school of " Ritualists " of a ceremonialism much more ornate than any which the most forward High Churchman had previously seen his way to exhibit. I am not in this conjunction praising or blaming any party; I merely point out that the gradual and peaceable assimilation by the Church mind of England of more artistic forms of worship on the older lines, of which the judgment of the Privy Council in the suits of Liddell *v.* Westerton and Liddell *v.* Beal, in 1857, was, so to speak, the Magna Charta, has, during the last ten years, given place to stronger claims and fiercer antagonisms. It may be a presumptuous, but it cannot be an unblessed, undertaking to interpose in the strife, and remind both sides that they are brethren. The worst fate that can befall the self-appointed mediator is personal failure. Two periods of even greater popular excitement, an excitement which culminated in rioting and positive danger to life and limb, have already marked the ceremonial revival. The first, as far back as 1843, came to a head in Exeter, and was due to the trivial question of white or black gown in the pulpit. The second, which raged through the end of 1850 and beginning of 1851, was provoked by the maladroit ingenuity of the Prime Minister, Lord John Russell, in writing a letter to the then Bishop of Durham, in which he grasped at imaginary political capital by connecting Pius IX.'s ill-managed revival of a Roman Catholic Hierarchy in England (which had bitterly irritated the national pride), with the increase of English ceremonial, as manifested in the newly-consecrated church of St. Barnabas, Pimlico. The Minister was incited, it must be owned, to this indefensible policy by an unfortunate Charge of Bishop Blomfield, who attempted to ride what he thought was a coming storm by tactics which only dissatisfied every party and increased the general uneasiness. I shall not travel over the wretched incidents of this anxious period. It is enough to remind a less turbulent, though more litigious generation, that the public peace was for a protracted period seriously menaced by rioting, which had its centre at, while it extended far beyond, the church of St. Barnabas. Then magistrates, members of the Legislature, and the classes of society in general, from whom sober counsels might have been expected, were all infected with the contagious spirit of unrest, till after a tumultuous time of meetings, protests, charges, both episcopal and archidiaconal, irritating leading articles setting off querulous letters, and all other forms of disturbance, the storm lulled as unaccountably as it had beaten up. The menaced ceremonial was only again heard of by the public in the courts of law, finally to be in the main sanctioned by the Privy Council in that judgment in the suits of Liddell *v.* Westerton and Liddell *v.* Beal, at which the last but one and the present Archbishops of Canterbury, Drs. Sumner and Tait, were the assenting episcopal assessors.

As I have already stated in the first Chapter, I shall make the corelation of book, building, and rubric my guiding principle. The tests to which, in subordination to the plain letter of the

Prayer Book, I shall put the various incidents of ceremonial will be those which I have already laid down in some 'Hints towards Peace in Ceremonial Matters,' which I published earlier in the year, namely:—

(1.) Compatibility with the spirit of the Reformed Church of England as a whole, in its widest and most tolerant aspect, as represented by all the leading Churchmen of the Reformation century (*i. e.* from 1547 to 1662).

(2.) Respect for primitive antiquity and the traditions of the Universal Church.

(3.) Capability of proof without reference to the practices of the mediæval and later Church of Rome —

To which I shall add, as a positive test, while unable to accept the reverse as conclusive of the incompatibility of the ceremonial with the already named conditions—

(4.) Legalisation by recent decisions either of the highest Court or of lower Courts, from which there has been no appeal.

At the same time regarding the general question as one of policy, or more properly of charity, I have no intention of insisting on even the most palpably legal ceremonial as obligatory upon clergymen or congregations who do not approve of it. The Public Worship Regulation Act may fix them with it. If so, it will be the work of those who forced that measure on, and not of the minority in either House of Parliament, who raised a warning voice against the evils of repeated litigation. In return for the desire not to oppress other schools within the Church of England, it is, I think, asking but little to claim that they, for their part, should not attempt to impose their yoke upon unwilling shoulders. There are various incidents of ceremonial, as to the legality of which, from the conflict of decisions, or the absence of any decision, a reasonable controversy may arise. In respect of these, if it can be shown, on the one hand, that there are plausible grounds for the assumption that they are legally right, and if, on the other hand, it can be demonstrated that they cannot be morally wrong, inasmuch as it will be impossible to show that they are contrary to the spirit of the Prayer Book, while they fulfil the other tests which I have laid down; then I plead in regard to these ceremonies that the principle of wise and charitable compromise, which ought to regulate the concerns of so large and complex a body as the Church of England, with its many parishes, and countless tastes, should win for those observances a cheerful recognition from parties which will thereby acquire an equitable right to claim from us—the High Churchmen—a similar recognition of their own allowable peculiarities.

There is a third class of ceremonies—those which at present stand condemned by recent decisions, but which were, so to speak, condemned by "the skin of their teeth," as irreconcilable with some specific enactment, canon or rubric, advertisement or injunction, but which no fair man can say are evidently inconsistent with the general framework of our worship, or contrary to the spirit of the Prayer Book; and which in particular cannot be repudiated as symbolical of the Church of Rome in its antagonism to our Communion. In regard to these ceremonies, when they cross my path, I should plead for a candid hearing, in order that—if it can be shown that they conduce to the edification of a proportion of Churchmen deserving of specific recognition—they might be henceforward authoritatively tolerated, under conditions which should prevent them from becoming offensive to persons of contrary tastes. There is, beyond all these, the indefinitely wide fourth class of things, either obviously contrary to both the letter and spirit of the Prayer Book, or so unpopular (whether on logical or illogical grounds) with the majority of the people, that it would be wrong in principle, or wrong from policy, to attempt their revival.

I have already, in my recapitulation of uncontroversial ceremonial, pointed out how the normal new English Church exhibits a nave and a chancel, distinguished from each other in their architecture and in their fittings; and that the chancel is, more or less carefully, appropriated to the direct performance of the service. I have also pointed out that the eastern portion of that chancel is habitually parted off for the Lord's Table and the celebration of the Holy Communion. In recurring to this type of sacred building, our Reformed Church visibly carries out that claim to continuity with the English Church from its beginning, and of identity with the Universal or Catholic Church of all ages, on which it bases its claims to the allegiance of its members, as is very clearly shown (not to burden my argument with a multiplicity of proofs) in this well-known passage of the thirtieth Canon :

"Nay, so far was it from the purpose of the Church of England to forsake and reject the Churches of Italy, France, Spain, Germany, or any such like Churches, in all things which they held and practised, that, as the Apology of the Church of England confesseth, it doth with reverence retain those ceremonies, which do neither endanger the Church of God, nor offend the minds of sober men; and only departed from them in those particular points, wherein they were fallen both from themselves in their ancient integrity, and from the apostolical Churches, which were their first founders."

I have, in my "English Cathedral of the Nineteenth Century," shown how the triple division of nave, of "Chorus Cantorum," choir or chancel, for the "saying or singing" of the daily offices, and of Bema, Apsis or Sanctuary for the Holy Communion, appears in modified forms, but yet in forms exhibiting a substantive identity of principle in the basilicas of the primitive and undivided Church, in the cathedrals, abbeys, and parish churches of the East and of the West after their unhappy separation, and in particular in those of England. Many other works exist which will give fuller information to the student who wishes to follow up this enquiry, and as it is not germane to my immediate object, I will not expatiate any further upon it.

It is certain that the Prayer Book can give no reflection, as a living mirror of worship, to the man who will not care to appreciate in what places and under what forms it must be carried out. To show this we need go no further than the earlier portion of its title-page, in which we read that it is "the Book of Common Prayer and Administration of the Sacraments, and other Rites and Ceremonies of the Church, according to the use of the Church of England." This description involves two facts—that there are prayers, and also that there are sacraments (besides the "other" occasional "rites and ceremonies"); and secondly, that the prayers must involve persons to lead and others to follow in the praying, and the "administration of the sacraments," persons to administer and persons to be administered to. This information as it stands is a dead letter, but when we learn that there are buildings so planned that those who are administered to, and those who follow the prayers, are conveniently arranged in one place, that those who perform the important office of leading these prayers are conveniently arranged elsewhere, that those who perform the still more important office of administering that sacrament, the participation of which is man's recurring duty, are conveniently arranged in a still higher place, in proximity to the furniture which the book later on prescribes for that rite, and that for the other sacrament of which each Christian is only once participant, convenient arrangements also exist in another part of the church, then the title-page of the Prayer Book, and with it the whole volume, becomes a living spirit. The remainder of the same title-page, with its references to the Psalter "sung or said in churches," and to the forms of "making, ordaining, and consecrating of bishops, priests, and deacons," only carries on the sentence which I have quoted to further particulars, and supplies additional reasons for the constructive peculiarities of our churches.

I have need to tarry very briefly over the ritual arrangements of the nave. These include five special features—the Font for Baptism, the Pulpit, sometimes the Lettern and

CHAP. II. FONT, PULPIT, LETTERN, LITANY DESK.

Litany Desk, and the seats. In' my first chapter I have quoted the eighty-first Canon, which prescribes that the font shall be of stone, and that it shall stand in the "ancient usual places." These three words mean that it is according to usual ancient tradition to be placed near the entrance of the church, in token that Baptism is the entrance into the Christian covenant. This order had, until the High Church movement, been habitually ignored for an indefinite period; now, on the contrary, I am glad to say that it is as habitually observed. It was a harmless and graceful old practice (though anything but a universal one) to make the font octagonal, with a double symbolical meaning, referring alike to the eight persons saved in the ark, and to the idea of an *eighth* day, the first of the new Christian week at the close of the week of the older dispensation. This symbol has much approved itself to modern builders. I pass from the font, only observing that its canonical position in the usual ancient place involves, whenever the baptism is performed according to the rubric after the second lesson, a ceremonious procession on the part of the minister down the church, which, if it had not been the direct and uncontrovertible inference from the words of the rubric and of the canon taken together, would, in all probability, not have escaped rather sharp criticism from anti-ceremonialists.

The pulpit, as it is never now used to block out the chancel, happily gives me nothing to discuss; and as the ornamental character, whether in the form of desk or eagle, of the Lettern as of the Litany desk, which sometimes stand in the nave, and sometimes in the chancel, is now beyond controversy, I gladly leave them, with this reference.

I must say a few words as to the seats. In the dull old times, the person who asserted that there was any principle involved in the design and arrangement of church seats would have been treated as a joker or a fanatic. Indeed, the awakening of the general conscience on the subject of pews and of free seats is a subject the moral importance of which is not to be measured by the simplicity of the language in which it may be described. I may fairly claim for the Cambridge Camden Society in its earliest days the merit of the most outspoken declaration upon pews, in the brief form of a paper of reasons against them. The abuse even in our churches is as yet hardly abated; but when it occurs it is felt to be a thing which calls for an apology; and, at all events, the seats are usually arranged so as to face the more sacred portion of the building. The denizens of the old square pews were a casual mob of listeners, carrying with them their worldly differences. Even where there are only uniform seats those who occupy them are visibly worshippers, and where these seats are open as well as uniform the nothingness of human distinctions in the sight of God is visibly set forth. In churches where galleries are found, the longitudinal arrangement of seats is an unavoidable necessity, and also I must add where there are deep transepts; but the plan which involves deep transepts is not a practical one for a church destined for our present English worship, in which, as far as possible, the altar should be visible by a united congregation from all parts of the building. In chancels or choirs the seats or stalls are longitudinal, because those who fill them are looked upon as taking a direct part in the performance of worship, and particularly in the antiphonal singing; and as college-chapels are, in fact, choirs, in them also the old practice of longitudinal seats has rightly been respected down to our own days.

I dare not attempt to disentangle the thorny question of appropriated seats. There is an extreme anti-pew party which denounces all appropriation. But these persons, I believe, push a right principle beyond the bounds of practical expediency. Proprietorship in seats is an abuse, but a temporary appropriation according to local and individual circumstances, and depending on the persons so placed being at church, may really be the carrying out of the direction to "do all things decently and in order." St. James denounced favouring a rich man, because he was rich, with the best place in church, and treating the poor man with contumely; but he does not say that the casual attendant, who may be not only poor, but arrogant, is to be at liberty, on account of his poverty, to push out the meek habitual worshipper, however wealthy he may be. At all events, I do not believe that rural parishes, as a rule, would get on without a certain fixity of seats; not as by right, but as ordered by the officers on whom the responsibility rests. In towns the case is different, and I can understand many cases in which an absolutely free church is a most potent engine of evangelization. I am disposed to be equally elastic upon the question of the division of sexes. It has certainly survived in various old-fashioned places, and in them it would be a kind of sacrilege to abolish it. There are also obvious reasons for its introduction into crowded town churches; indeed, in those which are absolutely free it is indispensable, at the risk of grave scandal. In some other country churches the attempt to break up the families would probably merely throw back church-going to the advantage of the conventicle, and perhaps even of the public-house. The form of the sittings, whether benches or chairs, was a few years since a matter of rather sharp argument, and the novel appearance of the latter led to the usual ignorant accusation that they were Popish; an assertion which was supported by the undoubted fact that the traveller in Roman Catholic France met them in all the churches; and which was not replied to as it might have been by the equally true assertion that the traveller in Roman Catholic Germany found benches in every church. Since, however, they have been introduced into the naves of our cathedrals this prejudice has died away, and persons are now pretty well satisfied that the advantages and disadvantages of the two ways of seating churches about balance each other. Chairs are actually the cheaper and the more manageable, except when (as is very often the case) they are converted into a bad and makeshift form of bench, by being lashed together to a long lath.; while benches conveniently seat the larger compact mass of worshippers.

I have now reached the chancel, including in the larger sense of the word the sanctuary, with which the remainder of this book will be mainly concerned, and I cannot more appropriately introduce the subject than by quoting the direction or rubric of the Prayer Book which points to its condition.

"The morning and evening prayer shall be used in the accustomed place of the church, chapel, or chancel; except it shall be otherwise determined by the Ordinary of the place. And the chancels shall remain as they have done in times past.

"And here it is to be noted, that such ornaments of the church, and of the Ministers thereof, at all times of their ministration, shall be retained, and be in use, as were in this Church of England, by the authority of Parliament, in the second year of the reign of King Edward the Sixth."

I shall have a great deal to say both in this chapter and in the further portions of my volume upon the second paragraph of this direction, commonly called the Ornaments Rubric, but I am at present mainly concerned with the words "and the chancels shall remain as in times past." To understand this order, or, indeed, any part of the Prayer Book, it must be recollected that the Prayer Book was no more absolutely a new book in 1549, when it appeared in its earliest form, than the Church which put it forth was a new Church. The old English Church had its succession of daily services, interspersed with Psalms and lessons, only more complex than the present arrangement, divided into seven or eight "hours" (for it admitted of either computation), written in Latin, and, as the prefatory matter to the Prayer Book declares, with its original character "altered, broken, and neglected, by planting in uncertain stories, and legends, with multitude of responds, verses, vain repetitions, commemorations, and synodals;" and also let me add by invocations of the Blessed Virgin and of the Saints, against which it is not possible to protest too strongly. This collection of services had for many centuries been termed in the Western Church the Breviary, while the Eastern had its similar but independent system. The Western Breviaries, while built on generally similar principles, were widely different in different countries, dioceses, and monastic orders. In England, among the other varieties, the Salisbury or Sarum "use" predominated, and next to that the one of York, and each had also a corresponding Missal. One characteristic pervaded all these books—they were in a dead language, and they had become the devotion not of the general people, but of the clergy only, taking that word in its broadest sense. It is still so to a preponderating extent in Roman Catholic countries, but it was, I believe, still more exclusively clerical in the Middle Ages, for, with the spread of education and the diffusion of translations, vespers at least have to an appreciable degree taken their position as a congregational devotion.

The English Reformers, with a bold ingenuity for which they have often received less than their due praise, conceived the idea of giving the Breviary back to the people as a vernacular and popular form of worship, and this they accomplished by boldly compressing those translated portions of the Sarum use, which they judged proper to retain, into an order of Morning and Evening Prayer; or, as it is also termed in the Prayer Book, continuing the old English names of two of the principal services, of "Mattins" and "Evensong," and by providing them with an order for reading the Psalms and with a lectionary, both framed on different and more simple principles than the order of Psalms and lessons contained in the Breviary. They added a Litany translated from old forms, they compiled a Communion Office from the Sarum Missal (mainly preserving in translation the old Collects, Epistles, and Gospels), and they went to the same traditionary forms for aid in the occasional offices, for instance preserving in the Marriage Service the vernacular words of wedding which had ever been used in the mother tongue. I take this opportunity of emphatically declaring that in my opinion the Reformers performed an act at once manifesting courage, prescience, and ability, when, in bestowing upon the English Church a vernacular Prayer Book, they vindicated the enjoyment of the daily services for the people.

It is hardly too much to say that in the possession of this compendium of formal devotion alike available for the public use of the whole congregation, and for the private prayers of each Christian soul, the Church of England enjoys a treasure of which no other community can boast. The Vesper Book of the Church of Rome is in its popular aspect comparatively a makeshift, and the various litanies now in vogue among the Roman Catholics fail in the elements of praise and of scriptural instruction. The length of the services in the Eastern Church renders them unfit as a whole for congregational use in the unabridged form. In the Lutheran churches the vernacular service is mostly confined to a popularising of the Communion service, which has lent itself with a bad facility to the abuse under which we have suffered of taking the earlier part of it as the completion of the normal Sunday service, and omitting the Communion itself. I may be pardoned for illustrating my position and proving the religious value of such a body of devotion, by a reference to recent occurrences. Those who may have most disagreed in the popular movement among Churchmen for the retention in its integrity of the Athanasian Creed as a practical constituent of the Prayer Book worship, must at least own that honest conviction lay at the bottom of the determination. It showed that men cared for something definite, and were not ashamed to own their conviction. Well, if there had not been a vernacular form of worship in England, and if the Athanasian Creed had not formed part of that form, it would have been as little known and as little cared about, as I find it in the various countries of the Continent. Whatever may be the benefit of "hearing Mass," it does not teach the Creeds, make the Bible familiar, or attune men's hearts to Divine psalmody.

In paying the tribute of just gratitude to the Reformers, I must at the same time express a very deep regret that in the recoil from the corruption of multiplied private Masses, the framers of the Prayer Book, or those into whose hands it came to carry out the work, took no sufficient precautions for securing in practice that the Holy Communion should, as in the earliest and best days of the Undivided Church, be recognised and established as the centre and moving influence of public worship, the act which at the least should hallow each succeeding Lord's Day. The rift in the lute was undoubtedly the rubric in the First Prayer Book of 1549, establishing the use of the earlier part of the Communion service as a customary devotion for Wednesdays and Fridays, coupled with the following one prescribing the same form when there were presumably on Sundays none to communicate with the priest. The exception gradually became a vicious rule, and this rareness of communions has most undoubtedly been a grievous shortcoming in our Reformed Church, operating as it has done for the bad, both in directly withholding the highest means of grace, and in encouraging the neglect of the "Holy Mysteries" on the too distant recurrences of their celebration. There is, indeed, no more hopeful sign in the revival of the last forty years, than the wide-spread and increasing exertions which have been made all over the country to wipe away this disgrace.

The First Prayer Book of Edward VI. published in 1549 was soon succeeded in 1552 by a revision made under the influence of those Swiss and other foreign Reformers, who had found not only peace, but honour and power in England. This book deviated in various ways from the old national models further than the one of 1549, which was exclusively compiled by English hands, and the comparative merits of the two Prayer Books cannot, I fear, be taken as one of the points which I have ventured to term uncontentious in the present Church of England, although it uses a form which is not identical with either of the earlier compilations. The accession of Mary swept both books away, and when Elizabeth came to the throne, a third Prayer Book was issued, mainly reproducing that of 1552, but with elements taken from that of 1549. A new edition of this book, put out early in James the First's reign, does not present enough of difference to entitle it to the title of a fourth book. The recognised Fourth Prayer Book is our present one, as edited by Convocation and passed by Parliament in 1662, consequent on the restoration of the Church and the Monarchy. The points upon which this book differs from its predecessor are in the direction of the more definite views of High Churchmen, and the leading spirit of the revision was the learned Bishop Cosin of Durham. We were happily but narrowly saved from a fifth Prayer Book in the time of William III., in which less definite doctrine would have been set out in more stilted phraseology.

These prefatory directions to the Prayer Book occupy an important place among the arguments which are alleged in defence of the most startling developments of Ritualism. Ritualists are fond of taking up the position that *omission is not prohibition*. The gloss placed upon that dictum is, that in order to show that any rite or ceremony in use in the Church of England before the Reformation is now unlawful, some direct prohibition of it since that period must be produced. Now, leaving this gloss for further enquiry, I believe that it would not be easy to disprove the dictum itself as an abstract proposition, but, as in the case of other abstract propositions, it leads on a very small way to establish or disallow any particular incident without a vast appendix of explanations and qualifications. It is of the nature of similar aphorisms, such as "The King can do no wrong," "Every Englishman's house is his castle," &c., the practical application of which on the part of persons not learned in the law is apt to lead to another wise saw, touching those who are their own lawyers, being quoted. But after all the question of the naked truth of the principle thus epigrammatically worded is of very slight interest to the actual discussion, for it is or is not valuable as a special and not as a general rule, and just according as it can be brought forward to establish or to disprove any specific observance. In this connection it is supported on two bases of argument, one of them relying upon the fact of the continuity of the English Church before and after the Reformation, and the other appealing to positive enactment.

The contrary view has been put forward in the most logical and authoritative shape in the Report of the Judicial Committee in the case of Martin v. Mackonochie, delivered in December 1868, which is known to have been written by Lord Cairns, in a passage dealing with Mr. Mackonochie's position at the Prayer of Consecration:

" This being, in their lordships' opinion, the proper construction of the rubric, it is clear that the respondent, by the posture or change of posture which he has adopted during the prayer, has violated the rubric, and committed an offence within the meaning of the 13 and 14 Car. II. cap. 4, sects. 2, 17, 24, taken in connection with 1 Eliz. cap. 2, and punishable by admonition under sect. 23 of the latter statute.

" It was contended on behalf of the respondent, that the act complained of was one of those minute details which could not be taken to be covered by the provisions of the rubric; that the rubric could not be considered as exhaustive in its directions, for no order could be shown in it requiring the celebrating minister to kneel while himself receiving the bread and wine; and that there was no charge or evidence against the respondent, that in kneeling after the consecration any adoration of the Sacrament was intended.

" Their lordships are of opinion, that it is not open to a minister of the Church, or even to their lordships in advising Her Majesty as the highest Ecclesiastical Tribunal of Appeal, to draw a distinction, in acts which are a departure from or violation of the rubric, between those which are important and those which appear to be trivial. The object of a Statute of Uniformity is, as its preamble expresses, to produce 'an universal agreement in the public worship of Almighty God,' an object which would be wholly frustrated if each minister, on his own view of the relative importance of the details of the service, were to be at liberty to omit, to add to, or to alter any of those details. The rule upon this subject has been already laid down by the Judicial Committee in Westerton v. Liddell, and their lordships are disposed entirely to adhere to it. 'In the performance of the services, rites, and ceremonies ordered by the Prayer Book, the directions contained in it must be strictly observed —no omission and no addition can be permitted.'"

A reaffirmation of this principle as to ceremonial, coupled with the assertion of a contrary one in reference to doctrine, is contained in the judgment in Sheppard v. Bennett, delivered in 1872:

"In the case of Westerton v. Liddell, and again in Martin v. Mackonochie, their lordships say, 'In the performance of the services, rites, and ceremonies ordered by the Prayer Book, the directions contained in it must be strictly observed; no omission and no addition can be allowed.' If the Minister be allowed to introduce at his own will variations in the rites and ceremonies that seem to him to interpret the doctrine of the service in a particular direction, the service ceases to be what it was meant to be, common ground on which all church people may meet, though they differ about some doctrines. But the Church of England has wisely left a certain latitude of opinion in matters of belief, and has not insisted on a rigorous uniformity of thought which might reduce her communion to a narrow compass."

It might be asked why the restrictions imposed on ceremonial ought not to be extended to doctrine, or the indulgence which is given to doctrine should not also include ceremonial, but I have no wish to press the question, and only desire very briefly to examine the rule as to the use of the Prayer Book which the Judicial Committee in the Mackonochie case borrowed from the judgment in the Liddell v. Westerton case, and which has been for the third time affirmed in the Bennett judgment. The test I shall put it to is the very simple and practical one of how far it is possible to work the Prayer Book under it, without the same kind of appendix of explanations and qualifications, for which I have contended are indispensable to make the maxim " omission is not prohibition " more than a dogma of the schools. I believe that the result of the con-

CHAP. II.   HOW PRAYER BOOK TO BE CARRIED ON?   51

siderations which I shall have to advance will be to show that both views are true in one sense and untrue in another. *Nemo tenetur ad impossibile* is the aphorism which I personally venture to contribute. The Duke of Wellington's question, "How is the King's Government to be carried on?" has passed into a proverb, and in its spirit I now ask, "How is the Church's Prayer Book to be carried on," if either the Privy Council or the ritualistic principle is to be mercilessly enforced? We are told that "no omission and no addition can be permitted." There is not much technical difficulty in working this principle as far as the prohibition of any omission goes; although the provisions of the Act of Uniformity Amendment Act, which passed three years after the delivery of this judgment, show that the burden which it would have placed upon the worship of the Church was not acceptable to Parliament, or to the Convocation on whose action that Act was based. But when we come to apply "no addition can be permitted" to "the provisions of the rubrics," difficulties begin to come into prominence. I take up the Morning Service, and I consult the rubrics to see where the Priest or Minister (as the officiator is variously called) is to stand, and what he and the congregation are respectively to do to carry it on. I am, I believe, helped through by the preliminary directions and the current rubrics as far as the answer, which occurs very early in the service, "The Lord's Name be praised," but there I read, in reference to the Venite, "Then shall be said or sung this Psalm following; except," &c. (the exceptions carrying on my difficulty), and in the very next rubric, "then shall follow the Psalms in order as they are appointed," &c. I refer back to the preliminary matter for further help, and I only find directions for the Psalms "to be read through once every month." I wish accordingly to have the Venite and the daily Psalms " said," " sung," or " read," as it may be, and I look to my rubric, to which I am not permitted to make any addition, for the way in which it is to be done. It is clear that Psalms cannot sing them-

E 2

selves. The persons whom the Prayer Book alone has recognised are the "minister" or "priest," and the "people." Further on we read of "minister, clerks, and people," and we are told of "quires and places where they sing." Under risk of this gloss being an "addition," and therefore unlawful, we may assume that the reference to persons called clerks, and to the "quires and places where they sing," inferentially lets in a plurality of ministers (the whole Prayer Book being otherwise cast in the singular number, and, therefore, seeming to condemn the services of more than one minister as being an "addition"), and authorises the presence of men who are specially entrusted with the musical part of the service, whether surpliced or not. On this assumption then a defence may be raised for the so-called Cathedral Service, which would otherwise appear to be an "addition" under the terms of the Privy Council. But we are still as far off as ever from the answer to the question—Who is to "read," or "say," or "sing" the Psalms? Is it the "priest," or "minister," or the "clerks," or the "people," any or all? Is it to be done in unison or alternatively, if by all, or, if only by the minister, then is he to read them right through like a lesson? On all these alternatives the rubric is silent; and surely then the adoption of any one of them can hardly be cleared of the charge of being an "addition," and, therefore, not "permitted." It would almost seem that in despair of being able to reach a way of reading the Psalms which would literally fulfil this direction, the persons responsible for the service would have to dispense with them; but if they did so, they would be guilty of an equally illegal "omission." The directions for reading the lessons are fairly explicit, but perplexities, similar to those which I have pointed out, attend the recitation of the Canticles; while the difficulty is not lessened by a specific direction being at length found when we reach the Creed, which is to be "sung or said" "by the minister and people." In this rubric there is no room either for omission or addition, but in contrast to it the

Psalms, as I have shown, are simply unmanageable, unless the order forbidding omission or addition to the rubric is itself read with the necessary omissions and additions. It is far from my purpose to frame an indictment of carelessness against the rubrics, but I must point out that difficulties, of a nature akin to those which I have already rehearsed, would attend many ordinary forms of carrying through the Communion Service if this principle of the Judicial Committee were pressed to its logical extent.

There is actually not the slightest sanction in the rubric for the custom, inherited by the reformed from the unreformed Church, of the Epistle and Gospel being read by ministers distinct from the principal minister or celebrant, and yet this practice is referred to by the Advertisements of the 7th of Elizabeth, and again in the twenty-fourth Canon (which mentions those Advertisements), in the use of the names "gospeller" and "epistler" (both of them vernacular, pre-reformational designations). Surely the Lords of the Council must, in this case, acknowledge that the divines of Elizabeth's and James's reigns admitted that "omission was not prohibition"? Again, there is absolutely no order in rubric, canon, or advertisement, for the habitual practice of reading the Epistle to the south, and the Gospel to the north, of the Lord's Table. It is simply the tradition of an old practice omitted to be sanctioned, but not prohibited to be used. In any case, the Epistle and the Gospel must be read at some spot, and I do not quite see how the selection of that spot can be construed not to be an addition to the rubric, and how, accordingly, the portions of Scripture can be read at all if all addition is unlawful, or passed over if all omission is equally to be prohibited.

I have been drawing my illustrations of the position that omission cannot always be taken as prohibition from our actual Prayer Book, but there is another which is so pregnant, if not conclusive, in the Prayer Book as it stood between 1552 and 1662, that I must adduce it. During all that period the Prayer of Consecration stood with no " manual acts "directed in it—with nothing to show that during the Prayer of Consecration the celebrant had to lay his hand on the bread or the cup—yet all know that during this period the celebrant habitually did so, or, according to all ecclesiastical theory, there would have been no consecration. When it is recollected that the space of time so singled out was that of Andrewes, Overall, Laud, Wren, Thorndike, Cosin, the absurdity of supposing that the manual acts were in abeyance would be egregious; yet every priest during these hundred and ten years who performed those manual acts would undoubtedly have been guilty of one of those additions, which, by the stern ruling of the judgment in Martin v. Mackonochie, would not have been permitted, and would, therefore, subject him to severe penalties.

I venture, accordingly, to think, with great respect for the Privy Council, that there are "additions" to the rubric which can hardly be held not to be permitted; for, as we have seen, the rigid enforcement of this rule would actually bring the service to a dead-lock. It follows necessarily that all omissions are not, as such, prohibitions. It does not, however, follow that everything which has not been directly prohibited must, therefore, be allowed; a form of putting the plea which I must honestly say appears to me to be needful, in order to justify certain ultra-ritualistic practices.

Those who have argued on the ultra side appear to have forgotten that the analogy of common and of statute law is applicable to the ceremonial law of the Church of England. Those who are conversant in making or administering law know in how many ways the common law has been altered, confirmed, expanded, or explained, by positive statute; and they also know how legislation, when it takes in hand a principle of the common law, makes it its own, and by specifically enacting, though in its sense, evacuates it, so to speak, as common law, and leaves it statute law instead. The reason of this is the continuity of the English State. It is because our living

English constitution is continuous with the English constitution of the days when that common law was the all-important legal system, and statute law did not exist, or was only creeping into importance, that Parliament dares handle that common law according to its discretion. It is just so, *mutatis mutandis*, with the Church. The continuity of the Church is a gage that it shall not abandon or tamper with any portion of the Faith once delivered to the saints, or with any needful element of apostolic discipline. Besides, the habitual practice of our Ecclesiastical Courts shows the authority which mediæval canons and constitutions still carry. Had the scheme of a recast of them, provided for in the Act of Submission, ever been effected, the case would have been different, but this, as is well known, fell through. It is also in ceremonial matters a presumption that omission is not prohibition. But inasmuch as the ceremonial, which lies beyond the forms which we know that Our Lord Himself prescribed is of ecclesiastical appointment, and as the Church has never reduced it to authoritative heads like its Belief, the degree of probability in either case is very different. We have on one side that vast body of ceremonious prescriptions which belonged to the Church at the time of its Reformation, and which, in pursuance of my analogy, I venture to term its common law, although, in truth, the larger portion of it was very precise, not to say minute and artificial, legislation; and on the other, that body of enactments which Church and State have jointly imposed upon the Church of England since the Reformation, and which I call its statute law. I have given reasons for my belief that this statute law cannot be applied to the conduct of divine service without some help from the traditionary common law. But having established the concession, I must limit it. It is idle to deny (whether the acknowledgment is or is not palatable) that, while the modern English Prayer Book has been formed on the Missal, Breviary, Manual, and Pontifical, of our pre-reformational Church, the alterations, and in particular the abbreviations, were of the most wholesale description. The whole spirit of worship was intentionally changed from an exuberant and complicated luxuriance, to a grave, if not austere, simplicity. The change may have been carried too far, or not far enough; it certainly was carried very far, and it stands out in all our actual services as a dominant characteristic. Here, at last, we have reached a guiding principle. It is one which requires learning, tact, and, above all, common sense, in its application. But, like others which I have already passed in review, it cannot be trusted to work itself. Nevertheless, it is a valuable contribution towards the settlement of a most delicate, difficult, and complicated, controversy. I shall, in handling the details in which I must later on interest my readers, have to show how I apply it. It is enough now to say that I believe that a main cause of the mistakes which ritualists have committed is, that they have forgotten how far our reformed service-books intentionally differ in the spirit, as well as in the text, of their ceremonial from the earlier rituals. The consequence of this forgetfulness has been, while advancing the dogma that omission is not prohibition, they have occasionally forgotten how much there is which, by having been omitted in connection with that which has not only been omitted but also prohibited, has thereby inferentially and indirectly, but not less certainly, been made partaker of the same prohibition. Many of the most startling incidents of the ultra-ritualistic rendering of the Communion Service are, in truth, *purpurei panni*, cut out of a much more gorgeous, lengthy, and complicated whole, and glued on to what is in itself a short and simple service, and which, therefore, hang on it with very indifferent grace or appropriateness. The idea, for instance, which finds its adherents, of reproducing the whole *coup d'œil* of the Sarum Mass, may, apart from all considerations of wisdom and legality, be in itself an interesting artistic and archæological experiment; but if it is to be fastened on to the words and sequence of our actual Communion Service, the result must be a spectacular failure, on which a great deal which it is hard to risk will have been staked. The claim must be regarded from a more serious point of view. Let us assume that the construction of the statutable title-deeds of the Church, on a more critical analysis than they have been subjected to for three hundred years, should yield the astounding result that the actual Church of England was really, in virtue of its own reformed formularies, the lawful trustee and promoter of almost all the exuberant ritual, which led to the recoil of the Reformation. After this assumption had been made, it would still be difficult to deny that the putting in use of these long-forgotten and really (to use the word inoffensively) revolutionary faculties, must, by all the laws of comity which govern human actions, be reserved as the special office of the Church in its corporate character, or at least of its responsible rulers. Long disuse may not, in effect, have repealed those dormant powers (although, under the most favourable construction their continuous existence can hardly be put higher than an inference), but it cannot be within the competence of any self-appointed person, whose power and responsibility are limited by some single parish, to make himself the interpreter in action of a system the continuance of which had been a sealed book to all our greatest divines of every party, ever since the Church of England had resettled itself upon its reformational basis. So long as the believer in such latent powers confines himself to his pen or his voice, and strives to persuade his brethren to claim their revival by regular means, he is clearly within his own rights. When he solves the tangled question for himself, by giving active vitality to general principles of a perfectly novel description, which have been asserted without having been proven or formally revindicated, he merges the sympathy due to the ingenious advocate of novel deductions in the aversion commonly felt for a gratuitous innovator.

In the meanwhile I have been summing up against an

extreme application of a maxim containing in itself the abstract assertion of a generally received truth before coming to close quarters with the demonstration which is chiefly relied on to establish the claims of ultra-ritualism. It is no doubt conceivable that the evidence may be so definite, and the argument so cogent, as to establish those claims in theory, although, for the reasons which I have just been urging, I do not think the justification exists for putting them in practice at the behests of the private judgment and personal taste of any incumbent. I desire to follow out the enquiry with perfect impartiality. After all abatements, the direction "and the chancels shall remain as they have done in times past" is a strong declaration of ritual continuity. Those who hold the most pronounced opinions as to the permission of what is termed advanced ritual, couple with it the later prescription, which I must repeat.

"And here it is to be noted that such ornaments of the church and of the ministers thereof, at all times of their ministrations, shall be retained, and be in use, as were in this Church of England, by the authority of Parliament in the second year of the reign of King Edward the Sixth."

The history of this direction, which comes, although in a slightly different form, from the Prayer Book of Elizabeth, is so briefly and clearly given in the Liddell *v.* Westerton judgment that I shall borrow the passage. It will be recollected that this judgment was the unanimous decision, in the year 1857, of one of the strongest courts which ever sat as a Judicial Committee comprising Mr. Pemberton Leigh (afterwards Lord Kingsdown, who drew it), Lord Chancellor Cranworth, Lord Wensleydale, Sir John Patteson, and Sir W. H. Maule, with not only Archbishop Sumner, but the present Archbishop of Canterbury, then Bishop of London, as assenting assessors.

"If reference be now made to the alterations in these matters introduced by the Second Prayer Book of Edward VI. and the subsequent Rubric to the Prayer Book of Elizabeth, the meaning will be sufficiently clear. The Second Prayer Book forbids the use of different vestments by the priest in the Performance of the different services, and enjoins the use of a surplice only; and does not expressly mention the paten, chalice, and corporas. After the overthrow of Protestantism by Queen Mary, and its restoration on the accession of Queen Elizabeth, a great controversy arose between the more violent and the more moderate reformers as to the Church service which should be re-established, whether it should be according to the first or according to the Second Prayer Book of Edward VI. The Queen was in favour of the First, but she was obliged to give way, and a compromise was made, by which the services were to be in conformity with the Second Prayer Book, with certain alterations, but the ornaments of the church, whether those worn or those otherwise used by the minister, were to be according to the First Prayer Book. In conformity with this arrangement, the Act 1 Eliz. cap. 2, was passed, by which the use of the Second Prayer Book was established, but it was provided 'that such ornaments of the church and of the ministers thereof shall be retained and be in use, as was in this Church of England by authority of Parliament in the second year of the reign of King Edward VI. until other orders shall be therein taken by the authority of the Queen's Majesty, with such advice as therein mentioned.'

"The Rubric to the new Prayer Book, framed to express the meaning of this proviso, is in these words:—'And here is to be noted that the minister, at the time of the Communion, and at all other times of his ministration, shall use such ornaments in the church as were in use by authority of Parliament in the second year of the reign of King Edward VI., according to the Act of Parliament set in the beginning of this book.' Here the term 'ornaments' is used as covering both the vestments of the ministers and the several articles used in the services; it is confined to such things as in the performance of the services the minister was to use. It will be observed that this Rubric does not adopt precisely the language of the statute, but expresses the same thing in other words. The statute says, 'such ornaments of the church and of the ministers, shall be retained and be in use;' the Rubric, 'that the minister shall use such ornaments in the church.'

"The Rubric to the Prayer Book of January 1, 1604, adopts the language of the Rubric of Elizabeth. The Rubric to the present Prayer Book adopts the language of the statute of Elizabeth; but they all obviously mean the same thing, that the same dresses and the same utensils or articles which were used under the First Prayer Book of Edward VI. may still be used. None of them, therefore, can have any reference to articles not used in the services, but set up in churches as ornaments, in the sense of decorations.

"It was urged at the bar that the present Rubric, which refers to the second year of Edward VI., cannot mean ornaments mentioned in the First Prayer Book, because, as it is said, that Act was probably not passed, and the Prayer Book was certainly not in use till after the expiration of the second year of Edward VI., and that, therefore, the words 'by authority of Parliament' must mean by virtue of Canons or Royal injunctions having the authority of Parliament made at an earlier period. There seems no reason to doubt that the Act in question received the royal assent in the second year of Edward VI. It concerned a matter of great urgency, which had long been under consideration, and was the first Act of the Session; it passed through one House of Parliament on January 15, 1549, N.S.; and the other on the 21st of the same month; and the second year of the reign of Edward VI. did not expire till January 28. In the Act of the 5th and 6th Edward VI. c. i. sec. 5, it is expressly referred to as the Act 'made in the second year of the King's Majesty's reign.' Upon this point, therefore, no difficulty can arise. It is very true that the new Prayer Book could not come into use until after the expiration of that year, because time must be allowed for printing and distributing the books; but its use and the injunctions contained in it were established by authority of Parliament in the second year of Edward VI., and this is the plain meaning of the Rubric."

By this quotation it appears that the vestments so called are in the opinion of the judges sanctioned by the "ornaments rubric." But they are not in question now. The argument of those who will not admit that "the authority of Parliament" implies the Act of Uniformity of Edward VI., which legalised the first Prayer Book of 1549, may be shortly summed up. Some have been doubtful on that which the judgment which I have just quoted takes for granted, namely, that the Act received the royal assent in the second and not the third year of Edward, but it is certain that it did not become operative in the use of the new book till "the Feast of Pentecost next coming" (June 9, 1549). Now this day fell incontestably in the third year of the reign, so they argue that the things which became law "by the authority of Parliament" on a particular day in the third year of Edward's reign cannot be the things which are referred to as in the Church of England by the authority of Parliament in the second year. It follows, therefore, in their opinion, that the rubric refers back to such ornaments as the Church of England possessed and used by the authority of Parliament variously signified, anterior to the promulgation of her first reformed Prayer Book, that is in her unreformed days. I am unable to accept this argument from two lines of reasoning:—First, Those who employ it hardly seem to appreciate in its fulness the very formal system by which from the origin of Parliamentary legislation the numeration of the sessions of Parliament, and in connection with those sessions of the various Acts passed during them, was so regulated as on the one hand to indicate the regnal year of the sovereign, and on the other to keep alive the unity (or to use a clumsy modern word the "solidarity") of the session itself. As long as there was a Scotch Parliament it numbered its statutes by the year of Our Lord; England never did so. The session, if it falls within a single regnal year of the sovereign, is the session of such a year of such a sovereign, and the different Acts which are passed during its continuance are successively numbered as "chapters" from "one" onwards, and are the Acts of that session so designated. But if the session runs over into another regnal year, it is then known as the session of such and such years of such a sovereign, while the consecutive numeration of the Acts or chapters runs, as before, continuously throughout the session. Supposing the rubric had spoken not of "the authority of Parliament" in the second year of Edward VI., but of "an Act" or "a statute" of the same year, there would, I believe, have been no difficulty, although the rubric would, like the statute of Elizabeth on which it is founded, have stood convicted of a somewhat inaccurate and incomplete phraseology. The lawyer or the judge who was sent to find out what were the statutes of "the second year of Edward VI.," namely, of that session of Parliament which by immemorial usage survived in its enactments under that appellation, would discover that there was no session, properly speaking, of "the second year of Edward VI." only, but that there was a session of "the second and third of Edward VI." He would then say, "I am landed either in a nonentity or in a description incomplete and inaccurate indeed, but yet sufficiently definite to furnish the desired identification without the possibility of any ambiguity. The only session of Parliament from first to last which ever can be quoted as 'the second year of Edward VI.' is one which was 'the second of Edward VI.' and something more besides, namely, the session of 'the second and third of Edward VI.,' being the only session of Parliament which ever occurred in that year, although it ran into another one. To that session, therefore, I will go." The man who reasoned in that way would find that there was a statute of that very Parliament which contained precisely the matter which he was led to expect; this of course would conclude the whole question in his judgment. But, as we know, the expression in the rubric is not "by statute in the second year of Edward VI.," but "by the authority of Parliament in the second year of Edward VI." Does this variation of phraseology so alter the value of the other words as to let in the interpretation which implies that the things legalised are those which were not enacted during that session? On this head I must speak somewhat decisively from a personal acquaintance with Parliamentary phraseology. I cannot conceive the use of the expression "by the authority of Parliament" in connection with the mention of a special session, except as a direct reference to the special statutes of that session. Those who read the words differently seem to agglutinate "by the authority of Parliament" ("authority" implying specific statutes, and "Parliament" the specific Parliament or session at a time when Parliaments usually lasted for only a single session) to "were in." The truth is that "in the second year of Edward VI." should be agglutinated to "by the authority of Parliament," and might be expanded as "by the authority of *the* Parliament *holden* in the second year of Edward VI." These are my reasons for the sense which I affix to the ornaments rubric drawn from its internal construction. If we look at the circumstances under which it was promulged, the difficulties environing any other interpretation are immeasurably increased. Bishop Cosin, indeed, in his Additional Notes to the Prayer Book, published in Nicholls's edition of 1710, included the provisions of the Act of Submission of the 25th of Henry VIII. among the things covered by the ornaments rubric previously to its last revision. The practical difference, after all, is only verbal, but I conceive that I am more accurate. The Act of Uniformity, as I believe, while it did not confirm the statute of Henry, did not affect it. The Act of Henry VIII. was then law, besides and in addition to that of Elizabeth, but not, as Bishop Cosin, writing in the reign of Charles I., would seem to imply in virtue of it. Nor is it at present valid, in virtue of the Act of Uniformity of Charles II. All of pre-reformational date, which the Church of England still possesses and can use under the Act of Submission, (considering how thoroughly its scheme of a reformation of canons fell through), she claims in virtue of that Act in itself, and not from any merely inferential references to it in any subsequent statutes.

The actual ornaments rubric, as we have it, grew out of prescriptions very similar in their practical results, though with a variation of wording, found both in a statute and in a rubric dating from the commencement of Elizabeth's reign of which the statute points to a possible subsequent modification. The balance of parties in the Reformed Church of England at that period between the more national or higher Churchmen, and the lower Churchmen who derived their inspirations from Zurich or

Geneva, was such, and the public exasperation at the cruelties with which Mary's reign had closed was so great, that Elizabeth was compelled, contrary to her own predilections, to accept the Prayer Book of 1552 as the basis of the settlement, with only some modifications referring back to the book of 1549. Is it conceivable that one of the chief of these modifications should have been so worded as to let in not the ornaments prescribed in 1549—which were few and simple compared with the gorgeous exuberance of the earlier Church, although somewhat more ornate than those of 1552—but actually that very gorgeous exuberance with a hardly more than nominal limitation? Would Elizabeth's councillors and prelates have dared such an experiment? Would that active and dreaded Low Church party, which had its mouthpiece in the episcopate and its wire-pullers in Switzerland, out of the reach of Elizabeth's regal authority, have kept silence at such an aggression? We know that they did complain very loudly of the ceremonial which was actually let in, but their complaints refer to specific ornaments in congruity with the ritual of 1549. They certainly would not have spoken out upon these, and kept silence at the much wider general permission had they suspected its existence. To come down a century, would the Convocation and the Parliament which brought back the Church in 1662 after the Savoy Conference, and in presence of a defeated but still powerful Puritanism, which retained Bayley and Prynne for its mouthpieces, have adventured so audacious a policy when they restored the ornaments rubric with a slightly varied phraseology? In his elaborate notes on the Prayer Book Bishop Cosin, the great leader of the decided Church party at this crisis, had explained "the authority of Parliament" as meaning the Act of Uniformity of Edward VI., and as retaining accordingly the ornaments mentioned in the First Prayer Book. To be sure, as I have pointed out, he also includes under this reference to the authority of Parliament the Act of Submission, which exists on its own independent Parliamentary authority; but this does not weaken the value of his evidence as to what he believed to be the ornaments which are at present specifically permitted. Can we suppose that Cosin, who had thus deliberately expressed his conviction upon the meaning of certain prescriptions, when they were still to all appearance firmly rooted in the Statute Book, would have, after their temporary overthrow, and at a time when he found himself, as concerned in their restoration, in a position of the highest trust in Church and State, have so decidedly shifted his ground and taken up a position which, even before the advent of the Commonwealth, he had felt to be untenable? After all, however, the meaning of these specific words in the ornaments rubric has really nothing to do with the general question of the value of the principle of omission not being prohibition. In whatever sense they may be taken, they remove a certain category of ornaments from the domain of the common to that of the statute law of the English Church. In one case an indefinite list of ornaments would be removed, and in the other a limited one. General principles in either case would still regulate all ceremonial which was not included under the ornaments rubric.

I cannot better sum up the discussion than by quoting some sentences from a pamphlet which Sir John Taylor Coleridge published in 1871, after an interpretation had been put upon the ornaments rubric by the Privy Council, in the case of Hebbert v. Purchas, contrary to that which was affixed to it by the then members of the same Court, in the case of Liddell v. Westerton:

"Now Mr. Purchas has been tried before the Committee for offences alleged to have been committed against the provisions of the 'Act of Uniformity': of this Act the Common Prayer Book is part and parcel. As to the vestments, his conduct was alleged to be in derogation of the Rubric as to the ornaments of the Church and the ministers thereof, which ordains that such shall be retained and be in use as were in this Church of England by the authority of Parliament in the second year of the reign of King Edward VI.

"The Act of Uniformity is to be construed by the same rules

exactly as any Act passed in the last Session of Parliament. The clause in question (by which I mean the Rubric in question) is perfectly unambiguous in language, free from all difficulty as to construction; it therefore lets in no argument as to intention other than that which the words themselves import. There might be a seeming difficulty in *fact*, because it might not be known what vestments were in use by authority of Parliament in the second year of the reign of King Edward VI.; but this difficulty has been removed. It is conceded in the Report that the vestments, the use of which is now condemned, were in use by authority of Parliament in that year. Having that fact, you are bound to construe the Rubric as if those vestments were specifically named in it, instead of being only referred to. If an Act should be passed to-morrow that the uniform of the guards should henceforth be such as was ordered for them by authority, and used by them in the 1st Geo. I., you would first ascertain what that uniform was; and having ascertained it, you would not enquire into the changes which may have been made, many or few, with or without lawful authority, between the 1st Geo. I. and the passing of the new Act? All these, that Act, specifying the earlier date, would have made wholly immaterial. It would have seemed strange, I suppose, if a commanding officer, disobeying the statute, had said in his defence— 'There have been many changes since the reign of Geo. I.; and as to 'retaining' we put a gloss on that, and thought it might mean only retaining to the Queen's use; so we have put the uniforms safely in store.' But I think it would have seemed more strange to punish and insult him severely if he had obeyed the law and put no gloss on plain words.

"This case stands on the same principle. The Rubric indeed seems to me to imply with some clearness that in the long interval between Ed. VI. and the 14th Ch. II. there had been many changes, but it does not stay to specify them, or distinguish between what was mere evasion and what was lawful: it quietly passes them all by, and goes back to the legalised usage of the second year of Ed. VI. What had prevailed since, whether by an archbishop's gloss, by commissions or even statutes, whether in short, legal or illegal, it makes quite immaterial."

The learned writer might have enlarged his illustration by assuming that, although the supposititious session which he calls the 1st of George I., was really the 1st and 2nd of that King, yet, as I have shown, the choice in that case must have been between a nonentity and a description not quite accurate or complete, but quite sufficient for identification. With this addition the analogy would have been absolute.

I now come to the direct investigation of the meaning of the direction that the chancels shall remain as in times past. This obviously refers, in the first place, to the furniture of the chancel, and only to the worship so far as it can be inferred from that furniture. I have already shown, in my recapitulation of uncontroversial advance, that all parties in the Church now accept a chancel distinct from the nave, especially devoted to the performance of divine worship, frequently seated with stalls or longitudinal seats for the use of the clergy and the choir, and terminating in a sanctuary, divided off for the Lord's Table and the celebration of the Holy Communion. These arrangements are the general fulfilment of the direction in question, but it has been ruled to legalise more. In the remainder of this chapter I shall only consider the furniture of the chancel proper, and leave the ornaments of the sanctuary which equally come under this rubric for subsequent consideration.

I had doubted whether or not, at all events since the Liddell *v.* Westerton judgment, to include among the uncontentious furniture of the Church, the "one partition" in our churches "for local distinction between the clergy and the rest," as the judicious Hooker felicitously describes it which previously to Hooker's writing Archbishop Parker had in his visitation articles ordered to be kept, and to which Cosin specifically refers in the Notes to which I have already called attention; as, however, this has formed the subject of one lawsuit in modern times, I preferred, on the whole, to mention it in this place. I suppose no better example of a moderate High Churchman of the old, thoroughly English, anti-Roman school, could be found than Bishop Beveridge, who was offered the bishopric from which Bishop Ken was deposed, and who accepted one from the Government of Queen Anne, when other High Churchmen, as thoroughly anti-Roman as he, but with stiffer opinions on some points, had retired from the Established Church and formed the Nonjuring Secession. Beveridge had, in 1681, to preach the sermon at the consecration of his parish church of St. Peter's, Cornhill, rebuilt by Wren after the Great Fire, and which is still in existence, and in the course of his discourse vindicated the propriety of the chancel screen for which St. Peter's was distinguished, in a passage which I may as well quote, as I adopt its statements in full:

"The Sacrament of the Lord's Supper being the highest mystery in all our religion, as representing the death of the SON OF GOD to us, hence that place where this Sacrament is administered was always made and reputed the highest place in the church: and therefore, also, it was wont to be separated from the rest of the church by a screen or partition of network, in Latin *cancelli*, and that so generally, that from thence the place itself is called the chancel. That this was anciently observed in the building of all considerable churches within a few centuries after the Apostles themselves, even in the days of Constantine the Great, as well as in all ages since, I could easily demonstrate from the records of those times. But having purposely waived antiquity hitherto, I am loth to trouble you with it now: but I mention it at present only, because some perhaps may wonder why this should be observed in our church rather than in all the other Churches which have lately been built in this city; whereas they should rather wonder why it was not observed in all others as well as this. For, besides our obligations to conform, as much as may be, to the practice of the universal Church, and to avoid novelty and singularity in all things relating to the worship of God, it cannot easily be imagined that the Catholic Church, in all ages and places, for thirteen or fourteen hundred years together, should observe such a custom as this, except there were great reasons for it.

"What they were it is not necessary for us to enquire now. It may be sufficient to observe at present, that the chancel in our

Christian churches was always looked upon as answerable to the Holy of Holies in the Temple; which, you know, was separated from the sanctuary or body of the temple by the command of God Himself; and that this place being appropriated to the Sacrament of the Lord's Supper, it ought to be contrived as may be most convenient for those who are to partake of that blessed ordinance."

Such screens were an habitual feature in our mediæval churches, in which, however, they were frequently used in combination with other ecclesiastical fittings with which they were not necessarily united. In the primitive basilica, as still in that of St. Clement at Rome, the *chorus cantorum* was flanked by two low stone pulpits (in the singular *ambo*, and plural *ambones*), the lesser one to the south, for the Epistle, and the larger and richer one to the north, for the Gospel. In process of time these two ambones were, in the mediæval Church, fused into one long transverse gallery, which in parish churches generally filled up the chancel arch, but in the large cathedrals, abbeys, and collegiate churches, was placed wherever the choir ended, which (as in the case of Westminster Abbey) was frequently some way down that part of the building which architecturally belonged to the nave. This gallery was destined for the singing at the High Mass, sometimes of the Epistle, and generally of the Gospel, with those accompanying canticles termed "Tract" or "Sequence," with which, in the pre-reformational uses, it was embellished; the Epistle being frequently said in a less conspicuous way within the choir, in token of its subordination to the Gospel. On the Continent this gallery was commonly termed the "Jube," from the first word of "Jube, Domne, benedicere" ("Bid, Sir, a blessing"), the set phrase in which the deacon invited the priest to bless the people from this elevation; but in England it was called the rood-loft, in reference to yet an independent use to which it was also put. There was a practice of the Western Church, since the earliest mediæval days, of setting up or suspending a large crucifix somewhere in the centre of the church, and as nearly as possible between the nave and chancel, which, in later times, was often accompanied by the figures of St. Mary and St. John, so as to produce a Crucifixion scene. Rood, I need hardly say, is old English for crucifix. The jube was of course handy to hold this crucifix, and the custom of placing it there became so common as to give to it its current English name of rood-loft, as well as that of rood-screen to the chancel partition, for in smaller churches, where there was no loft, the rood would stand upon the screen. Still there was no necessary connection between rood, jube, and screen. Abroad, where the taste for open spaces during the three last centuries has swept away so many screens, or prevented their erection in new churches, the rood is often suspended from the roof, or stands in mid-air upon a simple beam, while the reasons which Hooker and Beveridge allege for the retention of the partition have nothing to do with the place where, or the pomp with which, the Gospel is read. Accordingly, in the orders of the third year of Elizabeth, as much stress is laid upon preserving the screens as upon demolishing the lofts.

"It is thus decreed and ordained that the rood-lofts, as yet being at this day aforesaid, untransposed, shall be so altered that the upper part of the same with the soller be quite taken down, unto the upper parts of the vautes, and beam running in length over the said vautes, by putting some convenient crest upon the said beam towards the church, with leaving the situation of the seats (as well in the quire as in the church) as heretofore hath been used.

"Provided yet, that when any parish, of their own costs and charges by common consent, will pull down the whole frame, and re-edifying again the same in joiner's work (as in divers churches within the City of London doth appear), that they may do as they think agreeable, so it be to the height of the upper beam aforesaid.

"Provided also, that where in any parish church the said rood-lofts be already transposed, so that there remain a comely partition between the chancel and the church, that no alteration be otherwise attempted in them, but be suffered in quiet. And where no partition is standing, there to be one appointed."

Various chancel screens were accordingly constructed during the seventeenth century, among which, in addition to that at St. Peter's, Cornhill, I will only notice that which was put up in Wimborne Minster in James I.'s reign, and unfortunately taken away during a restoration of a few years ago, the one in St. John's Church, Leeds, which was erected in 1634, when the church itself was built, that in Brancepeth, Durham, made by Bishop Cosin, and the one at Ingestre Church, Staffordshire, which, together with the whole building, belongs to the reign of Charles II. Chancel screens, of course, fell into desuetude during the long Georgian torpor, and, as might have been supposed, they came in again with the Church revival. One was put up in the church of St. Barnabas, Pimlico, consecrated in June 1850, and was so far unlike earlier post-reformational screens that it bore a cross. This feature was undoubtedly a novelty, but it seemed to be one which was justified by the nature of things, and was in strict correspondence with the spirit of the 30th Canon, which defends the use of the cross in our Church in reference to the employment of the sign of the cross in the Baptismal Service. This cross bore the same analogy to the rood of the older Church that the Prayer Book does to the older services. Anyhow, Bishop Blomfield consecrated St. Barnabas' Church with its screen and cross. In a few months, as I have reminded a younger generation, a riot raged round the church, and in due time Mr. Westerton took the law of St. Paul's, Knightsbridge, and Mr. Beal of St. Barnabas'; the two suits being heard together, as they were in many respects identical, and in all congruous. Dr. Lushington, Chancellor of London, before whom they were in the first instance heard, sanctioned the screen at St. Barnabas', but condemned the cross. So did Sir John Dodson, the Dean of Arches. The Judicial Committee (composed as I have already pointed out) took a different view in March 1857, and, after a very elaborate discussion upon the use of the cross in our Reformed Church, concluded:

"Upon the whole, their Lordships, after the most anxious consideration, have come to the conclusion that crosses, as distinguished from crucifixes, have been in use, as ornaments of churches, from the earliest periods of Christianity; that when used as mere emblems of Christian faith, and not as objects of superstitious reverence, they may still lawfully be erected as architectural decorations of churches; that the wooden cross erected on the chancel screen of St. Barnabas is to be considered as a mere architectural ornament; and that as to this article, they must advise Her Majesty to reverse the judgment complained of. Their Lordships hope and believe that the laws in force respecting the consecration of any building for a church, and which forbid any subsequent alteration without a faculty from the Ordinary, will be sufficient to prevent any abuse in this respect."

During the seventeen years which have elapsed since this judgment, screens surmounted with crosses have been constructed in various churches, among which I need only mention the cathedrals of Lichfield and Hereford, the one in Ely Cathedral being of an earlier date.

This brings me to the close of the present chapter. I could wander on with artistic or archæological disquisitions upon the details of choir stalls, with their quaint misereres and aerial canopies, but I feel that such discussions are hardly germane to my immediate topic. The various forms which may be given to the great lettern from which God's Holy Word is solemnly proclaimed, may be a subject of proper interest to the man of religious taste, but this also would be an indefensible call upon my reader's patience when there are so many questions of immediate, and, I am sorry to add, controversial, interest still to be considered.

CHAPTER III.

Beveridge calls the Sacrament of the Lord's Supper the highest mystery in our religion — Precise definition of its doctrine not necessary to prove the honour due to its celebration — Distinctive Eucharistic dress — "Address against vestments and eastward position" — Mr. Scott Robertson — Difficult distinction — Surplice obnoxious to Puritans as symbolising sacramental doctrine — Vague assertions of a somewhat rhetorical protest — Voice of formularies speaking for themselves above suspicion — Communion Office speaking for itself on its relative honour compared with other services — Right on its own showing that the celebration should be especially dignified — Burden of proof of contrary on objectors — Inexcusable incaution of ultra-ritualistic language — Use of term Mass — John Evelyn, witness to old High Church view of Sacramental doctrine — Extract from his 'Rational Account of the True Religion' — Old Catholic conference at Bonn — Dr. Howson and Dr. Liddon agree on a statement of Anglican doctrine — Why cannot they agree to differ on the ceremonial showing forth their common doctrine?

I MUST repeat the sentence with which the quotation which I made from Bishop Beveridge in my last chapter commences.

"The Sacrament of the Lord's Supper being the highest mystery in all our religion, as representing the death of the SON OF GOD to us, hence that place where this Sacrament is administered was always made and reputed the highest place in the church."

If this is true of the whole chancel, much more true must it be of that part of it which stands in the closest proximity to the Holy Table of Our Lord, and at which the service of His Holy Communion is immediately performed; and, above all, must it be true of the Holy Table itself. I have now to speak of its construction and of its furniture, of the position and the dresses of the ministers who perform at it their appointed office, and of the various seemly accompaniments which the Church of England permits or enjoins for that sacred occasion. Some of these accidents of the Communion Office have, in connection with "ritualism," become the subject of sharp debate, but I shall be very careful, as far as possible, to regard the matter from a judicial rather than a polemical standing-ground. I shall in particular avoid engaging in the controversy upon the doctrine of the Eucharist as held in the Church of England. My abstention will not be because I do not fully appreciate the importance of this question. The accurate doctrine of the Holy Communion is, I am convinced, of the highest theological moment to our own Church, as it is to all which attach any value to purity of dogma. But the controversy lies beyond the subject of the present argument, in which the only point for consideration is whether or not the Sacrament of the Lord's Supper is, or is not, in the mind of the Church of England a rite of the highest majesty and importance, and as an act of worship one which transcends all other offices of prayer and praise, whether or not it is in Beveridge's words, "the highest mystery in all our religion."

If this premiss can be established, then the conclusion follows that it cannot be contrary to the mind of the Church of England to invest the celebration of that Sacrament with incidents of beauty and solemnity superior to those which she has to bestow upon her other services. Each of these incidents must stand and fall on its own merits, and will have to be separately examined. At present I am merely contending for the general principle. A "distinctive Eucharistic dress," to mention one matter of much present interest, may, or may not, be in itself in accordance with the positive ceremonial law of the existing Church of England, but—if it is not only consonant with the true spirit of that Church that a clergyman when he is reading prayers should wear something more (namely, a surplice) than when he is only teaching his Sunday School, but absolutely and penally enjoined upon him to do so; and if it is, again, as absolutely and penally enjoined upon him on the occasion of the celebration of the Holy Communion to wear the same, failing any other and more distinctive dress—then it cannot well be contrary to the spirit of the same Church that, when he is doing something still higher than merely reading prayers— namely, showing forth The Lord's death till He comes, that then his official garb should be something more stately than that surplice. This more stately dress may be forbidden by positive enactment, but certainly it does not stand condemned from any inconsistency with the spirit of the Church of England, or at all events with the spirit of that school in the Church which has made itself so conspicuously responsible for encouraging scrupulosity of feeling in favour of change of dress for different functions—I mean the one which insists on the black gown being substituted for the surplice when preaching man's sermons succeeds to praying the Church's prayers and reading God's Word.

I have been led thus early to insist upon the question of Eucharistic ceremonial, as one which ought in its broad details to be raised on the letter of the Communion Office, taken in its general and uncontroversial meaning; because I observe, to my great regret, that attempts are being made in a memorial signed by clergymen of position to place it upon an irrelevant issue, as a thing which is taken " by many persons " as " typifying and implying such a sacrifice in the celebration of the Holy Communion, and such a sacrificial character in the Christian priesthood as we believe are not in accordance with the teaching of the liturgy and articles of the Church of England." This, as will be at once seen, is a net with wide meshes, and one which is intended to sweep in a miscellaneous haul. The indefiniteness of this protest is increased because it is at second hand, so to speak, that it affixes the unfavourable interpretation to the rites of which it disapproves as being the meaning given to them "by many persons," and because it does not in so many words call either for the dress or for the eastward position, to be put down, not only that they should not be further legalised.

On the face of the document, however, it was plainly allowable to traverse this rhetorical figure, and assume that the words which I have quoted convey the memorialists' own criticism. But since the 7th of October the mask has been completely thrown off, for the 'Guardian' of that date contains a letter from Mr. Scott Robertson, the gentleman who has charged himself with the collection of signatures to this Memorial, soliciting them as to "the address against vestments and the eastward position." *Habemus confitentem reum.* Those clergymen, if any, who may have signed the paper merely supposing that they were petitioning in favour of a *status in quo* will have learned from its prime manager that they were protesting directly against vestments and the Eastward position altogether. I thank Mr. Scott Robertson for his candour. It might, perhaps, be difficult to trace the connection of the "eastward position" with "such a sacrifice," and of a "distinctive Eucharistic dress" with "such a sacrificial character" as the memorial protests against; or (as by the use of "such" the remonstrants predicate both sacrifice and sacrificial character in some sense in the Holy Communion and the priesthood) to adjust the precise extent of them which would correspond with the southward position, and with that surplice which is, although not an exclusively distinctive Eucharistic dress, yet one which is a distinctive dress for the performance by the minister of all the offices of the Church, of which the Eucharist is the highest and best, while not the distinctive dress wherein to preach. The disputants of the present day, and particularly those who cling to the preaching gown because it is not the praying gown, forget that there was a time extending over more than a century, when this surplice, that "rag of Popery," excited the fiercest animosity among the Puritans, both in their earlier days, while they still unwillingly conformed to the Establishment, and in their last phase after they had split into the Presbyterian and Independent persuasions. They resisted it, not because it was or was not the Eucharistic or the preaching dress, but because it was the most habitual garb in which the episcopally ordained priesthood of the Church of England performed sacerdotal functions, and which was therefore connected in their minds with sacramental doctrine. The fight began in the reign of Elizabeth. It raged through three reigns and down to the overthrow of Church and Crown. The controversy rose again just after the Restoration at the Savoy Conference; and even when the battle was hopeless, the aged but irrepressible Prynne could still pluck courage, after he had accepted royalty, to go on railing at surplices.

If the memorialists will show either that the language which the Church of England employs about the Communion Office, both as it is in itself and in comparison with other services, is so guarded, and so chary of seeming to exalt it above other acts of devotion, that the inevitable inference must be that she looks with disfavour upon any external symbol which appears to place that office upon a pedestal of superior dignity; or if, without attempting to uphold this somewhat daring proposition, they will analyse each controverted rite in succession, and prove from the authoritative language of the English Church that it has been forbidden, then I will respectfully accept their correction. In the meanwhile I decline to be entangled by the vague assertions of a somewhat rhetorical protest; and I will, for my part, endeavour to establish the contrary view by a process analogous to that which I contend it would be their proper duty to follow out. I will first rehearse the words of the Communion Office, and show in the Church's own language how much she honours the institution of Christ Himself, and having thus established the presumption that she cannot be averse to special forms and rites in its honour, I will, one by one, call those forms and rites to the bar of that Church of England.

The memorial as we have seen appeals to the "teaching of the liturgy and articles of the Church of England." All expositions of the teaching of a religious body, when translated into the language of the disputant, carry with them a certain suspicion that he unconsciously has transferred a flavour of his own private opinion into the recapitulation of authoritative formularies. One thing is beyond any suspicion, namely, the voice of those formularies speaking for themselves in so far as they are self-explanatory. In the present case the task is made more compendious because the memorialists themselves appeal to the direct teaching of the Church's own formularies. I shall go through the Communion Office, and quote successively every expression in the order in which it occurs, which can throw light, not upon the precise Eucharistic doctrine of our Church, but upon the relative honour and importance of the Communion Service in comparison with other rites.

The title of the service is, as all are aware, "the Order of the Administration of the Lord's Supper or Holy Communion." The use of that adjective of respect " holy " is so habitual, that it has, so to speak, merged itself into the substantive, and lost in general estimation its qualifying value; but it is curious to notice that no such distinctive adjective is employed in the title either of the other sacrament or of sacred rites, such as Confirmation or Matrimony, and yet the phrase "Holy Baptism" occurs in the very first prayer of, and twice again in, the Baptismal Office, while the term "Holy Matrimony" is not only incorporated in its Marriage Service, but stands out prominently in the proclamation of banns. No adjective of honour appertains to Morning or Evening Prayer or to the Litany, but "Holy Communion" occurs eight times in the prayers, rubrics, and exhortations of its own service, and "the Communion" only three times (in the exhortation where people are negligent to come, in the rubric to the third exhortation, and in that to the "Prayer of Humble Access"), until we reach the rubric after the conclusion of the regular office, and introductory to the occasional collects, where we find " no Communion," and afterwards " collects either of the Morning or Evening Prayer,

Communion, or Litany," in which and in the final collects, which are, so to speak, of a business-like character, the adjective is dropped in a double mention of "no" and a double one of "the" Communion, besides which we once find "Communion time" and once "a Communion." The first exhortation tells us of "the most comfortable Sacrament of the Body and Blood of Christ," of the gift of our Saviour "to be our spiritual food and sustenance in that Holy Sacrament," "the dignity of that Holy Mystery," "such a heavenly feast," "that Holy Sacrament;" again, in the second, or more urgent, exhortation we read of "this Holy Supper," and "the banquet of that most heavenly food." In the third exhortation "at the time of the celebration of the Communion," the title of the divine ordinance is expanded into "the Holy Communion of the Body and Blood of our Saviour Christ." The reception with "a true penitent heart and lively faith" of "that Holy Sacrament," is to "spiritually eat the flesh of Christ and drink His blood." It is to "dwell with Christ and Christ with us," to be "one with Christ and Christ with us." Further on we read of "Holy Mysteries." In the fourth short exhortation "Holy Mysteries" again occurs. In the "Prayer of Humble Access" the petition is, "Grant us, therefore, gracious Lord, so to eat the flesh of Thy dear Son Jesus Christ, and to drink His blood, that our sinful bodies may be made clean by His body, and our souls washed through His most precious blood, and that we may evermore dwell in Him, and He in us." I will not quote the Prayer of Consecration further than to remind my readers that in it the Holy Communion is termed "a perpetual memory of that His precious death, until His coming again." In the first of the alternative prayers after the reception the service is referred to as "our sacrifice of praise and thanksgiving," in manifest reference to the Greek name of the Sacrament Εὐχαριστία ("Eucharist," that is, "offering of thanks"), and responsively the worshippers offer themselves "a reasonable holy and lively sacrifice" to God. The "Holy Communion" is again spoken of, and then, while the worshippers " be unworthy to offer unto Thee any sacrifice, yet we beseech Thee to accept these our bounden duty and service." No one, I should think, would be so wedded to a theory as to assert that the expressions which I have quoted from this prayer are bounded to its exclusive limits, and do not include the whole service, particularly when it is recollected that in the First Prayer Book it followed immediately upon, and virtually formed part of, the Prayer of Consecration. In the second and alternative prayer, priest and congregation thank God " that Thou dost vouchsafe to feed us who have received these Holy Mysteries with the spiritual food of the most precious Body and Blood of Thy Son our Saviour Jesus Christ." Thereby we are assured of "God's favour and goodness towards us;" we are " very members incorporate in the mystical Body of Thy Son which is the blessed company of all faithful people," and we are " heirs through hope " of His " everlasting kingdom." Three times, as we have seen, the Communion is called a " Holy Mystery " or " Holy Mysteries." Whatever these words may import they must indicate something higher than, and different in kind from, the ordinary service of prayer, praise, and thanksgiving, and they seem almost sufficient in themselves to establish the corollary that to adorn the celebration of the Holy Mysteries with a beauty of external circumstance to which neither daily service nor litany can naturally lay claim, would be only to carry out the indication of her own mind which our Church affords, not only in these, but in the language which, as we have seen, she habitually employs all through the Communion Office.

These fairly and fully rehearsed, not picked and sorted, but taken in the order in which they occur in the service, are the expressions which the Church of England uses in its Communion Service to express her opinion of its value and dignity. Relying on these, as a true son of that pure and simple Church, in thorough devotion to her Reformation, out of no desire to ape Rome, nor any antiquarian longings after the use of Sarum or of York, but simply in the desire to conform to the spirit of my own actual Church, in the wish that her outward practice may correspond with her inward teaching; but, lastly, and most chiefly, out of deep deference to the sacred rite of our dear Lord's own ordinance, and loving thankfulness for the inestimable benefits which He has thereby been pleased to vouchsafe to all faithful believers, I contend that it is meet and right that the celebration of the Holy Communion should be environed with circumstances of beauty, dignity, and solemnity, which would be incongruous in the case of any other service however pious, healthful, or necessary that may be for the edification of the worshipper or the glory of God. Other services are in great measure of man's own planning. The Holy Communion is, in the words of the Articles, "ordained of Christ our Lord in the Gospel."

Those who may hold a contrary opinion, and contend that it is not in accordance with the teaching of the Church of England that Christ's especial ordinance should be honoured by any peculiar ceremonial, are bound to establish their point, for on them, and not on those who believe otherwise, rests the burden of proof; only I must insist that these arguments should take the shape of reasoning, and not of denunciation. Let them prove that those who hold otherwise are mistaken as to the intentions of the Church of England, not that they are versed in, and intent upon carrying out, the policy of Rome. Here again, at the risk of being tedious, I must repeat that I shall only plead for the higher ceremonial with which, as I fully hope to show, the Church of England intends that the celebration of the Holy Communion should be accompanied, as a pacific arrangement. Let the memorialists, or any other clergymen, refrain from its adoption if they like. If only the Lord's Table at which they serve be "honest" (that is, handsome and appropriate); if, as the Canon orders, it be ordinarily covered with "a carpet of silk or other decent stuff," and, at the time of celebration, with a fair linen cloth; and if, at the Prayer of Consecration, they stand where they believe the Prayer Book intends that they should stand—I ask no more. But, on the other side, I do claim, when priest and congregation, in sincere and hearty loyalty to the same Church of England, desire that higher exhibition of her prescribed order of Holy Communion to which they are convinced that they are entitled, that then they should, in due subordination to the godly rulings of the Ordinary, and in compliance with that great law of charity which forbids that even the weak brother should be offended, be permitted to worship God in the way which their conscience dictates as most conducive to His honour and their edification, and which I now venture to assume, as I trust to show, is in absolute conformity with the existing law of our Church.

I grant that writers of the ultra-ritualist school have, by the singular and inexcusable incaution of their language, given grave cause for suspicion as to the intentions of those who desire to establish a generous permission for a higher ritual in the celebration of the Holy Communion. But I do not admit that these errors of a few excited partisans are any sufficient reason for keeping the Church of England in leading-strings, supposing the end to which she desires to advance with firm and fearless tread, is one which is consistent with the spirit of her Reformation, wholesome for her people, and tending to the glory of Almighty God. One of the most perverse instances of this wilful desire to be suspiciously singular which characterises certain persons, is the practice of calling the Communion Service the " Mass." The word " Mass" in itself is colourless, for in its original form of " Missa," it was at the beginning a familiar, and hardly even an authoritative, name for the Holy Communion. caught up as it was out of the sentence with which the congregation were (to use the English word, which has the same root) dis*missed*— " Ite, missa est." Nor has it been in later times exclusively confined to the Roman Catholic Communion Service, for the title of our service in the first Prayer Book of Edward VI. is "the Supper of the Lord and the Holy Communion, commonly called the Mass," while in the Swedish Service the Sunday Communion Office is still named the High Mass. Still the word has been so identified with the Roman Church in the minds of the English people, that its abrupt readoption by persons who affect a singular phraseology could only be excused by some overpowering advantage or congruity in it which no other phrase would present. Can such be predicated of it? I venture to think the contrary. I have just explained the somewhat trivial origin of the word. So derived, it has never prevailed beyond the limits of the Western Church. In the East the Communion Service has always borne the more dignified and expressive name of "Liturgy" (Λειτουργία), that is, the great "work of supplication;" and Liturgy is a household word with us, although less properly applied to every set form of worship. "Eucharist," the great deed of praise and thanksgiving, is common to East and West, and familiarised among the theological writers of our Reformed Church. What excuse can there be, then, when we are already rich with names for the Holy Communion, so venerable, so expressive, so widespread, to go out of our way to borrow one which has long carried with it a secondary signification most likely to cause suspicion and misunderstanding among persons whose confidence it is our Christian duty to win; and which, after all, in its origin is so far less noble or accurate, or gratefully recognisant of the Author of all good things than Liturgy or Eucharist?

I have abstained from any attempt to express in words of my own that which I believe a loyal lay son of the Church of England may hold about these "Holy Mysteries." I shall not quote from any divine either of the High Church School of the seventeenth century, or of the modern revival. But there is a passage which I may be allowed to offer for what it is worth, proceeding as it does from the pen of a layman, famous in his own days and in all times since for the wisdom and moderation of his opinions. The writer whom I shall quote is one whose attachment to the Church of England was equally conspicuous in the days of Cromwell when he was arrested for partaking of the Communion on Christmas Day, and in those of James II., and who was afterwards a warm supporter of, and much trusted by, the Government of 1688. I need hardly explain that I am referring to John Evelyn, whose remarkable fate it has been to have left so many of his writings to a publication, not only posthumous, but postponed till the century succeeding that into which he had himself only just survived.

Among the manuscripts of Evelyn, preserved at Wotton, was one entitled "A Rational Account of the True Religion," commenced in 1657, and having the date of 1683 in one part of it, as well as a reference to the unhappy career of Bishop Parker of Oxford, and therefore the ripe labour of its author's long life. This work, after lying forgotten from the death of Evelyn in 1706 till 1850, was published in that year, but was not successful in attracting much attention. That year gave rise to so much contemporary excited literature on present Church difficulties, that it may easily be understood that a voice from the tomb would hardly make itself heard above the raging din of the Papal Aggression. The treatise, which commences with a vindication of natural religion, concludes with a careful digest of the doctrines of the Church of England as Evelyn understood them, and which he takes especial pains to discriminate from those of the Roman Church, against which he inveighs with peculiar eagerness. Of course he has to deal with our doctrine of the Holy Communion, and although this passage is somewhat long I venture to transcribe it as the confession of faith of a layman in days long before our present controversies had arisen, embodying the views which have been continuously current among the section of Churchmen holding what are known as High Church opinions. The prevalent deadness of the last century may have led to a wide and lamentable neglect of the Holy Communion evinced by its very infrequent celebration, and fostered by the scandalous selfishness of Bishops who seemed to take pains to make even the benefit of Confirmation difficult of attainment, but there were never wanting those persons whose heart was as that of Evelyn in their veneration for the Holy Mysteries. Indeed, it is the great extension of those whose belief he has summed up, coupled with the increasing appreciation of the beautiful and the dignified as the congruous accompaniments of God's service no less than of a refined secular life, which has led to the present instinctive demand among so many pious persons for a higher ceremonial within the allowable limits of the Church of England, utterly irrespective of the opinions or practices of that particular section of theorisers who have invented and who boast of the appellation "Ritualist."

At the same time there are many, I should hope, among those Churchmen who are unable to accept Evelyn's views as representing their own opinions, who may yet from heartily acknowledging that the Church of England has with no uncertain sound proclaimed the transcendent value and benefit of the "Holy Communion" far surpassing those of any other act of worship, admit that persons who desire that higher ceremonial within the permitted limits of undoubted allegiance to their spiritual mother have an equitable claim to have their plea considered, so that they do not wrong to the consciences of the other brethren. Judging from the antecedents of those whose signatures to the memorial have been published, I should gather that it might contain the names of clergymen who agree with, as well of others who would disagree from, the passage which I am about to quote from Evelyn. From those antecedents, at all events, it is impossible to conclude that they can be a homogeneous body in their Church opinions. I appeal accordingly to them to reflect whether it would not be a wiser and a more charitable act, instead of raising suspicions against their brethren by vague generalities about "such sacrifice" and "such sacrificial act," and—instead of attempting to limit the liberty in things non-essential of those whose principle and earnest endeavour is to leave their liberty unrestricted, and whose claim is not preponderance but toleration—to strive by generous concession and an equitable concordat to enable each great acknowledged party in that Church of England, which numbers such different phases of thought, to worship God in peace according to its own conscientious prepossessions.

But in the meanwhile I have not allowed Evelyn to speak for himself.

"The Church of Christ, truly reformed, holds, that the Supper of the Lord* is a Sacrament of our Redemption by the Death and Passion of Christ upon the cross, of which only the faithful, prepared, do receive the benefit. That the elements are made sacramental by consecration, fraction and distribution, and thereby convey the real body and blood of Christ after a heavenly, spiritual, and mysterious manner, but without any transubstantiation or change of the species, and therefore in no wise to be worshipped. That they seal to, and possess us of, an interest in all that Christ has, by His suffering and obedience, promerited for us.

"She holds, that both the wine, as well as the bread, ought to be received of all the communicants, laymen as well as priests, by Divine and indispensable institution.

"She holds, that the sacrifice of Christ upon the cross, once offered, was a full, perfect, and complete oblation, propitiatory and satisfactory, for the sins of all the world; and therefore needs no bloody repetition, or suppletory for quick and dead, as Papists pretend in their superstitious masses.†

"She holds, that after the words of consecration and efficacy of benediction of the elements, the symbols become changed into the body and blood of Christ, after a sacramental, spiritual, and consequently real manner; and that all worthy communicants receive Christ to all the real purposes and effects of His Passion, instrumentally conveying its influence and operation; bread in natural substance; Christ in sacramental. Nor are the symbols more really

---

* 1 Cor. x. 16, 17; Matt. xxvi. 29; Luke xxii. 19, 20; Mark xiv. 22; 1 Cor. xi. 23-34.

† Acts xx. 28; Rom. v. 6-9; Gal. iii. 13; 1 Cor. vi. 20; Acts x. 43; Heb. ix. 12-22.

given than really received; and so, as really, nourish the soul, as the elements do the body; the first substance being changed by grace, though remaining the same in nature; nor barely as bread and wine, naked figures, and figures only, but such as exhibit Christ Himself, and puts the worthy recipient into sure possession of Him, sealing and giving him federal right and title to all His promises and promerits. Wherefore Holy Church holds a *real presence;* (and so the Canon of the Church of England, *really and indeed;*) and no understanding person of her communion denies it: since a thing is not one jot less *real* for being spiritual ; and thus are the gifts and graces of God's Holy Spirit real and sensible graces, and not things ambiguous or unintelligible to those who are not altogether immersed in gross and material objects, which have no place in this sacred mystery.

"The Christian Catholic and Orthodox Faith affirms a real change, retaining the ancient and middle belief; but presumes not to determine the *mode* or manner, because nowhere revealed, nor any ways appearing; besides that, she has the possession of above twelve hundred years, from our Saviour's institution, to the contrary; exploding the gross and corporeal change, as now imposed by the Church of Rome.

"The Holy Church adores not the elements; but holds that the sacred elements, so set apart and consecrated, are an homage and (as may be said) an act of adoration; and the Church of England receives it in that humble gesture. Forasmuch as Christ is thus present in an extraordinary and mysterious manner, and with so great advantages. But this, her adoration, is to her Lord Christ alone, at the right hand of the Father, adoring His flesh and blood in the mystery and venerable usage of the symbols, which represent and impart Him to the soul of the worthy communicant.

"The Church of Christ truly reformed, as to the oblation in the Holy Sacrament, affirms with the ancients that it signifies only, Oblatum celebrare, et memoriâ revocare; or as St. Chrysostom calls it, 'Ἀναμνήσιν ; and that if Christ were really offered, He must as often be put to death; whilst the Apostle tells us plainly, He was but *once* offered :* so that, if sacrificed in a natural sense, when first instituted, it could not be propitiatory; seeing, then, His Father must have been reconciled before His Passion. Wherefore, the Church of England holds it representative and memorative only of that

---

* Compare Rom. vi. 10-21, with Heb. ix. 11-28.

which was after to be done, and now of what has actually been done. And she also holds it to be a sacrifice both propitiatory and impetratory; because (as Mr. Thorndike well observes) the oblation of it to Almighty God, with and by the prayers and praises of the Church, does render God propitious, by obtaining those benefits which the death and Passion of Christ do represent. And, therefore, in her offices for the Church militant, she beseeches God for the universal peace of the Church, and the whole state of Christians, and especially of those who then actually communicate."

I had written the first draft of this chapter when I read in the 'Times' of September the 18th the report of the conference held at Bonn, under the chairmanship of Dr. Von Döllinger, between the Old Catholics and the representatives of the Eastern and Anglican Churches, at which an article upon the doctrine of the Eucharist was adopted in the following terms:

"The Eucharistic celebration in the Church is not a continuous renewal of the propitiatory sacrifice offered once for ever upon the Cross, but its sacrificial character consists in this,—that it is the permanent memorial of it, and representation and presentation on earth of the one oblation of Christ for the salvation of redeemed mankind, which, according to the Epistle to the Hebrews (ix. 11, 12), is continuously presented in heaven by Christ, who now appears in the presence of God for us (ix. 24), while this is the character of the Eucharist in reference to the sacrifice of Christ, it is also a sacred feast, wherein the faithful, receiving the body and blood of our Lord, have communion one with another." (1 Cor. x. 17.)

It was especially stated that among the committee who drew up this statement, Canon Liddon and Dr. Howson, Dean of Chester, bore a prominent part, so that it may be taken most thoroughly to express the accepted doctrine of the Church of England on that most vital question, both as to the points on which the " sacrifice " and the " sacrificial character " of that sacrament, as held in the Church of Rome, differs from the " teaching of the liturgy and articles " of the Church of England, and as to the sense in which that " teaching " holds it to be a " sacrifice " and to have a " sacrificial character." Now it is a curious coincidence that amongst those who have made themselves prominent in claiming both by declaration and otherwise the distinctive Eucharistic dress and the Eastward position Canon Liddon holds a foremost place, while the Dean of Chester is one of the most prominent signers of the declaration on which I have just been commenting, against both those incidents of sacramental ceremonial. In the name then of Christian charity and of common sense, why cannot the parties in the Church of England agree to differ in their Eucharistic ritual? Dr. Liddon has expressed no desire to interfere with Dr. Howson's practice; why need Dr. Howson interfere with that of Dr. Liddon? Dr. Liddon may prefer the west side and the distinctive dress, Dr. Howson the north end and the simple surplice; but as both could combine in framing a document to embody the doctrine which the Church of England holds upon the "sacrifice" and the "sacrificial character of" the Eucharist, each may well leave the other to adopt the rites which most tend in his own eyes to carry out views on which they both agree.

CHAPTER IV.

The "Distinctive Eucharistic dress," under conditions, a ruled and uncontentious point — The dress ordered by Canons accepted in Hebbert v. Purchas — All that has to be decided is the conditions — Vestments of first Prayer Book pronounced legal by Liddell v. Westerton and Martin v. Mackonochie — Does Ornaments Rubric overrule Canons, or do Canons colour Ornaments Rubric? — Canons of 1604 in Latin and English — Canons on copes and surplices in Cathedrals — As High Mass is the highest Roman ceremonial, so Cathedral Communion is the highest English — Cope really ordered in Cathedrals at all Communions — Canons only define who is to be celebrant on principal feast-days — Elizabeth's Advertisements — Difficulty of understanding Canons otherwise — Point proved by wording of Latin Canons — Rubric of 1549 prescribes maximum and Canons the minimum — Descriptions of vestments — Early confusion of vestment and cope — Machyn's Diary — Tunicles — Meaning of "agreeably" — Anyhow the rite on principal feast-days the normal ceremonial — Dilemma from which no escape — Hebbert v. Purchas on a maximum and minimum — Blunder of not observing convertibility of alb and surplice — Canon on surplices, for benefit of ratepayers — Bishop Phillpotts's Helstone judgment — Privy Council argument would make daily service unlawful — Martin v. Mackonochie confesses Liddell v. Westerton — Purchas judgment attempts to escape by distinction between different ornaments rubrics — Meaning of "retain" — Peter Smart and Cosin — Cosin clearly held the rubrics of 1549 to be still valid — Elizabeth's Chapel before and after Advertisements — Her ceremonial Easter, 1593 — Bishop Andrewes' Chapel copied by Laud — Its copes — Archbishop Williams — Parish churches — Wolverhampton — No vestments ordered in Visitation Articles, because not wanted to throw burden on parishioners. Cope practically used in place of tunicle — Advertisements never received Elizabeth's signature — Additional notes to Prayer Book by Andrewes, Overall, and Cosin, published by Nicholls — Cosin on ornaments rubric — Overall on the same — Comparison of Cosin's notes — They show the elastic working of ornaments rubric in those days — Policy of Church leaders after Restoration — Impediments to enforcing ornaments rubric — Its retention proof of animus — They could not see adverse future — Put it on record for futurity — Present revival of distinctive dress proof that their policy was no failure — Cosin at Durham — Circumstances of his diocese and cathedral — His influence at least preserved copes at Durham — Evidence of Thoresby — Not disused till latter half of eighteenth century — Really "Protestant" character of ornaments rubric of 1549 compared with older rites — Pre-reformational dresses

— Rock's 'Church of our Fathers'—Changes of 1552 against spirit of Church of England, and a failure—Episcopal dress—Assumption of pastoral staff acceptance of vitality of rubrics of 1549—Revival of vestments not to be forced on against will of congregations—*Modus vivendi* must be reached—Different rites may be used at different times in same church—Early communions—Churches with several clergymen collegiate churches in spirit of canon—Vestments would no longer be burden upon ratepayers—Restriction to copes not satisfactory—Limitation of white vestments suggested—Vestments a link with Universal Church—Vestments in Scandinavia—Forester's description of Norwegian ceremonial—Question complicated by adoption of cope at Magnificat—Indefensibility of practice—Stole or scarf legal—Biretta—Want of tact in dealing with prejudices—Long and short surplices—Episcopal dress—Pastoral staff—Surplice or gown in pulpit—Mutilated Communion service—Prayer for Church militant.

IN fact the "distinctive Eucharistic dress" is, under conditions, a ruled and uncontentious point, by the conclusions reached by the Judicial Committee itself, sitting on the case of Hebbert *v.* Purchas, and all which still remain to be decided are the area of the obligation, and the character of the dress itself. That judgment, indeed, which was in an undefended suit, may not stand, but then the dress would still be legal in a more extensive way by the dictum in Liddell *v.* Westerton, supported by that in Martin *v.* Mackonochie and by the weighty authority of Sir J. T. Coleridge, which I have already quoted. I shall, with all respect for the Judgment which was last delivered, give my reasons for the belief that the earlier opinion rests on sounder reasons, but for my immediate purpose I will assume that the dress is legal only so far as the principles laid down in Hebbert *v.* Purchas carry it. The case stands thus. The rubric to the first Prayer Book of 1549 enforces the general use of a distinctive Eucharistic dress. This rubric was certainly abolished in 1552, and certainly revived in 1559, with a reference to possible royal orders in the future, after which date a more limited use of such a dress, namely, in cathedrals and collegiate churches, was recommended in Elizabeth's Advertisements, a document of very uncertain legal value; and again, in words which have (erroneously as I think) been read as limiting the days, no less than the places, of their use, in the Canon of 1604.

Fifty-eight years after that date the ornaments rubric of the existing Prayer Book received its present shape, and thus in the opinion of the high authorities just cited consolidated the state of ritual law as settled in 1549. The other view is that the language of the Canons has, so to speak, prospectively coloured the meaning of words revised and put into an Act of Parliament fifty-eight years later; so that " by the authority of Parliament in the second year of Edward VI.," simply means by authority of the Canons of 1604. This sounds strangely, but, even if it were the case, the Church and realm of England have given a sanction to a distinctive Eucharistic dress, which is as completely a declaration of principle, though it were only applicable to cathedrals and to principal feast-days, as if it applied to all churches and all celebrations. In the Church of Rome the most elaborate ceremonial is only used at High Mass, but it remains pre-eminently the ceremonial of the Church of Rome.

In fact the contention may be summed up in very few words. It is (1) whether 1604 intended to supplement or to supplant 1549, and (2) whether 1662, when it seemed to be looking back to 1549, was really arresting its glance at 1604. Either the Canon is to be read with the rubric, and is intended to define the minimum observance of it, on which the Church for practical reasons is disposed to insist, or it is to be read as superseding it, and is intended to lay down the maximum of ceremonial which, upon more mature reflection, the Church is willing to tolerate. Let us begin by supposing the latter to be the case.

The Canons, as is well known, exist in a double original, English and Latin. The Judicial Committee in Hebbert *v.* Purchas unfortunately overlooked the Latin text, and dealt with the English one as if it were conclusive of the meaning of the Canon, and was in consequence led to the conclusion that the cope was only ordered in cathedrals and collegiate churches upon the " principal feast-days." The Canons which bear upon the point are the 24th and 25th, and are in English as follows :—

XXIV. *Copes to be worn in Cathedral Churches by those that administer the Communion.*

" In all cathedral and collegiate churches, the Holy Communion shall be administered upon principal feast-days, sometimes by the bishop, if he be present, and sometimes by the dean, and at sometimes by a canon or prebendary, the principal minister using a decent cope, and being assisted with the gospeller and epistler agreeably, according to the advertisements published anno 7. Eliz. The said communion to be administered at such times, and with such limitation, as is specified in the Book of Common Prayer. Provided, that no such limitation by any construction shall be allowed of, but that all deans, wardens, masters, or heads of cathedral and collegiate churches, prebendaries, canons, vicars, petty canons, singing men, and all others of the foundation, shall receive the Communion four times yearly at the least."

XXV. *Surplices and Hoods to be worn in Cathedral Churches when there is no Communion.*

" In the time of divine service and prayers, in all cathedral and collegiate churches, when there is no communion, it shall be sufficient to wear surplices; saving that all deans, masters, and heads of collegiate churches, canons, and prebendaries, being graduates, shall daily, at the times both of prayer and preaching, wear with their surplices such hoods as are agreeable to their degrees."

The use of the surplice in parish churches is laid down in the 58th Canon, and as the words are not important at this point, but will be further on, I refrain from quoting them at present.

The current interpretation of the 24th and 25th Canons is that upon " principal feast-days " (a liturgical term of a somewhat indefinite character in this collocation, borrowed from the Sarum use, and in the actual English Church usually assumed to be the feasts for which a special preface is appointed) the Bishop, the Dean, or one of the canons or prebendaries, is to be " principal minister " or celebrant, and that then, and then only, the cope is to be worn. I cannot think this accurate, and even as the words stand in English I believe them to mean that in cathedral and collegiate churches the cope is to be the normal dress whenever there is a communion, but that "when there is no communion, it shall be sufficient to wear surplices;" and further, that on the "principal feast-days" the celebration shall not be devolved upon any minor canon or priest-vicar (a lazy habit too prevalent both before and since the Reformation), but shall be taken by the Bishop, the Dean, or some member of the Chapter. If the 24th Canon, *as it is in English*, were read alone, it would be patient of the former interpretation, but it cannot be read alone for it interprets itself "according to the advertisements published anno 7 Eliz.," and it has its rider in the 25th Canon.

The Advertisements of Elizabeth run as follows:—

"*Item.* In the ministration of the Holy Communion in cathedral and collegiate churches, the principal minister shall use a cope with Gospeller and Epistler agreeably; and at all other prayers to be said at that Communion-table, to use no copes, but surplices.

"*Item.* That the dean and prebendaries wear a surplice with a silk hood in the quire; and when they preach in the cathedral or collegiate church, to wear their hood.

"*Item.* That every minister saying any publick prayers, or ministering the Sacraments or other publick rites of the Church, shall wear a comely surplice with sleeves."

It will be observed that in these orders there is absolutely no reference at all to "principal feast-days," on the contrary the most general words of which the language is capable, "in the ministration of the Holy Communion," are employed. Moreover (thereby, as I contend, mitigating in practice, or as other controversialists would say repealing the rubrics of 1549 and 1559), they lay down that the cope is not to be used "at all other prayers to be said at the Communion-table," as it was to have been by one of the rubrics of the First Book. This brings us to "when there is no communion" of the 25th Canon. I am totally at a loss to understand how those who believe that the 24th Canon only orders the cope at the "principal feast-days" can interpret the regulation contained in the 25th Canon, that "when there is no communion it shall be sufficient to wear surplices." According to their view the Canons are (1) very precise in regulating the ceremonial on the three Sundays and the two other great days which are principal feast-days, and also upon all the other Sundays and holy days on which there may happen not to be a celebration (which, by the way, as to Sundays contravenes the letter of the unrepealed rubric at the close of the Communion service —"and in cathedral and collegiate churches and colleges where there are many priests and deacons, they shall all receive the Communion with the priest *every Sunday at the least*, except they have a reasonable cause to the contrary ")— but (2) they are absolutely silent as to the dress which has to be worn during that large margin of other Sundays on which the rubric just quoted is complied with by there being a celebration in such cathedral or collegiate church. This interpretation of the Canons is manifestly impossible, and so we are driven back to read the 24th Canon in its English form (to which alone the Judicial Committee in Hebbert *v.* Purchas referred) as primarily intended to define who should in cathedral and collegiate churches be the celebrant on "principal feast-days," and only incidentally reaffirming (as a reminder to that celebrant to keep up the level of ceremonial conformity) that he is to be dressed as Elizabeth's Advertisements order that every celebrant should be dressed at every communion in those particular churches.

I have hitherto confined myself to the English Canons because the Judicial Committee in Hebbert *v.* Purchas was pleased to do so; and I have found in them strong inferential reasons for my interpretation. In referring to the Latin Canons which those Judges overlooked, I find my inferences turned into certainty. The 24th and 25th Canons in Latin run as follows :—

XXIV. *Cœnæ in Festis solennibus administratio in Ecclesiis Cathedralibus indicta, & Cœnam administrantibus Caparum usus injunctus.*

"Per Cathedrales omnes et Collegiatas Ecclesias sacram Cœnam in Festis solennibus administrari volumus, nonnunquam per Episcopum (siquidem præsens extiterit) nonnunquam verò per Decanum, quandoque etiam per Canonicum vel Præbendarium (Ministrum ibidem maxime eminentem) eundemque decente Capa amictum, ac adjutum ab Evangelii et Epistolæ Lectoribus (juxta Admonitiones in septimo Elizabethæ promulgatas) idque iis horis, et cum illa prorsus limitatione, quæ in Libro publicæ Liturgiæ præfiniuntur. Proviso semper, ut nulla ejusmodi limitatio admittatur, cujuscunque tandem interpretationis prætextu, quo minus singuli Decani, Guardiani, Magistri, sive Præfecti Cathedralis cujusque et Collegiatæ Ecclesiæ, et cuncti etiam earundem Præbendarii, Canonici, Vicarii, minores Canonici, Cantores, reliquique de Ecclesiæ gremio universi, si non frequentius, saltem quater omni anno Sacramentum percipiant."

XXV. *Superpelliceorum et Epomidum usus, Cœna non administrata, in Ecclesiis Cathedralibus indictus.*

"In Cathedralibus et Collegiatis Ecclesiis, cessante Cœna Dominica, satis erit tempore Divinorum officiorum Superpelliceis duntaxat uti: nisi quod Ecclesiarum Collegiatarum Decani, Magistri, et Præfecti, itemque Canonici, ac Præbendarii (dummodo graduati) cum Superpelliceis Caputia gradibus suis respectivè congrua inter rem Divinam gerere tenebuntur."

I hardly know how to make the point more clear to those who feel Latin, than by nakedly reciting the words. For the sake, however, of those who may not be so familiar with that tongue, I offer a hard literal translation of the former part of the 24th Canon:—

"Throughout all cathedral and collegiate churches we will, that the Holy Supper be administered on solemn feasts, sometimes by the bishop (if so be he may be present) but sometimes by the dean, occasionally even by a canon or a prebendary (the minister [whoever may be] there most eminent), and [by] him clothed in a decent cope, and helped by the readers of the gospel and epistle (according to the Advertisements published in the seventh year of Elizabeth,) and that at the hours, and altogether with that limitation which are defined in the book of the public liturgy."

The clear accentuation in the Latin of the order in which successive dignitaries are to administer is remarkable compared with the English. The vague "sometimes," "sometimes," and "at sometimes," of the vernacular is replaced by a series of adverbs in a descending scale of urgency, very unmistakably indicating that the bishop is the most right man, and the canon or prebendary most nearly a makeshift (inferentially showing, too, that the minor canon or vicar-choral would be quite one). This phrasing of the order proves, as I contend, that its emphasis lay in the choice of celebrant upon the specific days, not in the character of his dress. On the other hand, the Latin term "in festis solennibus" carries with it a wider prescription of days than the English "principal feast-days," and might in itself, and still more when interpreted by Elizabeth's Advertisements and by the rubric, be ruled to cover every Sunday. Sunday certainly is a "solemn," though it may not be a "principal," feast-day. Again, "*Ministrum ibidem maxime eminentem*," standing as a distinct clause, has a significance not possessed by the English "principal minister," which, in its context, simply seems tautological. We have already been told that the Holy Communion is to be administered by bishop, dean, canon, or prebendary; and the Canon goes on to say that he is to wear a cope; it would, therefore, be mere definition to sum him up as "principal minister." But the Latin words as they stand have a further and a very definite meaning, namely, that on each occasion of a "festum solenne" the minister of the highest rank who may be present shall be the celebrant, to the exclusion of any other of lower grade; that the Dean is not to celebrate in the presence of the Bishop, nor the Canon in that of the Dean. The old rite had Pontifical Masses, and masses "coram Pontifice;" in the reformed rite the latter were to merge, at least on those days, into the former. On the other hand, the English words seem, in one particular instance, more precise than the Latin, because in this passage the Elizabethan Advertisements are literally transcribed in the English version. The Gospeller and Epistler (titles inherited from the pre-reformational vernacular) who are to assist the celebrant, are to do so "agreeably." This is a rather obscure adverb, and the Latin compiler evaded the difficulty by assuming that "agreeably" was intended in some way to qualify the "according" which immediately follows it (although in the English editions which I am using a comma is interposed), and translated both by the single preposition "juxta." I have very little doubt that in the Advertisements "agreeably" had a very solid and specific meaning of its own, which must, of course, have followed it when it was imported into the Canon, whether those who framed that document fully appreciated it or not. This meaning is not germane to the present argument, but it will become important later, so I reserve it.

The explanation of the Advertisements and Canons for which I contend is, that they express the allowable minimum of ceremonial which the Church of Elizabeth and James was, for politic reasons, willing to tolerate. The other side says that they intentionally supersede the rubric. In either view it must be allowed, on the most grudging interpretation, that these regulations are intended in cathedral and collegiate churches—"in the administration of the Holy Communion" according to the Advertisements, "in festis solennibus" according to the Latin, and, at all events, on "principal feast-days" according to the English Canon—to prescribe a ritual which, whether identical or not with that of the rubrics of 1549, is, at least, intended to represent it. But 1549 orders the celebrant to wear a vestment or cope when there is a Communion, and when only the first portion of the Communion Service is used, a cope by the following rubrics, of which one precedes and the other follows the Communion Office itself.

"Upon the day, and at the time appointed for the ministration of the Holy Communion, the priest that shall execute the holy

VESTMENTS OF FIRST PRAYER BOOK.

ministry shall put upon him the vesture appointed for that ministration; that is to say, a white albe plain, with a vestment or cope. And where there be many priests or deacons, there so many shall be ready to help the priest in the ministration, as shall be requisite; and shall have upon them likewise the vestures appointed for their ministry; that is to say, albes with tunacles. Then shall the clerks sing in English for the office, or introit, (as they call it,) a psalm appointed for that day."

"Upon Wednesdays and Fridays, the English Litany shall be said or sung in all places, after such form as is appointed by the King's Majesty's Injunctions; or as is, or shall be, otherwise appointed by his Highness. And though there be none to communicate with the priest, yet these days (after the Litany ended) the priest shall put upon him a plain albe or surplice, with a cope, and say all things at the altar appointed to be said at the celebration of the Lord's Supper, until after the Offertory: and then shall add one or two of the collects afore written, as occasion shall serve by his discretion: and then, turning him to the people, shall let them depart with the accustomed blessing."

The Advertisements and Canons only speak of a "cope." The "vestment" or chasuble had been of old the dress specially, though not quite exclusively, reserved for the celebrant, and the cope had been, according to all liturgical tradition, the much less considered dress which clerks in any "orders," "minor" or "holy," wore in choir and in processions. Both had become rich dresses and in this respect differed from the surplice, or that closer, tighter, form of surplice, the alb* (a dress which had itself become rich in colour, material, and ornamentation in mediæval days, but which was, by this rubric, recalled to its older linen simplicity). Accordingly the Edwardian Reformers swept away the distinction, and—allowing only the distinction between a richer dress for the celebrant, a dress less rich, the "tunacle" (of which I shall have

---

* When I speak in my own language of 'alb' or 'tunicle,' I spell them according to modern correctness. When | I quote the Prayer Book of 1549, I follow its spelling of 'albe' and 'tunacle.'

to speak further on), for the assistants, and a plain linen dress (alb or surplice) for other clerks—made the richest one in either form indifferently "the distinctive Eucharistic dress." I should as well explain that the "chasuble," or "vestment" (for the words are identical), is a dress which in mediæval times was wide, light, and gracefully falling, rounded, or else oval with pointed ends, and which was donned by the wearer putting his head through a circular hole in the centre; its form was, in fact, identical with that of the South American "poncho." In the modern Roman Church it has become scamped, distorted, and stiffened with buckram or pasteboard till it has reached a close likeness to a couple of fiddle-faces before and behind its wearer. The cope is also a dignified dress, in the shape of a large cloak, open in front, and clasped or tied over the wearer's chest. In explanation of this fusion of two dresses with very different antecedents, Dr. Littledale, a very learned writer, and one who is not likely to minimise a question of ritual propriety, believes that he has found evidence to show that in English country churches the cope sometimes served, before the Reformation, as the Eucharistic dress, and he has obligingly pointed out to me a curious passage in the most valuable gossiping Diary, from 1550 to 1563, of Henry Machyn, citizen of London, published by the Camden Society in 1848. Machyn, who was both a garrulous diarist and the very compliant royal undertaker during the reigns of Edward VI., "Jane," Mary, and Elizabeth, is naturally an authority of the first value in questions near akin to his craft. He enters under the year 1562, "The viij. day of September, whent throughe London a prest, with a cope, taken sayhyng of masse in Feyter lane at my lade" [blank] "and so to my lord mare, and after to the contur" [counter] " . . . . and the thursday after he was carried to the Masselsay" [Marshalsea]. This passage, written about midway between the dates of the Act and the rubric severally reviving the Rubrics of 1549, and of the Advertisements, demonstrates one of two things, either that this priest did say mass in a cope, or else that, in 1562, a chasuble was already called a cope. In either case, it leads to the inference that when the ritualists of Elizabeth's and James's days read of a "vestment or cope" in one of Edward VI.'s vestiary rubrics, and of a "cope" in another, and when they themselves used a "cope" only, they were not conscious to themselves of a variation of order. In all probability the word cope had, by that time, in common parlance superseded the older word vestment, as describing the Eucharistic dress. Some of the dresses worn as, and called, "copes," soon after 1559, may have been really chasubles, but by the seventh of Elizabeth cope had become the current word for the vesture worn at a particular time. If we admit this modification of vocabulary, and if we remember how little was the difference between the surplice and the "white albe plain" (which are, indeed, named as alternative dresses in the second Edwardian rubric), we shall be brought to the conviction that the dress ordered for the celebrant in cathedral and collegiate churches by the Advertisements and Canons was intended to be that of the rubrics of 1549, and the modification which those orders were intended to introduce was to limit the area of the compulsory application of those rubrics, and not purposely to limit their details. 1565 and 1604, in fact, believed that they were repeating in more concise and less formal language the arrangements of 1549, while only compelling them in given cases.

We have still to deal with the direction in this rubric that the assistants at the Holy Communion are to "have upon them the vestures appointed for their ministry, that is to say, albes with tunacles." By the unreformed rite, the deacon who read the Gospel wore over his alb a "dalmatic," while the subdeacon who read the Epistle used the "tunacle." Both these dresses were, in distinction to the chasuble, square-cut, and in mediæval times, at all events, of the richest designs and materials, the dalmatic being, by the way, the dress which the English Sovereign still wears at the coronation; only the tunicle used to be smaller and less rich than the dalmatic. It is, accordingly, another proof of the simplification which ruled the changes of 1549, that the more splendid dalmatic should be dropped and the tunicle alone preserved. Is it a very extravagant conjecture to suggest that the "agreeably" of the Advertisements which, after nearly forty years, puzzled the Latinists of 1604, was a compendious way of saying that, "agreeably" both to the rubric and to their relations with the celebrant, the Gospeller and Epistler were to wear tunicles, as agreeably to the same he was to wear a cope? If this is admitted the correspondence of the ceremonial which the rubric orders for all churches, and the Advertisements and Canons for cathedral and collegiate churches will be complete.

I have instances of the use of copes in places which were not cathedral or collegiate churches, between the accession of Elizabeth and 1662, but I look upon them as proofs that the rubric was considered of living authority, although a less ornate *modus vivendi* had been provided beside it, so I will deal with them when I quit the canons for the rubrics. Only I must, in passing, note that they include Bishops' chapels and the chapels of colleges, places which prelates such as Bishops Andrewes and Cosin, and Archbishops Laud and Williams, would not have mistaken for cathedrals and collegiate churches, and which were not mentioned in Canon 24, which lays down the necessary dress for the latter, nor in Canon 25, which lays it down for parish churches. This omission of an important class of places of worship contributes an inferential reason for the supposition that the canons were not intended to serve as the universal rule of vesture.

Whether or not, however, the interpretation of the canons which confines the use of the copes to principal feast-days in cathedral and collegiate churches, or that which would extend it to every celebration there, be the correct one, the principle established by the canon remains unaltered. In the unreformed Churches both of the West and also of the East, the

Holy Communion is celebrated on different days, or under different circumstances, with varying degrees of ceremonial magnificence. The Missa Cantata has ritual features which are absent from the Low Mass, and the High Mass those which are absent from the Missa Cantata. But the norm and exemplar of Roman ceremonial is always sought in the High Mass, and especially in the High Mass of some principal feast-day in some cathedral when the Bishop is the celebrant. With a similar instinct, the English canons have decreed that as a practical rule our highest form of ceremonial pomp in the Eucharist, the fullest and grandest exhibition of the mind of the English Church as to the honour due to the "Holy Mysteries"—simple, indeed, and austere compared with a High Mass, but of great dignity and beauty—shall be in some cathedral or collegiate church when either the Bishop or Dean, or only in the absence of either, some member of the Chapter shall be celebrant, whether the day be one of the few "principal feast-days," or any "festum solenne," Sunday be it, or any red-letter day of our reformed calendar.

I think I have shown that whether the recognition of a "distinctive Eucharistic dress" be or be not the recognition of "some sacrifice," and "sacrificial character" in the Eucharist contrary to "the teaching of the liturgy and articles of the Church of England," yet that that Church most assuredly, by the confession of both parties, and under the conditions of a dilemma from which there is no escape, orders such a dress irrespective of consequences. Further I have pointed out that among the ministers who upon the most narrow interpretation of such orders cannot evade the obligation of wearing it, Bishops and Deans stand conspicuous, and among them of course those Deans who have signed the declaration. 1 will now proceed to consider the relations of the ornaments rubrics and of the canons to each other, and in so doing, examine the argument of the Privy Council in Hebbert *v.* Purchas. The gist of the subject, so far as it deals with vestments, is contained in two passages of that document which I shall consider separately.

The first of these discusses the theory that the canons prescribe a *minimum* and the rubrics a *maximum* of ceremonial.

"Their Lordships remark further that the doctrine of a minimum of ritual represented by the surplice, with a maximum represented by a return to the mediæval vestments, is inconsistent with the fact that the rubric is a positive order, under a penal statute, accepted by each clergyman in a remarkably strong expression of 'assent and consent,' and capable of being enforced with severe penalties. It is not to be assumed without proof that such a statute was framed so as to leave a choice between contrary interpretations, in a question that had ever been regarded as momentous, and had stirred, as the learned judge remarks, some of the strongest passions of man. Historically all the communications between Archbishop Parker and the Queen and her Government indicate a strong desire for uniformity, and the Articles of Visitation after 1662 were all framed with the like object. If the minister is ordered to wear a surplice at all times of his ministration, he cannot wear an alb and tunicle when assisting at the Holy Communion ; if he is to celebrate the Holy Communion in a chasuble, he cannot celebrate in a surplice."

Before I deal with the argument itself I may observe that the learned judges seem to have rather involved themselves in superfluous difficulties, from not having taken sufficient pains to disentangle the names of the dresses of which they were speaking from their realities. They say "if the minister is ordered to wear a surplice at all times of his ministration, he cannot wear an alb and tunicle," and "if he is to celebrate the Holy Communion in a chasuble he cannot celebrate in a surplice." This would be true enough if alb and surplice were inconsistent and dissimilar dresses, but as it happens that the "white albe plain" which the rubric of 1549 substitutes for the more gaudy albs of the older rites, is in fact nothing more than a small tight surplice, and that a surplice when made small and tight, becomes and may be called an alb, the difficulty vanishes, as indeed it does in those very rubrics of 1549, in which the

CHAP. IV. VESTIARY ORDERS NOT INCONSISTENT.   105

synonyms " albe or surplice" occur in the order as to what the priest is to wear under his "cope" when there is no actual celebration. That learned and devoted partisan of pre-reformational ceremonial, the late A. W. Pugin, writing exclusively for his own communion, defines " surplice " in his 'Glossary of Ecclesiastical Ornament' as "a declension from the albe, which was the original linen vestment used by all who ministered at the altar. The surplice is in fact an *Albe enlarged* [sic] both in the body and the sleeves." If Pugin had been answering this judgment instead of anticipating it by more than a quarter of a century, he could not have more directly met its statements. Accordingly, if in compliance with one rubric of 1549 the priest wore and did celebrate in an alb when he celebrated in a chasuble, because one dress was underneath and the other above, and if by another rubric of the same book he could read the first part of the Communion Service in an "albe or surplice" and a cope likewise, so now he can " celebrate in a surplice " (if it is small enough, that is approximates sufficiently to the alb) when he "celebrates in a chasuble," for one dress will be underneath and the other one above, and in like manner the assistant will continue to "wear a surplice at all times of his ministration" even though he puts a tunicle over it. A man still wears his shirt when he has his coat on, but I proceed to the main argument of the passage.

The allegation slightly compressed is that the doctrine of a maximum and of a minimum is inconsistent with the fact that the rubric is a positive order under a penal statute, capable of being enforced with severe penalties, and that it is not to be assumed that such a statute was framed so as to leave a choice between contrary interpretations. The position here taken has the merit of being both clear and definite; the ritual law laid down in the canons is the surplice for the celebrant in all parish churches, and that in the old rubric of 1549 the vestment or cope and alb for the same. These orders seem inconsistent and to exclude each other; they cannot be cumulative; and the more modern statutory rubric must, therefore, be read in spite of its contrary appearance to mean what the canons say and nothing else. If we accept this ruling we must accept it in its totality. According to it the canons lay down certain rules as to the minister's dress without reference to any thing in the rubrics which may fall below or transcend their scope, and it cannot accordingly be assumed that the Act of Uniformity leaves a choice between contrary interpretations. It follows of course that any further prescription which the canons may contain as to any other incident of public worship, if only it be propounded in the same positive and definite form must be equally valid in supplying the authorised interpretation for the meaning of the rubrics legalised under the last Act of Uniformity. The canons order a certain dress which in comparison with the order which is certainly in the First Prayer Book, and appears to be in the actual one, must plainly be called a minimum; and as the canon does not in terms prescribe any choice, it must be held to govern the rubric which was made statute law by an Act of Parliament fifty years later. The canon which the Judicial Committee quote as superseding the ornaments rubric, is the 58th.

Ministers reading Divine Service, and administering the Sacraments, to wear Surplices, and Graduates therewithal Hoods.

"Every minister saying the public prayers, or ministering the sacraments, or other rites of the church, shall wear a decent and comely surplice with sleeves, to be provided at the charge of the parish. And if any question arise touching the matter, decency, or comeliness thereof, the same shall be decided by the discretion of the ordinary. Furthermore, such ministers as are graduates shall wear upon their surplices, at such times, such hoods as by the orders of the universities are agreeable to their degrees, which no minister shall wear (being no graduate) under pain of suspension. Notwithstanding it shall be lawful for such ministers as are not graduates to wear upon their surplices, instead of hoods, some decent tippet of black, so it be not silk."

It will be at once seen that this canon does not say, or even in terms imply, that the minister ministering the Holy Communion shall not wear a "vestment or cope," only that he shall "wear a decent and comely surplice with sleeves to be provided at the charge of the parish," which or the alb (by whomsoever it might be provided) he must, likewise, wear as his under vesture though he were attired in the most gorgeous cope or chasuble. The Judicial Committee imagined that compliance with it involved the impossibility of compliance with the rubric, because the minister celebrating in a chasuble could not also celebrate in a surplice at the same service. I have shown that the minister who did celebrate in a chasuble or in a "cope" must also celebrate in an under garment which might indifferently be called, as in one rubric, "albe," in another "albe or surplice," or as in the canons, "surplice." In fact, I believe the gist of the canon intentionally to be in the words to "be provided at the charge of the parish." The canon, like the Advertisements of Elizabeth, was a measure of indulgence, not so much to the minister as to the ratepayers. By the rubrics the parish was burdened to find "vestment or cope," "tunacle" or "tunacles." This obligation was wearisome, costly, unpopular, or difficult, in the many then poor, trackless, waste-lying parishes of our England, such as it was before drainage, road-making, or railways had contributed their civilising influences. So Convocation stepped in, not to say "you, Reverend Sir, shall not wear the parish cope if you find it," but "you parishioners need only be at charges to find the surplice." Bishop Phillpotts, many years before this judgment hit the nail on the head, when he was challenged by the parishioners of Helston to censure a clergyman for preaching in his surplice.

"On this particular, I have no difficulty in saying, that Mr. Blunt has been right since he has preached in his surplice. The sermon is part of the Communion service; and whatever be the proper garb of the minister in the one part of that service, the same ought to be worn by him throughout. The rubric and canons recognize no difference whatever. The rubric, at the commencement of 'The Order for Morning and Evening Prayer,' says, 'That such ornaments of the church, and of the ministers thereof, at all times of their ministration shall be retained, and be in use, as were in this Church of England by the authority of Parliament, in the second year of the reign of King Edward VI.'—in other words, 'a white alb plain, with a vestment or cope.' These were forbidden in King Edward VI.'s second book, which ordered that 'The minister at the time of the Communion, and at all other times of his ministration, shall use neither alb, vestment, nor cope; but being an archbishop or bishop, he shall have and wear a rochet; and being a priest or deacon, he shall have and wear a surplice only.' This was a triumph of the party most opposed to the Church of Rome and most anxious to carry reformation to the very furthest point. But their triumph was brief—within a few months Queen Mary restored popery; and when the accession of Queen Elizabeth brought back the Reformation, she, and the convocation, and the parliament, deliberately rejected the simpler direction of Edward's second book, and revived the ornaments of the first. This decision was followed again by the crown, convocation, and parliament, at the restoration of Charles II., when the existing Act of Uniformity established the Book of Common Prayer, with its rubrics, in the form in which they now stand.

"From this statement it will be seen, that the surplice may be objected to with some reason: but then it must be because the law requires 'the alb and the vestment, or the cope.'

"Why have these been disused? Because the parishioners—that is, the churchwardens, who represent the parishioners—have neglected their duty to provide them; for such is the duty of the parishioners by the plain and express canon law of England (Gibson, 200). True, it would be a very costly duty, and for that reason, most probably, churchwardens have neglected it, and archdeacons have connived at the neglect. I have no wish that it should be otherwise. But, be this as it may, if the churchwardens of Helston shall perform this duty, at the charge of the parish, providing an alb, a vestment, and a cope, as they might in strictness be required to do (Gibson, 201), I shall enjoin the minister, be he who he may, to use them. But until these ornaments are provided by the parishioners, it is the duty of the minister to use the garment actually provided by them for him, which is the surplice. The parishioners never provide a gown, nor, if they did, would he have a right to wear it in any part of his ministrations. For the gown is nowhere mentioned nor alluded to in any of the rubricks. Neither is it included, as the alb, the cope, and three surplices expressly are, among 'the furniture and ornaments proper for divine service,' to be provided by the parishioners of every parish."

I can, indeed, produce definite evidence in favour of the assumed compatibility of the maximum according to rubrics of 1549, and of the minimum according to the canons from an authority whose weight can hardly be gainsayed. Bishop Cosin, as I shall further show, very strongly insists in those notes of his upon the Prayer Book, published by Nicholls at the beginning of the last century, while dealing with the ornaments rubric as it stood between 1604 and 1662, upon the continuous legality of the vestments prescribed in 1549; and yet in another part of the collection, namely a kind of prefatory explanation of our Communion service, offered by Nicholls as a translation from the Latin, and apparently intended by the tone of its explanations for the information of foreigners unacquainted with our ritual, he says, "Now the order wherewith this holy rite is celebrated in our churches is after this manner: First of all it is enjoined, that the table or altar should be covered over with a clean linen cloth, or other decent covering; upon which the Holy Bible, the Common Prayer Book, the paten and chalice are to be placed. Two wax candles are to be set on; and the person who celebrates is to be arrayed with a solemn ecclesiastical habit, that is, a surplice and hood." This is clearly intended as a popular picture of what took place, and not as a rubrical or legal description of what ought to be done, or he would not have mentioned the Bible, which is nowhere ordered as part of the altar furniture, nor recapitulated the chalice and paten, which ought only to be placed on the altar at the offertory, though in so doing he gives an interesting glimpse at the habitual usages of the seventeenth century. So in writing a popular description, Cosin merely describes the popular minimum habit; but when discussing the ornaments rubric he lays down the legal maximum, thus proving that the incompatibility which the judges in Hebbert *v.* Purchas find has no place in his mind.

In the meanwhile I have wandered from my intention of showing that the rule laid down by the Judicial Committee leads to results of which the learned judges can hardly have thought. There are two prefatory orders to the Prayer Book, of which—after what has taken place this year in Convocation, and what must hereafter (however its deliberations may be directed) take place,—I cannot too earnestly say, that I trust they may never be tampered with, or the reasonable indulgence for difficulties no less than impossibilities which they offer, be extended to licence.

"And all priests and deacons are to say daily the Morning and Evening Prayer either privately or openly, not being let by sickness, or some other urgent cause.

"And the curate that ministereth in every parish church or chappel being at home, shall say the same in the parish church or chappel where he ministereth, and shall cause a bell to be tolled thereunto a convenient time before he begin, that the people may come to hear God's word, and to pray with him."

These directions as they stand seem simple enough, but if we turn to the canons we find two which, in what they enact, are hardly consistent with them.

XIV. *The prescript form of Divine Service to be used on Sundays and Holy-Days.*

"The common prayer shall be said or sung distinctly and reverently upon such days as are appointed to be kept holy by the Book of Common Prayer, and their eves, and at convenient and usual times of those days, and in such place of every church as the bishop of the diocese, or ecclesiastical ordinary of the place, shall think meet for the largeness or straitness of the same, so as the people may be most edified. All ministers likewise shall observe the orders, rites, and ceremonies prescribed in the Book of Common Prayer, as well in reading the Holy Scriptures, and saying of prayers, as in administration of the Sacraments, without either diminishing in regard of preaching, or in any other respect, or adding anything in the matter or form thereof."

XV. *The Litany to be read on Wednesdays and Fridays.*

"The litany shall be said or sung when, and as it is set down in the Book of Common Prayer, by the parsons, vicars, ministers, or curates, in all cathedral, collegiate, parish churches, and chapels, in some convenient place, according to the discretion of the bishop of the diocese, or ecclesiastical ordinary of the place. And that we may speak more particularly, upon Wednesdays and Fridays weekly, though they be not holy-days, the minister, at the accustomed hours of service, shall resort to the church or chapel, and warning being given to the people by tolling of a bell, shall say the litany prescribed in the Book of Common Prayer; whereunto we wish every householder dwelling within half a mile of the church to come, or send one at the least of his household, fit to join with the minister in prayers."

A person ignorant of the judgment in Hebbert *v.* Purchas might suggest that the Prayer Book laid down the maximum and these two canons the minimum, and that while the Church solemnly warned her ministers of their duty to say publicly "not being let by sickness or some other urgent cause," and "being at home and not being otherwise reasonably hindered," "daily the Morning and Evening Prayer," she repeats her order more thoroughly and peremptorily, and with the determination of being obeyed, but only as to "such days as are appointed to be kept holy by the Book of Common Prayer, and their eves," and also as to Wednesdays and Fridays in respect of the Litany; but that the last thing the authors of the canons of 1604 would have dreamed of, would be to make the public use of daily Morning and Evening prayer penal. Any such theory would be rejected by the man who adopted the principles of the Purchas judgment, for by applying its positions to the present case he would find "that the doctrine of a minimum" of "public" worship, "represented by" the Morning and Evening Prayer on holy days and eves, and the Wednesday and Friday Litanies of the canons, with a maximum "represented by a return to the" direction to say daily Morning and Evening Prayer publicly when practicable of the rubric, "is inconsistent with the fact that the rubric is a positive order, under a penal statute, accepted by each clergyman in a remarkably strong expression of assent and consent, and capable of being enforced with severe penalties. It is not to be assumed without proof that such a statute was framed so as to leave a choice between contrary interpretations in a question that had ever been regarded as momentous, and had stirred, as the learned judge remarks, some of the strongest passions of man." "If the minister is ordered" to say Morning and Evening Prayer on holy days and eves only, he cannot say it daily; "if he is" to say the Litany only on Wednesdays and Fridays "he cannot" say the whole Morning and Evening Prayer on those days.

The respectful listener who had followed this argument to its close would, I believe, be prepared to hear as its conclusion, that the "positive order under a penal statute" must override the feebler monitions of any canon, and that the minister with the choice of two ways of acting must follow that order which is "capable of being enforced with very severe penalties." He might be a little surprised to learn after all that the solution proposed for this difficulty was, that as there could be no maximum and minimum, minimum and maximum must be the same thing, and "daily" be read to mean "such days as are appointed to be kept holy by the Book of Common Prayer, and their eves."

I have now to see how so amazing a result could have been reached, and shall come to still closer quarters with the Purchas judgment. I must refer my readers back to the second chapter, page 58, where I quote from the judgment in the Liddell case, a passage in which the Judicial Committee of that day, after pointing out the variations between the ornaments rubric of Elizabeth, the corresponding passage of her Act of Uniformity, and the ornaments rubric of the present book, which I need not, therefore, repeat, sum up by saying, "The rubric to the Prayer Book of January 1, 1604, adopts the language of the rubric of Elizabeth. The rubric in the present Prayer Book adopts the language of the statute of Elizabeth; but they obviously mean the same thing, that the same dresses and the same utensils or articles which were used under the First Prayer Book of Edward VI. may still be used."

The Judicial Committee in the case of Martin *v.* Mackonochie by the mouth of Lord Cairns, while it did not specifically refer to the minister's dresses, so thoroughly and unreservedly accepts the entire interpretation of the ornaments rubric given in Liddell *v.* Westerton, that it must be held to accept this portion of it.

"The rubric, or note, as to ornaments, in the commencement of the Prayer Book, is in these words:—

"'And here is to be noted that such ornaments of the church, and of the ministers thereof, at all times of their ministration, shall be retained, and be in use, as were in this Church of England, by the authority of Parliament, in the second year of the reign of King Edward VI.'

"The construction of this Rubric was very fully considered by this committee in the case of Westerton *v.* Liddell, already referred to; and the propositions which their Lordships understand to have been established by the judgment in that case may be thus stated:—

"First. The words 'authority of Parliament,' in the rubric, refer to, and mean the Act of Parliament 2 and 3 Edw. VI., cap. 1, giving Parliamentary effect to the First Prayer Book of Edward VI., and do not refer to, or mean canons or Royal Injunctions having the authority of Parliament, made at an earlier period.

"Second. The term 'ornaments' in the rubric means those articles, the use of which in the services and ministrations of the Church, is prescribed by that Prayer Book.

"Third. The term 'ornaments' is confined to those articles.

"Fourth. Though there may be articles not expressly mentioned in the rubric the use of which would not be restrained, they must be articles which are consistent with, and subsidiary to, the services; as an organ for the singing, a credence table from which to take the sacramental bread and wine, cushions, hassocks, &c."

"In these conclusions, and in this construction of the rubric, their Lordships entirely concur."

The method which the authors of the Purchas judgment adopt to get rid of the strong weight of adverse decisions, is to magnify as if essential those differences between the successive editions of the ornaments rubric and Elizabeth's statute which former Judicial Committees have pronounced to be of such slight moment.

"The Learned Judge, in the court below, assumes (Appendix, p. 74) that the Puritan party at the Savoy Conference objected to *this* rubric, whereas it was the rubric of James that they were discussing. Upon that, the Puritans observed that, 'inasmuch as this rubric seemeth to bring back the cope, alb, and other vestments forbidden by the Common Prayer Book, 5 and 6 Edward VI., and so for reasons alleged against ceremonies under our eighteenth general exception, we deem it may be wholly left out.' The rubric had been in force for nearly sixty years, and they do not allege that the vestments had been brought back; nor would a total omission of the rubric have been a protection against them. The bishops in their answer show that they understand the surplice to be in question, and not the vestments. (Cardwell Conferences, 314, 345, 351.) But the Learned Judge through this oversight has overlooked the most important part of the proceedings. The bishops determined that the rubric 'should continue as it is.' But after this they did, in fact, recast it entirely. It must not be assumed that alterations made under such circumstances were made without thought, and are of no importance. The rubric had directed the minister to 'use at the time of the Communion, and at all other times of his ministrations,' the ornaments in question. The statute of Elizabeth did not direct such use, nor refer to any special times of ministration, but it ordered simply the retaining of the ornaments till further order made by the Queen. The bishops threw aside the form of the old rubric and adopted that of the statute of Elizabeth, but added the words 'at all times of their ministration,' without the words which had in all former rubrics distinguished the Holy Communion from other ministrations; a mode of expression more suitable to a state of things wherein the vestments for all ministrations had become the same. The change also brought in the word 'retained,' which it has been argued, would not include things already obsolete. Whatever be the force of these two arguments, the fact is clear that the Puritans objected to a rubric differing from this; and that after their objections, the rubric was recast, and brought into its present form."

I can hardly better answer these pleadings than by referring back to the quotation from Sir J. T. Coleridge's pamphlet on the judgment, which I gave in my second chapter, page 65, and to Bishop Phillpotts' long anterior summing up of the question which I have lately cited. It would require very strong arguments to demonstrate that any canons, however weighty, could have the prospective effect of altering the plain meaning of a statute passed fifty-eight years posterior to them, and claiming to legislate directly upon their very subject matter. With great personal respect for the prelates and jurists who sat in Hebbert *v.* Purchas, I do not believe that they have succeeded in their difficult task, though, in the words of Sir J. T. Coleridge—which I should not have dared to use if they had not been a quotation from one so courteous, grave, and venerable—they may have "punished and insulted severely" men who were trying to carry into action that which, in 1857, they had learned was the law at the mouths of Archbishop Sumner and Archbishop Tait.

I cannot, however, pass from the subject without recording my decided opinion that the meaning and spirit of the word "retain" is exactly the reverse of that which has been assigned to it by the learned judges in the above passage. Surely "retain," derived from "re," "back," and "teneo," "I hold," and therefore identical with the common composite verb "I hold back," implies and figures the act of grasping at and keeping upright—of preventing from falling over—something which is in danger of slipping back and being lost, something which just risks becoming "obsolete," as the Eucharistic dress might have done if the Convocation in 1662 had not "retained" it in the words of the statute of Elizabeth. Having written this sentence, I referred to Bailey's translation of Facciolati's and Forcellini's Lexicons, and I found this respectable authority explaining "retineo" almost in my words, as "*to hold or keep back or in, stop, detain*, κατέχω, tenco ne abeat, ne elabatur, retro tenco." How far this etymology may help the meaning of the ornaments rubric for which I am contending, I leave to others to determine, but the attempt which has been made to supplant it, and to set up a narrow interpretation of the canons as a maximum law in its place, by fine distinctions as to the meaning of "retain," must, I think, be regarded as a rather weak attempt to sustain a position much in need of arguments. Besides, if the argument had any value at all upon the supposition that "retain" was a word found out and introduced in 1662 to represent the then present state of matters, it clearly would have none when applied to the directly contrary state of facts in 1559. "Retain" is the word used in the Act of Elizabeth, which had for its scope to *bring back* the ornaments of the minister and of the church, which had been in use in 1549 (as with much more from time immemorial), and had only become obsolete in 1552; so actually the Privy Council call upon us to affirm that a word which had been introduced into an Act of Parliament with one specific meaning in 1559, is to be held to have been imported from that very Act into a new rubric in 1662, with the direct intention of signifying the absolute contrary. "Retain," which was in 1559 devised to mean preserve, and revive that which had fallen into disuse, is in 1662 to mean reject it because of that very disuse.

   I have hitherto been considering the Eucharistic dress from a contentious standing ground, and discussing it in its legal aspect. I shall now, as briefly as possible, throw together a few facts, showing that the ornaments rubrics of the First Book of

CHAP. IV. CONTINUITY OF HIGHER USE. 117

Edward VI.—revived by the statute, and the complementary ornaments rubric of Elizabeth, qualified by the Advertisements of that Queen, and by the canons of 1604, but also drily revived by the ornaments rubric of the same year as the canons, and again as drily revived by the actual ornaments rubric—has not been a dead letter in the Church of England. Of course, the Eucharistic use of the surplice only has been since 1552 the enormously preponderating practice. Any attempt to shirk or minimise that fact would only weaken the argument on the other side, and expose the man who dared to adopt such a line of controversy to the merited reproach of sophistry and disingenuousness. What I contend for is, that continuously alongside of this use of the surplice, down at least to the days when the chill fogs of the eighteenth century were beginning to gather, another use continued, and was intended to continue, and that as that use is still as legally valid as it was at any former moment of its greatest prevalence, it has never ceased to be a living instrument in the hands of the Church, to be again actively employed when men's hearts have been moved to crave for the boon, not as of constraint, not universally, but wheresoever it may lead to the glory of God and the edification of the people.*

During the sixteenth and seventeenth centuries, neither religious nor political toleration, in its present sense, was understood or practised. So this, like other questions, assumed a pugnacious complexion. It can only be by wilfulness or mismanagement if it does so now, when all which is asked for is allowance even for that which those who make the request believe to be legal.

In selecting my evidence I shall not make a large use of a

---

* My friend and brother Ritual Commissioner, Lord Harrowby, in a letter which has provoked a good deal of newspaper comment, has assumed an unanimity against the vestments in the Commission, which he was far from being warranted in asserting. The word used as to them in the First Report was 'restrained,' and it is undoubted that a weighty section of the Commission did sign the report, because the word used was 'restrain' and not 'prohibit.'

class of quotations which have been much employed in the controversy—passages from the railing pamphlets of Puritans, in the days before the laws of literary courtesy had been established. I rather abstain from doing so for fear of seeming to overstate my own case and substitute diatribes for proofs. If the tirades of those vehement gentlemen are to be taken at all to the letter, it would seem as if what would now be termed "very advanced ritual" had overspread the land in the days of Elizabeth, and again of Charles I., to an extent for which I believe there is not very conclusive historical evidence; so I forego the advantage of the inferences which I might draw from their writings, in order to rest my case on circumstantial instances. For another reason I shall not produce all the references which I have before me to copes in cathedrals, during what I have designated the Reformation century. Their use in those churches is confessed on both sides, though one side quotes it as evidence of conformity to the ornaments rubric, and the other to the Advertisements and Canons.

There is, however, one episode in the campaign which the Puritans continued to carry on against the continuance of copes in the cathedrals, which is so valuable for the light which it throws upon the legal question of the abiding validity of the ornaments rubrics of 1549, that I must deal with it at a little length. I shall again, and not for the last time, have to bring Bishop Cosin on the scene. He was at the height of his early activity, working as Prebendary of Durham, in concert with Dean Hunt, and other like-minded members of the Chapter, in adorning the service of his cathedral, when an adversary appeared in the person of a senior Prebendary, by name Peter Smart, whose character, unconsciously photographed by himself in his long-winded accusation against his colleagues, would require Sir Walter Scott to do it justice. Even in that age of literary ill-manners, unwearying iteration, and garrulous prolixity, the "Articles or Instructions for Articles" which this "elder brother," as he boorishly styled himself, drew up, would pass as a masterpiece of all which is not graceful in composition. These, which he brought in 1630 against " Mr. John Cosin, Mr. Francis Burgoine, Mr. Marmaduke Blaxton, Dr. Hunt, Dr. Lindsell, Mr. William James, all learned clerks of the cathedral church of Durham," in the High Commission Court of York, turned to poor Smart's disadvantage, as it led to his imprisonment and sequestration, and, finally, to his deprivation, as he neither would recant nor pay costs. Ten years later he was able to repeat his charges before Parliament with a different result.

The copes, with other ornaments of the Church and the ministers, appear over and over again in this paper, which has lately been printed for the first time, and at length (with the exception of one page happily lost), in the first volume of Bishop Cosin's Correspondence, edited, for the Surtees Society, by the Rev. G. Ornsby, which appeared in 1869. But the only passage which I shall give is the following:

"16. Item: we article and object against you, Richard Hunt, John Cosin, Francis Burgoin, that you having scornfully abused and disgraced the gratious Font of regeneration (though lately you have carved it and trim'd it as the Pharises did when they had slain the prophets; to make them amends they bestowed white sepulchres upon their dead carkasses), and having erected an high altar (as you call it) as farre from the congregation as possibly you could, thither you ascend dayly, and upon Sundays and Holydays in copes, to say part of Morning Service, and 2 or 3 prayers after sermons, for the saying of which prayers copes are put on again, contrarie to the example of all Cathedrall churches in England, and contrarie to the express words of the Canons, which command no praiers to be said at the Communion-table in copes, but in surplices, save only at the Administration of the Holy Communion, fanatically and phantastically thinking, and making seely seduced girls beleeve, that the service, and praiers said at the Altar in the east, and in copes, are more holy and effectuall then those that are said at the Communion-table, or Deske in the body of the church or chancell, yea though the people heare not a word with understanding (as is done at Mr. Burgoyn's Altar in Warmouth Church, and Mr. Cosin's in Branspeth").

The singular value of this statement is at once apparent. Peter Smart, looking to the Advertisements and Canons only, and interpreting them as narrowly as possible, contends that, according to them, the use of the cope at the Lord's Table is permissible "only at the administration of the Holy Communion," and that at other times, when the first part of the Communion Service is read, surplices only should be used. Dean Hunt and Dr. Cosin, on the other hand, pass over these documents, and falling back on the later of the two ornaments rubrics of 1549, used copes on these occasions. It is no question as to which party was, in this particular respect, more liturgically in the right. Perhaps I should be more inclined to agree with Smart on this head than in other of his sayings and doings, for there is a manifest incongruity in decking out that empty shadow of a reality, the truncated Communion Office—so unhappily introduced in the Book of 1549—which is to end in nothing, with the trappings of a real celebration. The question is as to what state of the law this action of theirs bears witness. If the Advertisements and Canons had superseded these ornaments rubrics, then Smart would have been right in his view of the law, and the remaining chapter would have committed an illegality. If, on the contrary, they were sustained in what they did—and they were sustained—then we have got a direct conclusion, many years after the canons, as to the dress of the minister, contained in the Prayer Book of 1549, being held to be still in full force as against them, and so the reasonings of the Purchas judgment are shown to be fallacious.

Much of Smart's anger arose from the active part which his brethren took in restoring to the service of the Sanctuary some very costly copes of pre-reformational date, which, as I will show further on, were the same which continued in use in Durham Cathedral till some period between the middle and the end of the last century, and which still exist to prove what a vexatious meddler he was. It happens, however, to be on record that the cope which Dr. Cosin himself wore was of plain

ELIZABETH'S PRIVATE CHAPEL.

white satin, and may have been his property, although there is a reference to an old white satin one in the following passage of the Acts of the Chapter of Durham, dated June 12, 1627, and in Cosin's own handwriting, three years before Smart's intervention, which is published in the Cosin correspondence:—

"It is further agreed that the three vestments and one white cope, now belonging to the vestry of this church, shall be taken and carried to London, to be altered and changed into fair and large copes, according to the Canons and Constitutions of the Church of England. And that allowance shall be made to the treasurer of the money that shall be expended therein, by the direction of the Lord Bishop of Durham."

I much wish when the Archbishop of Canterbury inquired of the Bishop of Lincoln, during the late debates in Convocation, whether Cosin himself ever wore vestments, that the Bishop could have answered the question by the statement of this specific fact.

The use of copes upon days when the mutilated Communion service was alone used is, as we have seen, a proof that the rubrics of 1549 were still in force after the publication of the Advertisements. The use of copes in places of worship other than "Cathedral and Collegiate Churches," would be direct evidence to the same effect, and of this we have ample proof. I shall not refer to the use of them in the well-known private chapel of Queen Elizabeth, at the beginning of her reign, about which so many bitter complaints, written in the correspondence between the Puritan Bishops and the Zurich reformers, which has been published by the Parker Society. I do not abstain for fear of the rejoinder that as Elizabeth thought herself, and was thought, above law, and as the ordinary jurisdiction of the episcopate could not reach her chapel, therefore what she, still a young woman, headstrong and inexperienced in the art of reigning, might or might not please to do in an apartment which she regarded as, so to speak, her own spiritual boudoir, was of little moment in a controversy touching the general condition of the great public Church of England. I am not careful to enter on these considerations, simply because I have a respect for chronology. Unwilling as I am to accept the canons of 1604 as colouring an Act of Parliament fifty-eight years after, I can hardly bring myself to deal with doings of Elizabeth, as interpreting Advertisements of hers, full four years later, although I may myself believe they could throw some light on the animus of that proceeding. Whatever else Elizabeth was, she was the "supreme governor" in all ecclesiastical causes, and the value of the ritual in her chapel was enormous, not only as setting an example, and, to borrow a phrase of her own, as "tuning the pulpits," but as showing what were the feelings as to ceremonial of those who had the best opportunities of knowing what their own Advertisements meant, that is, of those who had had a hand in framing them. As to the ceremonial in Elizabeth's earlier regnal period, it happens, as I have said, that the correspondence in which Sampson here, and Peter Martyr, in Switzerland, were principal letter-writers, took place in 1560, before the publication of the Advertisements, and it is therefore only so far evidence as helping to show the animus of their compilers. As, however, we learn that Elizabeth, in 1570, still retained that crucifix in her chapel, which was, with its other ornaments, so great a trouble to the Zurich party, and as there is an incidental description of the fittings of that chapel in 1565, shortly after the Advertisements, with a list of altar-plate and hangings of a fabulous richness, it is at least more probable that she did not dispense with the copes, although that description being one of the fabric and not of the officiators, the occasion of describing them did not occur.

But all this is conjecture. I have before me an authentic narrative, unprinted and unknown till two years since, of the ceremonial in Elizabeth's chapel, after she had been hardened by thirty-four years Queenship—after she had seen Grindal replace Parker on the throne of Canterbury, and Whitgift Grindal—after she had given her love to Dudley, that fosterer of the Puritans—after she had, by the defeat of the Armada, met and overthrown the power of Papal Europe. We now know that she kept Easter in 1593, in her chapel, in this guise.

"The moste sacred Queene Elizabethe upon Estre day, after the Holy Gospell was redde in the Chaple at St. James, came down into her Majestes Travess; before her highnes came the gentlemen pencioners, then the Barons, the Bushopps, London and Landaffe, th Erls and the ho: Councell in their colors of State, the Harolds at Arms, the Lord Keeper bearinge the Great Seal himselfe, and the Erle of Herefford bearinge the sword beffore her Majestie. Then her Majesties Royal person came moste chearfully, havinge as noble supporters the Right Honorable th Erle of Essex, Master of her Majestes Horse, on the right hande, and the Right Hon. the Lord Admyral on the lefte hand, the Lord Chambrelen to her Majestie (also nexte beffore her Majeste) attendante al the while. Dr. Bull was at the organ playinge the Offertorye. Her Majestie entred her Travess moste devoutly, there knyelinge: after some prayers she came princely beffore the Table, and there humbly knielinge did offer the golden obeysant, the Bushop the hon. Father of Worcester holdinge the golden bason, the Subdean and the Epistler in riche coaps assistante to the sayd Bushop: which done her Majestie retorned to her princely travess sumptuously sett forthe, untyl the present action of the Holy Communion, contynually exercysed in ernest prayer, and then the blessed Sacrament first receyved of the sayd Bushop and administred to the Subdean, the gospeller for that day, and to the Epistler, her sacred person presented herselfe beffore the Lord's Table, Royally attended as beffore, where was sett a stately stoole and qwssins (cushions) for her Majestie, and so humbly knielinge with most singuler devocion and holye reverence dyd most comfortablye receyve the most blessed Sacramente of Christes bodye and blood, in the kinds of bread and wyne, accordinge to the laws established by her Majestie and Godly laws in Parliament. The bread beinge waffer bread of some thicker substaunce, which her Majestie in most reverend manner toke of the Lord Bushop in her naked right hand, her setisfyed hert fixinge her semblant eyes most entirely uppon the woorthye words Sacramental pronounced by the Bushop, and that with soche an holye aspecte as it did mightelye adde comfforts to the godlye beholders (wherof this writer was one very neare): and likewise her Majestie receaved the cuppe, havinge a moste princely lynned clothe layd on her cushion pillowe and borne at the four ends by the noble Erle of Herefford, the Erle of Essex, the Erle of Worcester, and th Erle of Oxford: the side of the sayd clothe her Majestie toke up in her hande, and therewith toke the ffoote of the golden and nowe sacred cuppe, and with like holy reverend attention as beffore to the sacramentaon words, did drinke of the same most devoutly (all this while knielinge on her knies) to the confirmation of her faythe and absolute comfforte in her purged conscience by the holy spirit of God in the exercise of this holye Communion, of her participation of and in the merits and deathe of Christe Jesus our Lorde, and the perfecte communion and spiritual ffoode of the verye bodye and bloode of Christe our Lord Saviour: and so retorninge to her sayd Travess their devoutly stayed the end of prayers, which done her Majestie Royally ascended the way and stayrs into her presence, whom the Lord blesse for ever and ever. Amen.

Ant. Anderson, Subdean."

This curious extract is taken from 'The Old Cheque-Book or Book of Remembrance of the Chapel Royal, from 1561 to 1794. Edited from the original MS. preserved among the muniments of the Chapel Royal, St. James's Palace, by Edward F. Rimbault, LL.D. Printed for the Camden Society in 1872.' Thus, twenty-eight years after the Advertisements, Queen Elizabeth had vestments in her Chapel Royal, which was, in strictness, neither a cathedral nor collegiate church, and in so far conforming to the rubrics of 1549, disobeyed those recommendations.

Let me now adduce some instances of copes in the private chapels of Bishops, and in those of colleges, neither of which fall under the permissions of the Advertisements and Canons. Prynne and his party, in ransacking Archbishop Laud's papers for materials to use against him at his trial, found a plan of the private chapel of the famous Bishop Andrewes (who lived from 1555 to 1626, and was Bishop successively of Chichester, Ely, and Winchester from 1605 to 1626), with an inventory of its furniture, both of which Laud copied in his successive chapels at Abergwilly, London House, and Lambeth. The plan is engraved and the inventory printed in 'Canterbury's Doom;'

and by the latter we find that Bishop Andrewes had provided five copes and five surplices for the use of his chapel. In accordance with these arrangements Dr. Heywood, Laud's chaplain, confessed to have used a cope in the Archbishop's chapel, which the latter acknowledges, while justifying himself by an appeal to the canon, which I think would hardly hold good; although, if admitted, it negatives that interpretation of the canon which limits the use of copes to the Bishops, Deans, Canons, and Prebendaries of and in the specific cathedrals, if a chaplain could wear one in a chapel. In 1626 the then Bishop of Durham, Neile, consecrated Dr. Francis White Bishop of Carlisle in the chapel of Durham House, London, and it is noted that the Epistle and Gospel were read by Archdeacons Cosin and Wickham "in the King's copes," which were, of course, borrowed for the solemnity. Dr. Cosin, when Master of Peterhouse, Cambridge, gave copes to the still existing chapel, which he built for the use of the college, to replace as such the adjacent "Little St. Mary's," which had previously been both college chapel and parish church. The next instance which I have to produce is rather curious. Archbishop Williams, according to his Life by Hackett—

"also repaired one side of Lincoln College in Oxford, and built a chapel there, where the Mysteries of our Saviour Christ while He was upon earth, being neatly coloured in the glass windows, made a great and solemn appearance. The screen and lining of the walls is of cedar-wood. The copes, the plate, and all sorts of furniture for the Holy Table, being rich and suitable."

An *argumentum ad hominem* is not the highest kind of logic, but an *argumentum ab homine* may have great weight, and there are people who may think that one gift of copes from Williams to a place neither a cathedral nor collegiate church is more helpful in an argument on the ornaments rubric than a score from Laud would be.

I am unable to find definite instances of the use of copes in parish churches during the period with which I am dealing, unless the following passage referring to 1640 from Heylin's *Cyprianus Anglicanus* should be accepted, though it does not exactly say where these unfortunate divines wore their copes.

" The like [persecution by the House of Commons] happened also unto Heywood, Vicar of St. Giles's-in-the-Fields; Squire, of St. Leonard's in Shoreditch; and Finch, of Christ Church. The articles against which four and some others more, being for the most part of the same nature and effect, as, namely, railing in the Communion table, adoration toward it, calling up the parishioners to the rail to receive the Sacrament, reading the second service at the table so placed, preaching in surplices and hoods, administering the Sacrament in copes, beautifying and adorning churches with painted glass, and others of the like condition; which either were to be held for crimes in the clergy generally, or else accounted none in them."

There are a great many violent denunciations in Puritan pamphlets against clergymen for wearing copes, and even chasubles, but I adhere to my principle of not adducing general allegations as evidence. But I believe that, as there can be no smoke without fire, the revival of ceremonial in the earlier part of the seventeenth century must have been characterised by the use in various places of a distinctive Eucharistic dress. Those who adopted one began to find as religion became political that this was hardly a safe practice, and so very naturally, and after the long interval of the Commonwealth, the record of their actions had perished. I throw out of the category the very curious account of a gorgeous ceremony, which I must, I suppose, call the " opening " (as no bishop was there), of a new altar in Wolverhampton Church in 1635, at which four copes, borrowed from Lichfield were worn; for Wolverhampton Church was till very recently (though only titularly) a collegiate church. I freely and at once admit that, in the large collection of visitation articles of the seventeenth century published in the second report of the Ritual Commission, no trace exists of a vestment higher than the surplice being insisted upon. This is quite consistent with the policy of the obligatory minimum (out of regard to the rate-payers, who must have paid for the copes),

CHAP. IV. COPES IN SUBSTITUTION FOR OTHER VESTMENTS. 127

which I believe actuated those ecclesiastical dignitaries during that period who were High Churchmen, while Low Churchmen would, of course, take great pains not to refer to the subject. Visitation articles never did go beyond the obligatory, and particularly would they not have done so in days when the duties of Churchwardens and the obligations of Churchmen were so much more stringent and more sharply defined than in this liberal age, even before the abolition of compulsory church-rates.

It will have been noticed that in the accounts of Queen Elizabeth's Easter, of the consecration of Bishop White, and of the service at Wolverhampton, which I have quoted or referred to, the use of more than one cope is expressly indicated, and that in the first two cases it is directly stated that they were worn by the Gospeller and the Epistler. The like phenomenon seems to have marked those ceremonials in cathedrals which I have forborne from quoting. This ornate ceremonial on the face of it appears to be neither consistent with the rubrics of 1549, the Advertisements, nor the Canons, in all which the one vestment or cope for the celebrant, with tunicles for the assistants in the first named, is all which is ordered. Several reflections may be made upon this fact. Generally, no doubt, it affords another instance of that reasonable principle of omission not being prohibition, without which the conduct of divine worship according to the actual rubrics would come to a dead-lock. More specifically two or three explanations may be offered. According to that somewhat rough and ready not to say inaccurate way in which I believe the rubric of 1549 was carried out, as a vestment or cope seems very early to have become in practice a cope only, so may the precise meaning of "tunacle" have become forgotten or disregarded, and the word assumed to mean merely some kind of rich dress, which would be very well supplied in the familiar form of another cope. It might also be that "agreeably," which so evidently puzzled the compiler of the Latin canons in 1604, was interpreted as "similarly," and the Advertisements concluded to order copes likewise for the Epistler and Gospeller, who represented the other assistant clergy, who are named in the rubric. Besides the processional character of copes had never quite been forgotten, so far as their use in the great procession of the Chapter of Windsor on St. George's Day, and on principal State occasions. The sanction for such processions can nowhere be found in our present rubrics, but though it was omitted it was not held to have been prohibited.

My argument has not led me to discuss the absolute legal value of Queen Elizabeth's Advertisements. Low Churchmen generally try to put it at the highest, in spite of the more than great doubt whether they had ever received the Queen's signature, while High Churchmen reckon their validity at much less. Since the passing of the Act of Uniformity of 1662, I regard this as a purely antiquarian question, and of no practical value whatever. I am writing with a copy of the original edition of the Advertisements in my hand, and I must say that the internal evidence, considering how courtly were the days in which they were published, seems overpowering that the Queen had little or nothing to do with them. The "in virtue" of the "Queen's letter commanding" them is mentioned on the title-page, but no posterior approbation signified, and they are at the end merely stated as "agreed upon and subscribed by" Archbishop Parker and the Bishops of London, Ely, and Rochester, "Commissioners in causes ecclesiastical," and by the Bishops of Winchester and Lincoln "with others." Cardwell erroneously prints the two latter as if also Commissioners. The cool dispassionate summing up of Cardwell is that "although the Queen was the person really responsible for these Advertisements, she did not sufficiently give her sanction to them at the time. Their title and preface certainly do not claim for them the highest degree of authority." Strype, indeed, infers that they subsequently received the royal sanction; but Cardwell doubts, and observes that Parker's and Whitgift's way of talking of them seems to negative their royal authority. Of course if they never did receive the royal authority, the last vestige of an argument against the abiding force of the ornaments rubric of 1559 falls to the ground.

I have reserved for the close of this particular examination what is, perhaps, the most valuable body of opinions which we possess, considering from whom they emanate, upon the ornaments rubrics. They are contained in the series of 'Additional Notes upon the Prayer Book,' reprinted in Dr. Nicholls' folio edition of it, which appeared in 1710, and as to which he explains that their component parts are separate collections of notes by Bishop Andrewes; by Bishop Overall as "supposed," and, as I believe, now accepted; by Bishop Cosin (in two collections); and by a Dr. Mills. Nicholls is careful to distinguish the respective authorships. Cosin explains, "and the chancels shall remain as they have done in times past," by "that is distinguished from the body of the church by a frame of open work, and furnished with a row of chairs or stools on either side." The then ornaments rubric on which Cosin comments is not the one we now possess as remodelled with Cosin's own co-operation upon the statute of Elizabeth, but that earlier form of it which the general consent of learned men, with the exception of the Judges in Hebbert *v.* Purchas, accepts as in respect of vesture "meaning the same thing." Cosin sums up the effect of the ornaments rubric with much precision. I have already had occasion to refer in the second chapter to what he says about the 25th of Henry VIII., and need not, therefore, repeat my remarks.

"*Such Ornaments, &c.*] Without which (as common reason and experience teaches us,) the majesty of him that owneth it, and the work of his service there, will prove to be of a very common and low esteem. The particulars of these ornaments (both of the church and of the ministers thereof, as in the end of the Act of uniformity) are referred not to the fifth of *Edwd. VI.* as the service itself is in the beginning of that Act, for in that fifth year were all ornaments taken away (but a surplice only) both from bishops and priests, and all other ministers, and nothing was left for the church but a

K

font, a table, and a linen cloth upon it (at the time of the Communion only) but to the second year of that King, when his first service-book and injunctions were in force by authority of Parliament. And in those books many other ornaments are appointed; as, two lights to be set upon the altar or communion table, a cope or vestment for the priest and for the bishop, besides their albs, surplices and rochets, the bishop's crosier-staff, to be holden by him at his ministration and ordinations; and those ornaments of the Church, which by former laws, not then abrogated, were in use, by virtue of the statute 25 *Henry VIII.*, and for them the provincial constitutions are to be consulted, such as have not been repealed, standing then in the second year of King *Edw. VI.* and being still in force by virtue of this rubrick and Act of Parliament."

I need not follow him in quoting the rubrics of 1549, which I have already given; he recites them fully, and as accepting all their provisions. In a following note he does not so much as condescend to notice the Advertisements or Canons, but boldly puts forward the revived ornaments of the First Prayer Book as the then existing law.

"These ornaments and vestures of the ministers were so displeasing to *Calvin* and *Bucer*, that the one in his letters to the Protector, and the other in his censure of the Liturgy, sent to Archbishop *Cranmer*, urged very vehemently to have them taken away, not thinking it tolerable that we should have anything common with the Papists, but show forth our Christian liberty in the simplicity of the Gospel.

"Hereupon, when a Parliament was called, in the fifth year of King *Edward*, they altered the former book, and made another order for vestments, copes, and albs not to be worn at all, allowing an archbishop and a bishop a rochet only, and a priest and deacon to wear nothing but a surplice.

"But by the Act of Uniformity the Parliament thought fit not to continue this last order, but to restore the first again, which since that time was never altered by any other law, and therefore it is still in force at this day.

"And both bishops, priests, and deacons, that knowingly and wilfully break this order, are as hardly censured in the preface to this book concerning ceremonies, as ever *Calvin* or *Bucer* censured the ceremonies themselves. Among other ornaments of the Church also then in use in the second year of *Edward VI.*, there were two lights appointed by his injunctions (which the Parliament had authorised him to make, and whereof otherwhiles they make mention, as acknowledging them to be binding) to be set upon the high altar, as a significant ceremony of the light which Christ's Gospel brought into the world; and this at the same time when all other lights and tapers superstitiously set before images were by the very same injunctions, with many other abused ceremonies and superfluities, taken away. These lights were (by virtue of this present rubrick, referring to what was in use in the second of *Edward VI.*) afterwards continued in all the Queen's chapels during her whole reign, and so are they in the King's, and in many cathedral churches, besides the chapels of divers noblemen, bishops, and colleges to this day. It was well known that the Lord-Treasurer *Burleigh* (who was no friend to superstition or popery) used them constantly in his chapel, with other ornaments of fronts, palls, and books, upon his altar. The like did Bishop *Andrews*, who was a man who knew well what he did, and as free from Popish superstition as any in the kingdom besides. In the latter end of King *Edward's* time they used them in *Scotland* itself, as appears by *Calvin's* Epistle to *Knox*, and his fellow-reformers there, anno 1554, Ep. 206, where he takes exception against them for following the custom of *England*."

Bishop Cosin in subsequent notes repeats the same arguments, with a special reference to Judge Yelverton, with whom he had been brought into collision through the meddling of Peter Smart, " which is a Note wherewith those men are not so well acquainted as they should be who inveigh against our present ornaments in the Church, and them to be innovations, introduced lately by an arbitrary power against law; whereas, indeed, they are appointed in the law itself. And this Judge Yelverton acknowledged and confessed to me (when I declared the Matter to him as I have set it forth) in his account at Durham, not long before his Death, having been of another Mind before."

The following note by Bishop Overall is inserted among those of Cosin.

"*As were in use.*] And then were in use, not a surplice and hood, as we now use, but a plain white alb, with a vestment or cope over it; and therefore, according to this rubric, we are all still bound to wear albs and vestments, as have been so long time worn in the Church of God, howsoever it is neglected. For the disuse of these ornaments we may thank them that came from Geneva; and in the beginning of Queen *Elizabeth's* reign, being set in places of government, suffered every negligent priest to do what him listed, so he would but profess a difference and opposition in all things (though never so lawful otherwise) against the Church of *Rome* and the ceremonies therein used.

"If any man shall answer, That now the 58th Canon hath appointed it otherwise, and that these things are alterable by the discretion of the church wherein we live; I answer, That such matters are to be altered by the same authority wherewith they were established; and that if that authority be the Convocation of the Clergy, as I think it is (only that), that the 14th Canon commands us to observe all the ceremonies prescribed in this book, I would fain know how we should observe both canons."

Bishop Overall's earlier testimony is not a mere anticipation of that of Cosin, for he belonged to a more ancient school, which, like himself, had already begun to take a prominent part in Church affairs during the reign of Elizabeth, the school to which Hooker himself belonged, and of which Bishop Andrewes was the great practical leader, and he had himself personally a share as member of Convocation in the work of making the very canons which he rated at so much below the rubric. Cosin on the other hand belonged to the second school of Laud, and Wren, and lived into the still later one of Thorndike, Sanderson, Pearson, and Gunning. Overall was born in 1559, became bishop in 1614 and died in 1619, having left an indelible mark upon the English Church as author of the admirable second part of the Church Catechism upon the Sacraments. From Overall some recognition of the canons in regard to clerical vesture might have been expected, but as we see he simply puts them on one side, and appeals to the ornaments of 1549 as those which ought still to be worn, I

CHAP. IV. ELASTIC WORKING OF ORNAMENTS RUBRIC. 133

shall not weaken the force of such testimony by any remarks of my own.

I cannot pass from these very important extracts without calling attention to what might at first sight appear to be a discrepancy between Cosin's opinions and practices. We see him in his writings advocating with no compromise the ornaments rubrics of 1549 as the ceremonial law of the Church of England, with their choice between vestment and cope, and their prescription of alb and tunicle; we see him in practice both celebrating in a cope, and acting at Bishop White's consecration as Epistler in a cope. This circumstance appears to be an additional proof of the position, which I have been all through this chapter contending for, that the High Churchmen of the reformation century regarded the ornaments rubrics of 1549 revived in 1559 as formally binding though dispensable in parish churches, but that they understood and worked them in a very elastic, not to say unantiquarian, manner, compromising for the various forms of richer vesture by the one habiliment, the cope. I am not now saying this either to their praise or dispraise, but solely in the interest of what I believe to be historical truth. At the same time, those who may have first begun this more lax handling of the ornaments rubrics in Elizabeth's days—clergymen who must themselves have often been present at, if not taken part in, High Mass before 1549—had a precedent in the rubrics of the unreformed uses, which vary the general prescription of dalmatic for the deacon and of tunicle for the subdeacon, by ordering that the two latter officiators were to wear chasubles at mass during certain portions of the year, and albs only at the same during other portions. To persons who had once been familiar with this rule, there was nothing absolutely repugnant in seeing Gospeller and Epistler arrayed in the same dress as the celebrant, or in seeing on the other hand the celebrant only wearing a distinctive upper dress, while generally speaking this usage must have tended to break down the feeling in favour of the chasuble as the exclusive dress of the celebrant, and one which was, therefore, invested with a unique character of sanctity. Thus from the position of familiarly recognising the chasuble as a dress which others besides the celebrant might wear, it would not be so great a step to accept the cope as one in which the priest might rightly celebrate, for the supplementary use of the chasuble would, as I have shown, have somewhat divested that particular vesture of its peculiar prestige. This is independent of the theory to which I have already adverted, that in some country parishes the cope was the celebrant's vesture before the Reformation, while it tends to explain that confusion, either of vestment or of name, involved in Machyn's talking of the priest who had been taken in a cope saying mass.

Nothing less than forgetfulness of history could have given currency to the argument which is so often brought forward in face of Cosin's own vindication of the ornaments rubric, that he and the other revisers of 1662 could not have intended that rubric to imply that which common sense and common grammar say that it must imply, and which Cosin himself has written that it did imply, because they do not seem to have taken steps to put it in operation after the Restoration. The Prayer Book had been restored upon the collapse of a rigid Presbyterianism and a tyrannous Independency under which all the decent ceremonial of the Church had been submerged. These rival religionisms were down at the time, but so little were they extinguished that at the Savoy Conference preceding the revival of the Common Prayer, the bishops had to fight for the most rudimentary elements of ceremonial point by point; a fixed form of prayer, the sign of the cross in baptism, kneeling at the Communion, the use of the surplice, were all impugned, and each had to be vindicated. It was a victory to have carried these, which might have been imperilled by any immediate attempt to put much beyond them into practice, added to which the clergy, pinched by poverty, and so many of them exiles for years from home and duty, could not have had much heart for what they may have thought the more recondite questions of ceremonial. Still less would the parishioners have had much inclination towards supplying the lacking vestments out of the rates, which was the only way in which they could be legally provided. In face of all this it was an act of conviction and of courage to place on record so emphatic a declaration of that which the then leading churchmen believed to be the more perfect way. As to Cosin indeed recent researches at Durham have completely dissipated this worn-out theory, for they have brought to light his suggestions for the revision of the Prayer Book, some adopted and others not, among the latter of which was a proposal to particularise the vestments. As to the Church party generally of those days, so far from the little practical use which they made of their verbal success being any proof that they could not have meant what they said, it would be more philosophical to own that their saying it under such circumstances proved that they meant it. They appealed to God and to futurity. They cast their bread upon the waters and they trusted to find it after many days. It might be sooner or later, but in God's good Providence it would come. Times and seasons were against them then; but how could they forecast that, for they had no gift of prophecy? All things—in spite of present troubles and difficulties, the still strong and now exacerbated influence of extreme Puritanism, and the poverty of the restored clergy—seemed consistent with a more serene to-morrow. They could not tell that the restored King would be so unmitigatedly worthless and vicious, or that any serious feeling which might underlie his lust and selfishness would be pledged to the Roman Church. They could not foresee Charles II.'s childlessness and the perversion of his brother; they could not guess that England would have to turn to a foreigner and a Calvinist to pick up her sceptre. In the reigns of the sovereigns who had gone before, the Chapel Royal had been accepted as the model of the more stately ceremonial. They might reasonably have hoped that Charles II. would have conceded this little (which would have cost him no trouble) to a Church to which they still believed that he would yield a respectful allegiance in return for its self-sacrificing devotion in the days of trial. If the Royal Chapel had been as that of Elizabeth and her successors, this fact alone would have made it patent to all men, that in continuing the ornaments rubric they were not paltering with unreal words. The cathedrals also had been schools of splendid worship, and they might have looked to such a cathedral as St. Paul's in London, to revive the bygone glories. How could they forecast that in three years London would be desolated by the plague, and in four that St. Paul's itself would be burnt down, not to be restored to worship till after a generation? Even as it was, the fact that they did continue that rubric, and that now more than two centuries after their day that act of theirs has fostered a desire for a distinctive Eucharistic dress, proves that their prescience was neither failure nor mistake; that they did indeed labour for futurity, and that futurity may yet enjoy the fruit of their exertions.

But, after all, the charge brought against them, either of total immediate failure or of personal neglect to give effect to their legislation, conveniently forgets the fact that the man who was the leading spirit in the revision of 1662, was the one man in England who did secure the continuance of the Eucharistic dress in the church over which he presided. I have already expressed my regret that, when one in a high place enquired whether that man ever wore a vestment, he had not received the reply, "Yes, we even know the colour and the material of his cope." This was Cosin, before the Commonwealth head of a house, archdeacon, prebendary, and dean. Did Cosin, after the Restoration Bishop of Durham, shrink from his earlier practice? Let those who desire to show that he had not the courage of his own convictions, ransack his visitation articles and boast that Bishop Cosin of Durham, that great ceremonialist, never thought of pressing any dress more significative than a surplice upon the clergy of his diocese. I should think not; Cosin would not have been the wise man whom the world took him for if he had borne thus hardly upon the poor country parsons of his moorland and mountain diocese, a land of which the mineral wealth was yet undiscovered. It would not merely have been that in so doing he would have disturbed the well-recognised concordat of the minimum which Churchmen before him had ratified and of which the canons were the standing settlement, but the men whom he would have oppressed would not even have been those parsons, men who had just crept back to their homes from years of privation. Declaimers on the anti-ceremonial side argue as if it was the minister who had to buy the officiating dress. The smallest smattering of acquaintance with things as they are should have made them understand that this is a responsibility which devolved upon the parishioners. The 58th Canon limited the legal obligation of those parishioners to finding a surplice, and now controversialists will argue that Cosin and other bishops of his school did not believe in the ornaments rubric, because they did not try to force parishes into expenses from which that canon had relieved them.

The remains of the bishop which have recently been published show to what a miserable condition Church and society had been reduced north of the Tees. There was one church in which he had the right to demand more, the church of which he was Prince Bishop, and in which he had fought his own early battle for the honour of the sanctuary. Even there he was still harassed by Puritan opposition, but he persevered, and Durham Minster, as we know, alone of the Churches of England, continued to use its copes till late into the last century. Of Cosin's later work at Durham, his son-in-law and archdeacon, Dr. Granville, who ten years after his death was promoted to the deanery of Durham, and whose correspondence has been recently published, asserts that "a weekly celebration" there "was the only considerable matter in our cathedral or diocese which Bishop Cosin left unaccomplished;" and this defect Dean Granville himself was able to supply. Cosin clearly wished it; and this fact shows how little to his taste could have been that gaudy presentment of a service which was not communion about which Peter Smart troubled him.

As to the ceremonial of Durham after Cosin's death, that outspoken old Puritan, Ralph Thorseby, who visited it in 1680, eight years after the great bishop's time, complains of the "exceedingly rich copes and robes." Thorseby returned to Durham on January 1, 1680-1, and (as the next day was a Sunday) "in the forenoon went to the minster: was somewhat annoyed at their ornaments, tapers, rich embroidered copes, vestments, &c. Dr. Brevin,[*] a native of France, discoursed on the birth of Christ." Sunday, January 2, was not a "principal feast-day," and yet the copes were worn at Durham on that day so late as 1681, which is a corroborative evidence for the reconciliation of the ornaments rubric with the 24th Canon, which I offered early in this chapter, and which Bishop Cosin's own practice at Durham as prebendary seems to strongly confirm. An often repeated anecdote attributes the disuse of copes at Durham to the pettishness of Bishop Warburton, who would not tolerate the disturbance of his wig by one of them. He dashed down his cope, so it was said, and no other dignitary of the cathedral cared afterwards to put one on. This story, like others of the same kind, seems to have a substratum of truth, and yet to be wrong in the absolute facts, and in the present instance these facts prove the even stronger hold which the Eucharistic dress had upon the Chapter of Durham, in spite of the chill of the eighteenth century. The real circumstances of the transaction are thus stated by Mr. Ornsby in a footnote to the first volume of 'The Correspondence of Bishop Cosin,' from which I have already quoted:

---

[*] Dr. Brevint, a native of Jersey, a well-known theologian.

"The copes which formed the subject of so much bitter invective on the part of Smart are still preserved, as is well known, in the library of Durham Cathedral. Additional interest attaches to them from the fact of their having been worn at the celebration of the Holy Communion in that cathedral down to a comparatively recent period. An unpublished diary, kept by Gyll, a local antiquary, who was Attorney-General to Egerton, Bishop of Durham, has the following entry respecting their discontinuance:—' 1759: at the latter end of July or beginning of August the old copes (those raggs of Popery) which had been used at the communion service at the abbey ever since the time of the Reformation, were ordered by the d. and ch. to be totally disused and laid aside. Dr. Warburton, one of the prebendaries, and Bp. of Gloucester, was very zealous to have them laid aside, and so was Dr. Cowper the dean.' No such order, however, appears amongst the Acts of Chapter; and, indeed, it may well be supposed that some hesitation might be felt as to the formal enrollment of an order which directly contravened one of the canons of the Church, however little individual members of the body might be disposed to render obedience to its requirements. Silently, however, the use of the copes was abandoned about that time, or shortly afterwards, and they are only cared for now as interesting relics of a by-gone time."

This narrative is confirmed by a statement published in the 'Gentleman's Magazine' of 1804: "In the vestry of Durham Cathedral are five ancient copes, which were until these twenty years worn at the altar on festivals, and other principal days of the year." Yet persons point to Bishop Cosin as a leader among those who abandoned the distinctive Eucharistic dress at the last settlement of the Prayer Book, and they cite the existing ornaments rubric as the document by which that abandonment was effected. Durham Minster was the one church in which the use of copes after the Restoration was persistent and long-continued, doubtless from the enduring influence of Cosin. But it was not the only one for which copes were provided after that date. The copes still preserved at Westminster, and used on very high state solemnities, are of the time of Charles II.; and Blomefield in his

'History of Norfolk,' says of Norwich Cathedral, after describing the destruction by the rebels of its five or six old copes, "the present cope was given at the Restoration by Philip Harbord, Esq., then High Sheriff of Norfolk."

The really "Protestant" character of the settlement of 1549, even if it had been taken literally, and not with the relaxations which those who observed it from Parker down to Cosin permitted themselves, has never, during recent discussions, been insisted upon as fully or clearly as historical accuracy demands. This is not astonishing, for it has been the policy of both sides in the controversy to inflate its ceremonial magnificence. Ultra-ritualists, of course, would gladly make it carry as much as it can possibly bear, while writers of a Puritan turn have played into their hands from the wish, by proving it to be obnoxious in a Romanising sense, to obstruct any return to its prescriptions. The true way, too, of testing it is not to consider it in comparison with subsequent usage, or with the more monotonous outward forms with which practice has made our age familiar, but to see what was the body of old inrooted ceremonial which its framers desired that it should replace, and to trace how it was understood by those who had practically to work it at its first promulgation, and after its revival by Elizabeth. The opponents of the High Church revival (encouraged, it must be owned, by the untenable and provocative assumptions of the extreme right) argue as if the Prayer Book of 1549, in its ceremonial aspect (with which alone I am now concerned), was a half-measure, a timid, faltering, first step, which had to be completed, and its shortcomings rectified, by the really consistent and thorough work of 1552; and this view of things has been encouraged in quarters from which we might have hoped for more accurate knowledge. Now, then, what does the Prayer Book of 1549 order? In answering this question I must again quote its rubrics, but the extracts are not long, and the repetition will tend to clearness. They lay down the surplice as the one general vesture for all clergy

CHAP. IV. EDWARDIAN AND PRE-REFORMATIONAL DRESSES. 141

throughout their ministrations with two specific exceptions: (1) that "upon the day and at the time appointed for the ministration of the Holy Communion" (which double prescription of time I read to mean that the dresses in question are not to be used at the preliminary Mattins or Litany), "the priest that shall execute the holy ministry shall put upon him the vesture appointed for that ministration, that is to say, a white albe plain, with a vestment or cope. And where there be many priests or deacons, there so many shall be ready to help the priest in the ministration as shall be requisite, and shall have upon them likewise the vestures appointed for their ministry, that is to say, albes, with tunacles." To which direction in another place is added as a kind of rider, "And though there be none to communicate with the priest, yet these days"— namely, on Wednesdays and Fridays—"(after the Litany ended) the priest shall put upon him a plain albe or surplice, with a cope, and say all things at the altar (appointed to be read at the celebration of the Lord's Supper) until after the offertory." And (2) "Whensoever the Bishop shall celebrate the Holy Communion in the church, or execute any other public ministration, he shall have upon him, besides his rochette, a surplice or albe, and a cope or vestment, and also his pastoral staff in his hand, or else borne or holden by his chaplain."

This is the first time I have referred to the last-quoted rubric, for nothing in my late discussion happens to have turned on it. But what is the system which these few and simple orders replace? I shall take my description of the pre-reformational ceremonial, reduced to the briefest possible language, from 'the Church of our Fathers, as seen in St. Osmond's Rite for the Cathedral of Salisbury,' published between 1849 and 1853, by the late Dr. Rock, a very learned Roman Catholic divine. I need not extract what he says of the origin of the alb and surplice; these, as we know, are modifications of the same white linen dress, the surplice being the later form, and so called (*superpellicium*) because worn over the furred gown of the clerk. The Prayer Book of 1549 allows of one use of the cope, that is, as the alternative dress for the vestment or chasuble which was exclusively worn by the celebrant in the older English Church.

"While offering up the unspotted Sacrifice of the Mass, the priest must ever be clad, together with the rest of his sacred attire, in a chasuble. For processions, as well as at every part of the liturgy during the year more immediately connected with them, the rubrics, according to the Salisbury use, direct the chief celebrant, at least, to have on a cope; so, too, under the same ritual feeling, in collegiate and cathedral churches, and the wealthier religious houses, the canons, the monks, and friars, and as many as possible of the elder clergy, were arrayed in silken copes at the principal services on each Sunday and holyday marked for walking in any kind of solemn procession.

"For a like reason was it, moreover, that the 'rectores chori,' or rulers of the choir, who, on account of their office, had to be so often moving to and fro as they led the singing, not only bore richly ornamented staves in their hands, but from the Anglo-Saxon, and all through the English period, were vested, too, in copes, the most beautiful which their churches happened to possess."

No modern English dignitary has claimed to wear the "furred amys," unless, indeed, the university hood may be said to represent it, so I need not quote Dr. Rock's description of this dress. Under his cope or vestment the celebrant of the reformed Prayer Book is only to wear a "white albe plain," a less conspicuous dress even than the usual full-sleeved surplice, while the mediæval priest, besides the stole (which, as all persons know, has asserted for itself a traditional position in our actual Church) bore upon his wrist a maniple, "often made of the richest golden stuffs," while as to the alb, although

"Linen of the finest quality continued to be, as now, the material of which it was then always made for common use, on great occasions, and in the larger churches, it was to be seen formed, not only entirely of silk, but sometimes even of velvet and cloth of gold. But this was not all; for though white was of course its usual colour, yet do we find a green, or blue, or red, or black alb to have been occasionally worn; and albs were not called by the name of one or the other of these dies because their apparels only were of that colour, but because they were tinted throughout red, blue, or green, as the case might be."

Nor were even these gorgeous albs what is technically known as "plain," for on to them were further stitched "apparels" which

"were of three sorts; some were merely pieces of the self-same tissue of which the chasuble had been made; others were formed of some rich stuff, of silk, or cloth of gold, and adorned with needlework after an elaborate but befitting design; the third, and most beautiful, the storied kind, exhibited the figures of saints and passages from the New Testament, done in embroidery."

Finally, round his neck the priest suspended the "amice," which

"during the English period at least of our Church, was always beautiful, often truly gorgeous; generally the same rich tissue which supplied the apparels for the alb, furnished another for the amice belonging to it; small but glowing enamels set in elaborate embroidery were, in many instances, to be observed sewed on to it; and not unfrequently might be seen around the neck of an old English bishop, an apparel to the amice made from sheets of the purest beaten gold, thickly studded with pearls and sparkling with precious stones."

By the ritual of 1549, those priests and deacons who are "ready to help the priest in the ministration," which, of course, covers Gospeller and Epistler, and those who might further aid in distributing the consecrated elements, "shall have on them likewise the vestures appointed for their ministry, that is to say, albes with tunacles." In the mediæval English Church the celebrant at High Mass was assisted by a "deacon" and a "subdeacon," who were in reality priests, though acting for the occasion in the lower capacities. The deacon who read the Gospel was, except on the particular occasions to which I have referred, vested, over his alb, in a "dalmatic," which "corresponded in colour with the sacerdotal chasuble, and like it, was overspread with beautiful embroideries and ornaments in gold." The subdeacon, to whom was assigned the Epistle, wore the tunicle, "which was, in outline, the same as the diaconal garment, and differed from it only by being smaller in all its dimensions, and decked with fewer and less conspicuous ornaments." What also was the richness of the alb which was common to deacon and subdeacon I have already shown. Of course, in an ante-reformational High Mass there was no communion of the laity, but there were clergy in the stalls joining in the choral worship, and, above all, cantors directing the chanting. Their rich vesture in copes has been described in my first quotation from Dr. Rock. The substitute in Edward VI.'s book for this bewildering pomp of garb, was the single cope or vestment for the celebrant, the tunicles for his assistants, and then the plain linen surplices for all other clerks. The principle of the "distinctive Eucharistic dress" was maintained in this arrangement, but that was all. Perhaps the most significative proof of the rigorous spirit of simplification which ran through the whole process of reform, was the indifferent toleration of the chasuble, heretofore in theory (although, as we have seen, with a capricious exception) the distinctive Eucharistic dress of the celebrant, and of the cope, hitherto the less honoured vesture of the clerk in the choir, or joining in a procession. This was as much as to say, "We maintain the higher honour of the 'Holy Mysteries' above the ordinary service, and so we assign to them a higher dress; but among the various types of existing higher dresses we are indifferent." The direction that a "cope" only should be used when there is no actual celebration, but only the first part of the service read, is, I am disposed to believe, not an intentional distinction, but merely a shortened reference to the ruling rubric.

Dr. Rock, in a footnote to the passage which I quoted from his description of the cope, speaks of this change of Eucharistic dress with a bitterness which is natural from his point of view. I need not repeat his words, though I may refer to them to show how groundless is the charge of Romanising brought against the ornaments rubrics of Edward VI. The omission of all reference to the richer dalmatic, and the authorisation of the less conspicuous tunicle, no less than the change of the alb from elaborate richness to rigid simplicity, all tell the same tale. Such, as contrasted with the elaborate and oppressive splendour of the middle ages, was the simple dress which our reformers at first prescribed for the Holy Communion, and which, in theory at least, was, as I have argued, revived by Elizabeth, and continued in 1662. It was, if considered in its details, an extreme change; but it preserved the idea of special appointments for the highest rite of our religion, and was, accordingly (apart from more solemn considerations), wisely devised as a pacific compromise between the very different opinions which acquiesced in the change of 1549. Our statesmen and bishops then were not dealing with "members of the Establishment" and "non-conforming brethren," but with the whole people of England, of whom the larger, though not the more thinking, portion would be persons who had not been much troubled by growing corruptions, but who would be, no doubt, signally disconcerted at too violent a change in the outward circumstances of a worship which few of them in those pre-educational times were competent to follow in their Prayer Books, supposing them to possess such volumes, as the farmers and labourers of those days, of course, did not.

The plan had hardly been tried, when the strong pressure of foreign intolerance was brought to bear upon our rulers, and a novel ritual was dictated which killed the moderate settlement of 1549, and left to God's minister, celebrating His Holy Mysteries at His Board, no better or other dress than that in which he was vested while leading the Morning and

Evening Prayer. Whatever may have been the abstract merits of this new order of things, it certainly was not (I must respectfully submit) so consistent as that of 1549, with the conspicuous honour paid all through the Prayer Book to the office of the Holy Communion, not only according to the forms of 1549 but according to those of 1552; and I have with me the expressed judgment of the Elizabethan Reformers, who while they substantially reinstated the Prayer Book of 1552, married to it the vesture of 1549. Viewed merely as a concession on the part of those who did not wish for the success of what was afterwards called Puritanism, the change was a failure. It did not in the least content the revolutionary party, but by accustoming them to the surplice as the only vesture, it merely led them to concentrate on that most harmless dress an opposition which was so persistent and so rancorous that it was not quelled within the Church till after the lapse of a hundred and ten years.

In order to simplify my examination of the differences between the pre-reformational vestments and those of Edward VI.'s first book, I have hitherto no further referred to the episcopal garb therein laid down than by quoting the rubric respecting it. I may observe that the same distinction exists between the dress of the bishop as of the priest before and after the Reformation; for while the Edwardian Bishop is only to have "besides his rochette a surplice or albe, and a cope or vestment," his predecessor would also have worn a dalmatic beneath his chasuble, while his albe would have shone in all the splendour of "apparels," and his neck would have borne the weight of the gorgeous amice. The pastoral staff would have been common to both; and in this connection I must observe that I cannot understand why it is that so few of those Bishops who have revived the pastoral staff should not have also reassumed the "cope or vestment," for the same rubric which makes one legal also enjoins the other; while there is no Bishop, I suppose, who would not gladly escape from that uncouth and illegal dress, which he has alike to wear in the House of God and in the Parliament House. Two or three Bishops, it is well known, have recently worn copes; but they have only done so under the conditions of the 24th Canon, as interpreted in the more limited sense.

Strongly as I have insisted upon the legality of the Eucharistic dress, in the terms of the rubrics of 1549, and convinced as I am of its congruity with the framework and spirit of our services, I should be very much wronged and pained if I were supposed to be arguing that, in the present condition of Church feeling, every incumbent would be justified in reviving it at his own motion, and without consulting the feelings of his congregation. Such a course would be alike impolitic and uncharitable. Churchmen have, for so many generations, gone on in the practical appreciation of the surplice, and the surplice only, as the Eucharistic, no less than the ordinary ministerial dress, that to vast multitudes the return to rubrical correctness would carry with it the aspect of simply being an innovation. Other edifying improvements in the conduct of our public worship have been carried out between incumbent, flock, and ordinary; and in proportion as they have been thus effected they have proved successful, while the cases in which they have given offence have ordinarily been those in which these three factors of a pacific solution have not been brought together, or have only met to disagree. If some clergymen have been too rash and autocratic in the way in which they have driven on this and other changes, and if some congregations have been too suspicious where they were confronted by nothing worse than a loyal, if not always a discreet, zeal for the improved worship of the Church of England, our Bishops, it must be owned, have, for their part, been somewhat backward in mastering the claim of the Eucharistic dress. The recent debates in Convocation have, however, shown that this apathy is wearing away, and with the question now so rife, I am convinced that peace will never be reached except by way of some *modus vivendi*, which will permit of the use of the Eucharistic dress in parish churches, under the control of the ordinary, in cases and under conditions which shall save it from being saddled on recalcitrant clergymen, or forced on unwilling congregations, while it is secured to such as appreciate it.

This end may, of course, be reached in many ways, and perhaps in no parish or congregation will it be desirable that exactly the same course should be adopted as in the adjacent one. There will be on one side the long list of churches in which no change ought to be thought of, and on the other there may be one of those in which any omission of the distinctive dress would give offence. There ought to be little difficulty with either of these classes, the trouble will be with the large intermediate one of churches where there are two parties; but here common sense may readily reach an adjustment. The number of churches in which the clergyman is not single-handed is immense; and there is such a thing as giving and taking occasional help with the intention of meeting the varying susceptibilities of priest and people. Above all, it is a pure fallacy to assume that the same service need always be performed with the same rites at each recurrence of it in the same church. In places where the adoption of the distinctive dress would edify a notable portion of the congregation, and yet offend some tangible number, as well as in those its disuse would make a similar division, arrangements might, I am convinced, be very often arrived at by which, on different days or at different hours, either way of celebrating the Holy Communion might be employed.

The good practice of early communions, which we originally owed to the Oxford party, but which has now happily been embraced by all Church parties, offers an obvious and a convenient opportunity for varying ceremonial. Those who worship at 11, need not concern themselves with what has taken place at 8 or 9, and those who have had their own way at that early hour may well concede much which they cannot appreciate to their less active fellow-parishioners. Sometimes, of course, the earlier morning would see the more plain, and the later morning the richer service. There might be cases of churches where only a single Sunday celebration was possible, and in which, on the first or some other specified Sunday in the month, no special dress would be worn; in other cases the more ornate service might be reserved for that day. In some places, too, it might be convenient not to interfere with old Sunday forms, but to permit developments on such Holy days as fell inside the week.

There is a plea, of no legal value I am aware, but of a very decidedly equitable description, which I venture to urge upon those who most strongly believe in the Purchas judgment, and are therefore most decidedly convinced that a distinctive dress is not lawful in a parish church, but is so in a cathedral or collegiate one. At the time when the canons were passed, the parochial system had not reached that state of administrative development which makes it now so powerful an engine of evangelization. In the towns the population had not outstripped the capacity of the churches, and in the country the parishes were poor and sparsely populated, while the existence of pluralities combined with the shock of the reformational changes to keep the supply of clergy down to the lowest possible level. It was, in short, an age whose peculiar condition of civilisation made it one of striking contrasts, of the highest intellectual culture in London, the Court, and the Universities, and of something like savagery in the remote counties. The organization of the churches of large parishes under an incumbent, and a well-drilled staff of curates, which is the boast of our days, was not then even heard of. The question was not, as it is now so happily, how many clergy to the church, but how many churches to the clergyman. The only churches in which there was anything like corporate action were those cathedral and collegiate churches, and therefore very intelligibly, as regarded the actual condition of affairs, the canons took care that in these should be secured a higher type of worship. They ordered that these should be models of ornate ceremonial, both because those foundations were manned with a sufficient staff, and because they had their own revenues to provide the apparatus. The parish churches then were not merely undermanned, but hardly manned at all, too often dependent on the fragmentary ministrations of some poor drudge curate on whom devolved the duties of several non-resident rectors. So far, too, were these churches from having any superfluous revenues, that in many cases it would be a hard fight to scrape together what was needful for the barest necessaries of worship by the never popular method of local taxation. But we see where the private benefactor did come in, as at Abbey Dore and at St. Giles's in the Fields, that there was no scruple in the adoption of a rich ceremonial. But now, although not legally, yet practically and in the spirit of the canons, large full-manned parish churches, such as those of Leeds, of Doncaster, of Ludlow, of Tenbury, of St. Peter's Pimlico, of St. Michael's Paddington, and others, which I could name, are collegiate churches. They are churches in which there is a will and a way to carry out Divine worship in the heartiest and the most unsparing fashion. The vestments or other ornaments, however costly, which they might like to adopt, would not be charges upon any rates, but the freewill offerings of those who pleased to spend their own money upon them. It would, therefore, be in the fullest compliance, not with the letter but with the spirit of the Advertisements and of the canons, if churches of this kind were to be allowed (as in other cases with due conditions) to claim the privileges reserved for collegiate churches. I cannot believe the canons would have been so restrictive if they had contemplated such churches growing up. This, too, is another proof that those who framed them had no idea of superseding the ornaments rubric, if, in fact, they thought they were providing for just the cases in which they believed that rubric likely to be carried out. Financial considerations appeared to them to have made the ornaments

CHAP. IV.   SAFETY-VALVE MUST BE OPENED.

rubric an impossibility except in a certain class of churches; so they took care in that class to give it new life by specifically re-enacting its main provisions, although in different language. As to the remaining churches they did not repeal the ornaments rubric, but confined themselves to re-enacting its obligatory minimum provision of the surplice, and left its other orders to take care of themselves. The churches of the kind for which I am pleading, when situated in large towns, would have to be considered rather as to their congregations than as to their legal parishioners. The fact that in large towns, London for example, the congregational system for worship, as distinct from the civil accidents of a parish, has grown up alongside of the parochial, is one which has forced itself upon the attention of all who have studied the religious problems of the day, and most of them have accepted it. Still of course parishioners have rights, which, if they press them, it is impossible to ignore. It might, accordingly, sometimes happen that such a church would offer a plain ceremonial to its legal, and a higher one to its voluntary, congregation.

I have said enough on my own part in the way of suggesting some terms of compromise. It is for our bishops and for Convocation to take the condition of Church matters into their serious consideration. Unless a safety valve is opened the pent up vapours may find some angry and inconvenient escape. At all events the memorials which have come from the side which desires some practical acknowledgment from headquarters of the distinctive dress, only plead for a *modus vivendi*, which shall allow of the two types of ceremonial. It has been reserved for their opponents to put into circulation the one which whispers prohibition, and yet among the leading signers of that paper are dignitaries whose duty it is under either construction of the existing law—either under rubric or under canons—to assume the Eucharistic dress, and one of whom, as is well known, has not feared to do so.

Among the limitations suggested, are some which have

reference not to time and place, but to the shape, the colour, and the texture of the dress in itself. Some persons, for instance, have looked at the preponderating evidence for the way in which the cope (whatever may have been in the earliest reformational days included under that name), supplanted the vestment, and has indeed continued in use, under certain conditions, down to our time. Witness the copes at Westminster Abbey, which were worn (as I myself saw) at the Queen's Coronation, June 28, 1838. Their proposal accordingly would be to limit the Eucharistic dress, as a protest of distinctive Anglicanism, to its form of cope. I do not, I confess, think that much would be gained by this. The associations which might have made some persons fear the retention of the vestment three centuries back have long passed away, and the good side of the early traditional connection of that dress with the Eucharistic rite in no Romanising or transubstantiationalist connection, but as the great Christian mystery, may be said to have asserted itself instead. But chiefly it may be urged that practical experience has (as I am informed) shown that the vestment is a more convenient dress than the cope for the special object of celebration, inasmuch as the latter rather weighs upon the arms and the former, if light and flexible, does not offer any impediment.

Limitations as to colour and material claim a fuller consideration. The most earnest advocates for the revival of the Eucharistic dress unite in acknowledging that a white linen chasuble would fulfil all necessary conditions. To such a form of vestment there could hardly be any objection. Few people indeed would, I believe, distinguish it from a surplice. At the same time where a richer material would not give offence, it would be only congruous to honour God with the offering of more costly gifts. Bishop Cosin, as we have seen, used to wear a white satin cope. If the white linen vestment would, as I believe, be accepted in many cases with absolute indifference where it was not actually popular, so a vestment of white

Chap. IV. LIMITATION TO WHITE VESTMENTS. 153

silk or satin or of merino, could not excite the comments which the sudden substitution of varied colours for the habitual whiteness of the long familiar surplice might very naturally provoke. If such a settlement could cordially be reached, it would be puerile and vexatious for any one to stand out in respect of colours, which are not of the essence of the Eucharistic dress, and are not so much as mentioned in the ruling rubrics of 1549.

I have all through this discussion purposely confined myself to the question of the legality of the distinctive dress, according to the existing rubrical and ceremonial laws of England, and to its conformity with the teaching and Liturgy of that Church, as shown in her authorised formularies. I may now before parting with the subject, and in conformity with the rules which earlier in this book I laid down for myself as my guide in considering each successive rite or ceremony, say that to thoughtful Churchmen the use of such a dress has a value beyond that of dry legality, as a link which associates us in England with the practice of the Holy Church Universal from very early ages. I have said enough on the Western Church. Distinct Eucharistic dresses of great richness and dignity have from a remote antiquity characterised the Greek Communion. So they have the Armenian (in which the Eucharistic vesture has the form of a cope), as well as the other separated churches of the East. Vestments are also preserved in the Protestant churches of Scandinavia. I could multiply evidence on this head, but I only think it necessary to quote from a pleasant description of a Sunday service at Lillehammer, Norway, in 1848, given in Mr. Thomas Forester's travels in that country, which were published in 1850. I produce this statement only as evidence, and not as wishing my readers to approve of the ceremonial therein described. The non-assumption of the vestment till after the reading of the Epistle and Gospel, as if they were not important portions of the Communion service, not to say the non-use even of the surplice during the reading of the Gospel, was a ritual blunder which it is not necessary to be a 'Ritualist' to condemn. After describing the Church of pine logs, the men and women sitting on separate sides, the chancel screen reaching to the roof, the altar covered with a white cloth, and the reredos gaudily painted and gilded with carvings of the Last Supper, the Crucifixion, our Lord Ascending and in Glory, and of the Apostles,

Mr. Forester proceeds:—

"When I entered, the priest was giving the benediction to a number of young persons kneeling at the altar-rails, placing his hand on the head of each in succession. I failed to comprehend the nature of the office he was thus engaged in. Was it confirmation? The rite is especially regarded in the Norwegian Church, and the preparation of the candidates for it is attended to with particular care, but I had been led to believe that the performance of that rite is reserved exclusively to the bishop. The priest was habited in a black gown with close sleeves; over this, the young people being dismissed, he endued himself with the assistance of the precentor, in a surplice very much resembling that used in our churches. He then turned to the altar and chanted the collect for the day; after which followed the epistle, the people standing. He then divested himself of the surplice, and retired to the sacristy behind the altar, while the people sang one of those *Bede-psalmer*, or prayer psalms, which form the staple of their share in the public worship, four of them being introduced into the services of each day. Meanwhile the priest had ascended the pulpit, and the singing being concluded, offered a short extempore prayer, followed by the Lord's prayer. He then read the Gospel for the day, the people standing. It being the fifth Sunday after Trinity, it was (like that of our own Church) taken from a chapter of St. Luke, which relates the miraculous draught of fishes. Some of the present accompaniments to the recital of that striking narrative gave it a peculiar interest.

" At the conclusion of the sermon, the priest gave the benediction, making the sign of the cross with the fore-finger, the people standing and receiving it with great reverence. The occupiers of the galleries then departed, but the whole of the congregation in the body of the church remained. The office of baptism was then administered. Its forms very nearly corresponded with those of the English

Church. The infants were wrapped in long mantles of figured silk, tied in front with knots of white ribbon. At the conclusion of the service, the women who carried the children went in turn round the back of the altar, and coming to the south side, laid an offering of money upon it, making a reverence to the priest; the same ceremony was also performed by six or eight men, who advanced in succession from the body of the church. The office of baptism was followed by the celebration of the Holy Communion, the congregation still remaining. Preparatory to this, the priest having returned to the altar, the precentor invested him, over the surplice, with a rich vestment or cope," [not a cope] "of crimson satin embroidered with a broad cross of silver tissue before and behind.* Kneeling before the altar, he prayed for a short time in silence. Then standing with his face towards the altar, he chaunted some versicles in a low voice, the choir responding. The prayer of consecration followed, also chaunted in low measured tones of fine modulation; in the course of which he passed his hand over the elements on the altar, and took the patina and chalice in his hands. The communicants had now approached, and were kneeling at the rails, the women separated from the men. The sacrament was administered by the priest inserting the consecrated wafer into the mouth and holding the chalice to the lips, saying, in a low voice, to each, 'This is the true body (blood) of our Lord Jesus Christ!' Dette er Jesu sande † Legem. Dette er Jesu sande Blöd. Having completed the circuit of the rail, standing before the altar with the cup in his hand, he gave a short address to the communicants, who then retired and gave place to others. The choir continued singing while the administration was taking place. When all had communicated, the priest again chaunted some collects, the choir responding, and then gave the benediction to the people, making the sign of the cross, as he had done before at the conclusion of the sermon. He then laid aside the surplice and cope, which the precentor having placed on the altar, and advancing to the chancel gate, recited some prayers; while the priest himself communicated, kneeling in front of the altar.

"The bell in the steeple then rang, and the people departed. The number of the communicants was about ninety, the general con-

---

"* I had seen them of velvet with gold embroidery, but the colour was invariably crimson."—*Note in original.*

"† Sand, true, right, certain, sure.—*Dictionary.*"—*Note in original.*

gregation being from four to five hundred. Almost all had books containing the Bede-Psalmer and prayers. Nothing could exceed their grave and reverend demeanour during the whole of the service."

The vestment controversy has, in the hands of some ultra-ritualists, been complicated by a very strange revival of pre-reformational ceremonial in the conversion of the simple saying of the Magnificat in the evening service, into a spectacle of complicated gorgeousness. This rite, after it had been for several years advocated in print, and I believe practised in some churches which boast of their 'advanced' ritual, has been forced into general notice, by being made the frontispiece of the last published volume of directions for the performance of divine service, according to the principles of ultra-ritualism, in which the vesture of copes is represented with a prominence which is more emphatic than artistic. After this open challenge, it has become the duty of those who wish to develope the beauty of holiness in our Church within the limits of Prayer Book law, to speak their whole mind upon the subject. In order that I may be quite fair in my description of the rite, I shall give it in the very words (somewhat abridged) of the book to which I have referred :—

"On great occasions, when there are many clergy present, and the stalls are all filled, and solemn vespers are being sung, the officiant, vested in cassock surplice and cope of the colour of the day, attended either by two clergy in albs and dalmatics, also of the colour of the day, or by two acolytes, may occupy a position, with his attendants, on the south side of the sanctuary—not in the sedilia, but on stools or forms placed in front of the sedilia. . . . . It was formerly the old English custom to use incense at the Magnificat, and to light tapers at the antiphon-lectern, or near the altar. . . . . On Sundays and festivals incense should be used at evensong during the singing of the Magnificat, and additional tapers may be lighted."

A diagram is here given of the places of the various clergy, vested it will be remembered, and assistants at this ceremony.

"The officiating priest having had the thurible and incense-boat brought to him by two acolytes, may silently bless the incense in the following terms." . . . .

Then follows a ceremonious form of blessing, and the recapitulation of the elaborate censings of the altar, of the clergy and assistants, and of the congregation.

I must confess to a preliminary difficulty in discussing the question, from the inability under which I labour to put myself in the position of persons who have reached a conviction that this particular ceremonial can in any way be justified under our existing ritual system. In meeting them I seem to be transported into a sort of fairy land, in which those well-understood conditions of cause and effect, premiss and conclusion, which govern ordinary discussion, have no place. Alive as I am to the exceeding incaution of the proceeding, I will not harbour the suspicions of persons who would connect this peculiar honour shown to the Magnificat with that Mariolatry which has under the present Papacy reached its last and worst extreme. I fully recognise the loyalty to the Church of England of those who advocate and practise it, I accept their interpretation of it as exclusively intended to show forth the Incarnation; and I cannot contradict the assertion that they have persuaded themselves into its compatibility with the rubrical law under which we are all living, and in virtue of which they have the right to minister. But, after these concessions, I find it as hopelessly impossible as before to frame even a plausible argument for the legality of the rite. I do not go beyond legality, for if it is illegal, and if, as I believe, it is never likely to be declared legal, there is little use in discussing its edification. Still less will there be if, in addition to being illegal, it is also in the highest degree impolitic, as tending to bring other rites, which have a very strong claim to be formally accepted as legal, into disrepute, from the superficial resemblance existing between the practices, from both of them involving the use of the restored vestments. I must, in the first place, enquire whether there is any apparent sanction in the Prayer Book for environing the saying of the Magnificat with a pomp of circumstances superior to that which is bestowed upon the other Canticles of morning or evening service. I will not burden these pages with lengthened proof, for any one can satisfy himself as to it by looking at his Prayer Book. Only I must point out that there is, perhaps, an accumulation of proof in the form of the rubric specially referring to the Magnificat. If we take the analogous places in the morning service, we find a separate rubric devoted to the saying of the Psalms, including, by the way, the direction for the use of the Gloria after every Canticle except the Te Deum. Then the use of the Te Deum itself is enjoined in the rubric which orders the first lesson. But in the evening service, the Psalms, first lesson, and Magnificat, are in one rubric, the Psalms being ordered to be "said or sung;" and the Magnificat prescribed by the elliptical expression "And after that Magnificat (or the Song of the Blessed Virgin Mary) in English as followeth." Of course then, according to the rubric, it has to be "said or sung" like the Psalms, with neither more nor less observance. But that is not all, for there is an alternative, " or this Psalm, except it be on the Nineteenth day of the month; when it is read in the ordinary course of the Psalms." Therefore the "Cantate," as far as the rubric orders anything, is to be used under circumstances exactly parallel with those which govern the use of the Magnificat, and if any peculiar ceremonial legally environs this Canticle, it would be hard to prove that the man who bestowed the same on the alternative Cantate was more than inconceivably eccentric and wrong-headed.

Here, however, comes in that wonderfully elastic principle that omission is not prohibition, and it is argued that, because the Prayer Book contains no prohibition of the minister interrupting the evening service between the first lesson and the Magnificat by a series of ceremonious censings, and superadding a cope to the vesture legally appointed for him, therefore such proceedings lie within his own uncontrolled arbitrament. My only appeal against such reasoning must be to the natural sense of the congruous which is possessed by any person of average understanding, for it is intangible by any more formal argument. There are only two possible theories of vesture in the Church of England—that which holds that the canons override the ornaments rubric, and that which holds that the canons are overridden by that rubric. We may be pretty sure that no one would appeal to those who hold the former view, to defend this use of the cope. What comfort do they get from the rubrics of 1549, supposing them to be still in force? We need not again travel over the vestments which they prescribe at the celebration of the Holy Communion, nor refer to the cope, which is directed by the same book to be worn at the altar when the former portion of the Communion Office is used. The vesture of the clergy at the other offices is laid down in the "Certain Notes" to which I have already referred, at the end of the Prayer Book proper. The order there given is very brief and perspicuous, "In the saying and singing of Mattins and Evensong, Baptizing and Burying, the Minister, in Parish Churches and Chapels annexed to the same, shall use a surplice;" then follows a further order for hoods in cathedral churches and colleges, and the somewhat more vague exception, "But in all other places every Minister shall be at liberty to use any Surplice or no." What can be clearer than this?—The vestment or cope, albs and tunicles, being ordered for the clergy who celebrate the Holy Communion, or begin the Communion Service, those who execute the subordinate duty of saying mattins or evensong are to use surplices. The critic, driven to a strait to find some argument which should make these rubrics harmonize with the new practice, might probably opine that the order to wear a surplice meant one to wear a surplice, and anything else besides that the wearer fancied. At all events our book leaves us with the oracular pronouncement that "it is proper, and quite in accordance with the terms of the rubric of Edward VI.th's First Prayer Book, to wear a cope of the proper colour of the day at Solemn Vespers, viz., on the Evensongs—both First and Second—of Sundays and Festivals." I think it is more respectful both to the ingenious author and to my own readers to leave this assertion to speak for itself.

There is no analogy between it and the principle for which I have been contending that the order to wear the surplice in the 58th Canon is not inconsistent with the orders elsewhere to superadd the vestment or cope at certain times. Here there are two distinct vestiary prescriptions, both of them laid down at different times by the reformed Church of England, which it is, at least, respectful to reconcile. But as to this modern claim, the reformed Church of England, through the mouth both of its own Prayer Book and of its canons, orders one and one only dress at this particular time; and yet it is contended that each clergyman may of his own mere motion add another. The same stretch of words would justify the clergyman who was less ritualistic in topping his surplice with a great coat if the weather happened to be cold. I should not have dwelt at such length on the disproof of so untenable a ceremonial, had it not been for its inconceivable impolicy. The claim to wear a "distinctive Eucharistic dress," rests as I have shown, on very strong grounds; the one to wear a "distinctive dress" at the Magnificat, on none at all. But if ritualists will persist in lumping together the two practices in their demand for vestments, it will only be natural for the world to estimate the value of the whole claim at that of its weakest member, and to push aside the solid requisition as the lawless caprice of a knot of extravagant innovators. I have for my own part no hesitation in saying that the most gratuitous obstructors of the "distinctive Eucharistic dress" are the men who give rein to their own fancies in the utterly indefensible ceremonial which they have heaped round the saying at evensong of the Magnificat.

I may as well in closing this chapter dispose of every

question relating to ecclesiastical dress, whether or not it is directly connected with the Communion service. Every church goer is familiar with that vesture composed of a long strip of silk passed round the neck, and hanging down on each side, which low and old-fashioned Churchmen wear broad, and term a *scarf*, assigning some conventional reason for its use, but which upon the persons of High Churchmen shrinks into notable narrowness, and vindicates in name and shape its title to be the continuance of the ancient stole. There is not a word of reference to either stole or scarf in any post-reformational rubric, advertisement, or canon; and yet it is too well established and too generally accepted ever to be dislodged. Does not this fact teach a lesson of moderation to contending parties? Here at least the stern law of the Mackonochie case has not been held to, and never can prevail. Among the introductions which ritualism so called justifies under its general rules is that of the soft quadrangular cap, called the " biretta," which is ceremoniously put on and off by the Roman clergy during different periods of their ministrations, according to the comparative liturgical solemnity of the passing act of worship. The one point in which Mr. Purchas found mercy with the Judicial Committee, was the possession of a biretta, because it could not be proved that he wore it in service time. This head dress accordingly is legal, as goloshes are also, only it has not required the Arches Court and the Judicial Committee to allow our clergy to procure those. But upon the ritualistic use of the biretta, not as a covering but as a symbolical act of worship, which is moulded on the Roman rite, I have, putting on one side the question of its legality, only the right to allege my own feelings. There may be persons to whom it is edifying; to myself it is simply disturbing, and it seems to invest the service with a peculiarly alien character. The old familiar teaching of man's nothingness and the glory of God, derived from the spectacle of the bareheaded clergy, in this respect humbling themselves like the simplest of their flock before the Divine Majesty, is lost in a novel and intricate symbolism of which self-assertion appears to be an element. The practice is certainly void of any post-reformational recognition. The canons no doubt allow the use of a "night-cap or coif" in church to those only whose health forbids them to go bareheaded; but the *rationale* of this cap is that it should be so low and unconspicuous that the wearer of it is still assumed to be bareheaded. The *rationale* on the other hand of the ritualistic biretta, which has nothing to do with health, is that it should be conspicuous, and that it should be known when its wearer had it on and when off.

The question of the biretta may be a very small one, but it is one of many other small questions in which the ritualists have shown themselves deficient in tact, and careless in ascertaining the drift of popular feeling, even when that feeling may be prejudice. Many small things may combine in a large whole, and a prejudice, if harmless, ought always to be enough respected at least to be taken into account by men whose duty and whose desire is to mould public opinion. At the risk of offending them, I must say that the tact of the ritualists has not been commensurate with their learning or devotion. They have erred both in what they have insisted upon as if essential, and in the manner in which they have worded their insistance. The latter mistake is, I make no doubt, a very natural one with persons who are so accustomed to hear each other talk in a technical language about matters which are familiar to them, that they quite forget when they have to go down into the forum, that their very vocabulary is not merely unintelligible (for this would be comparatively unimportant) but just so half-understood, as to give the wrong and mischievous impression upon the points on which definite ideas on both sides are essential. Want of tact in what is done is in some respects less excusable than want of tact in what is said, although the latter may often do more mischief; for the number of persons who can read an incautious speech, flying from one newspaper to another, is much larger than those who can witness an incautious act. An instance of this want of tact on one side, and of the vexatious manner in which it has been taken up on the other, has latterly been helping the papers through the dull season. A noble lord who has held high office contrived in a Church defence speech so effectively to advocate Church dissension, that the secretary of the Defence Institution had to apologise. However, the point which the incautious speaker took hold of, trivial as it was, was just one of the things as to which a finer sense of tact would have saved the attacked section of High Churchmen from exposing themselves to attack about. The fervour of a clergyman's loyalty to the Church of England, does not depend on the length or breadth of his surplice, although when he means to put a "vestment or cope" over that surplice, he must, as I have shown, have it small and tight. But when he has no such intention, he simply goes out of his way in exchanging the old familiar full and graceful surplice, for the little scamped article in vogue in certain churches. His doing so only tends to excite distrust and suspicion upon a matter wholly non-essential, and which may prove a very serious impediment among that large class of persons who judge by the eye and by first impressions to his influence and usefulness in things which are really of the highest everlasting importance. As a further argument against the tight surplice which may tell with some minds, I shall quote what that stout Roman Catholic ceremonialist, A. W. Pugin, said about it in his 'Glossary of Ecclesiastical Ornament,' published thirty years ago. After explaining that the surplice is in fact an "*albe enlarged* both in the body and the sleeves," he continues:—"It will be readily seen, therefore, that there is but one true form for the surplice, that which it had from the commencement, *long* and *ample*" [the italics in both places are Pugin's] "much resembling the one figured in every plate of the Roman Pontifical; and which it has only lost within a comparatively short period, in consequence of its real use and intention being forgotten."

So actually these short, cramped, and singularly ugly surplices which have become in 'Punch' and similar authorities the very type of the ritualist and which, strange as the assertion may be, have I believe much contributed to make the ignorant believe that the clergymen who wear them are not really a portion of the whole clergy of the great Church of England, but a sort of independent, if not antagonistic sect, are by the authority (which it were easy to supplement by a thousand instances) of the great reviver in the Anglo-Roman Church of the ceremonialism of the Church of Sarum, A. W. Pugin, a modern and a reprehensible innovation, in confirmation of which he quotes (though I do not care to repeat it) the authority of a Pope of the fourteenth century.

With regard to the episcopal dress, it is much to be desired that the rubrics of 1549 should speedily be acknowledged as possessing binding authority, so as to establish a dress for our Bishops, when officiating, which might be a little more seemly than the ungraceful garb which fortune, and no binding Church law, has condemned them to wear. The practice lately introduced, in manifest compliance with the canons, of relieving the dingy dress by the use of the Doctor's hood, has rather improved the attire. Nothing, however, can make it graceful, and as long as the sleeves are what they are, nothing can make it dignified. This reform will be more easy to the Bench, as they have already in part adopted the pastoral staff from the Book of 1549. I should almost be tempted to say that they had given their pledge to the Church to carry out not only the reform of their own dress, but that of the whole clergy. The re-adoption by the Chief Shepherd of the shepherd's crook, is, by right-minded persons, generally felt to be appropriate and edifying. Still there might have been a question on legal grounds as to the opportuneness of the step, had it been a purely volunteer improvement. It is, on the contrary, a direct instalment of that ritual of 1549, which, as I believe, our ornaments rubric points to. But the Bishops who have, in using the staff, pronounced for the legality of the ornaments of the minister of 1549, cannot wish it to be said that they have stopped at a point which tends to their own amplification, and are unable to help the clergy committed to their charge to make a corresponding use of the same law. As to the Bishop's dress in general, no possible affections cling to it; while the Archbishop of Canterbury, not long since, took a bold step in the way of reform when, with some of his suffragans, he officiated at an episcopal consecration in Westminster Abbey in his red convocational robes.

Only one more question relating to dress remains to be considered, and that is one which appears to me to be of the very slightest importance, although in an earlier stage of the Church movement it excited an amount of popular indignation which, in one cathedral city, culminated in disgraceful rioting, and in London brought on a clerical rebellion against Bishop Blomfield —I mean as to the dress in which it is right for the preacher to appear while occupying the pulpit. The acrimony with which, some thirty years ago, High Churchmen pressed the surplice, and Low Churchmen the gown, as the proper vesture for preaching, seems simply inconceivable, and it is possibly still more so that so many of the latter still continue to persuade themselves into there being some principle at stake. I suppose the true interpretation of this otherwise inexplicable and hardly creditable episode in the history of the Church movement is, that it affords an example of the truth that "the fathers have eaten sour grapes, and the children's teeth are set on edge." It was a folly which owed its origin to a great blunder in a remote and very different age. I have already referred to the deplorable suggestion in the Prayer Book of 1549 of the mutilated Communion service—the "ante-Communion service," as it is absurdly termed as if every word of the whole service, from first to last, was not the Communion service. I have always refused, as in this book, to use the term, and I remember suggesting in the Ritual Commission, as a substitute, to call it the "non-Communion service"—a service with no communion to give it significance. This wretched suggestion led to the custom of concluding the non-Communion service at the end of the prayer "for the whole state of Christ's Church" (now a "Church Militant here on earth"), a prayer to which Mr. Gladstone unaccountably points as the most "Protestant" one in the Prayer Book in his late article on Ritualism, but which is really, when taken in connection with the celebration which ought to follow, the representation of the oblations and of the great intercessory prayer of the ancient Liturgies, and which in the Prayer Book of 1549 actually formed the first part of the Consecration Prayer. In time the burden of returning back to the altar for a few minutes more of service after the sermon, only to use a prayer which, when taken without its Eucharistic belongings hardly did more than repeat petitions already offered up in the Litany, led to the omission of the prayer for the Church Militant and to the ordinary Sunday morning service ending with the sermon. Then came in the foppish fashion of the preacher changing his surplice for a smart silk gown. Bishop Blomfield and those who acted with him, instead of boldly urging a return to weekly communions, tried to reimpose the obsolete unreality of the mutilated service, with the prayer for the Church Militant not omitted, and of course pressed the continuous use of the surplice, to avoid the intolerable nuisance of so many changes of dress. This change further involved the offertory, and that carried with it giving. So the forces of the worldly, the lazy, and the stingy were arrayed against the double imposition of a longer service and of an appeal to their pockets, and Churchmen maintained but badly their untenable position. Now that all earnest High Churchmen are united on more frequent communions, and on the unreality of beginning a service which is to be left off before its true end is reached, they may well look back with amazement at the miserable surplice war.

The judgment, otherwise so dear to Low Churchmen, in

Hebbert v. Purchas, has attached their favourite practice of preaching in the black gown with illegality. But while very ready to put down their brethren's vestments, they have not been so forward in putting off their own black gowns. It would really seem as if there was some natural proclivity in the innermost mind of an English Churchman for change of raiment in church and a silken garb, when we see men who cry Popery at the assumption of vestment or cope between Litany and Communion service, so stoutly standing out for the change of the modest linen surplice into the rich and rustling silk gown between Nicene Creed and sermon, even at the cost, on communion days, of having again to strip it off. As far as convenience has anything to say to the matter, the practice which maintains one dress all through the Communion service (surplice or vestment) is obviously more practical than one which involves, whenever there is a celebration and only one priest, a triple vestiture. In referring to the change of surplice to gown, I must note another humorous feature in the case, namely, that during that early controversy the irregularity of the hymn between the Creed and the sermon, which was introduced to fill up the pause, was a matter of strong remonstrance from the High Church side, while in the later days the practice of introducing voluntary hymnody into the Communion service is a subject on which Low Churchmen please to go to law with the advanced party. The change of dress for preaching after the afternoon service clearly involves less inconvenience, although then, as in the morning, the retention by the preacher of the dress in which he has prayed is a more simple proceeding.

CHAPTER V.

Position of celebrant — The protest against tolerating this even more unreasonable — Shepherd leading his flock — Sanctioned by Mackonochie judgment. — Eight reasons for it — Purchas judgment — Remonstrance of 4761 clergymen — Sir J. T. Coleridge — Lord Cairns in House of Lords 1874 — Present rubrics — Comparison of rubrics touching position in 1552 and 1662 — New rubric of 1662 before Prayer of Consecration — Question not merely of priest's position, but of that of Holy Table — Rubrics of 1549 — "God's Board" and "Altar" in 1549, "God's Board" and "Lord's Table" in 1552 Altar and Lord's Table — Omission of "Altar" at foreign dictation — Holy Table and Altar equivalent in Greek liturgies — If Altar is Romanism, then Romanism more ancient than I admit — Βῶμος and Θυσιαστήριον — Communion Table not in rubrics — Bride never taken to the Communion Table — Altar in Canons of 1640 — Liddell v. Westerton on Credence — Lord's Table in 1552 put longways — Elizabeth's injunction of 1559 — Clumsy compromise — Consequent varieties of ritual — 82nd Canon — Bishop Andrewes and Laud — The north side became west side — Extraneous circumstances prevented those who secured altarwise place of table from settling celebrant's position — Bishop of Lincoln on celebrant's position — Andrewes' Chapel — Cushion and the cross marked on plan — Positive evidence against Bishop of Lincoln's suggestion — North side became now west side — Cosin and Wren — Wren on trial for his life adopted secondary reason — Laud adopted the same course — Wren and consecration of Dore Abbey Church — Lord Scudamore — Wren's suggested alteration in Prayer Book in 1661 — No contradiction to his previous practice — Wren's share in Scotch Prayer Book of 1637 — His suggestions of 1661 correspond — Wren and Laud's policy explained — Heylin's attempt to justify altarwise position of table by throwing over the priest's position — Hostile evidence of Bayley in 1661 — Present rubric before Prayer of Consecration — Due to Cosin — History of its growth — Condition of things in 1662 — Discovery of Cosin's original draft — Judges in Purchas's case quote Visitation Articles of Cosin which never were published — Ne pueros coram populo Medea trucidet — Real meaning of breaking bread before the people — Celebrant looks with, does not turn his back to, his people — Bishop of St. Andrews — Bishop of Lincoln — Basilican usage — Great wrong done if eastward position forbidden.

THE position of the celebrant is the other point on which the Memorialists protest against toleration with, if possible, even less reason than they show in their resistance to the distinctive Eucharistic dress, for if they had their own full way they would inflict much more active annoyance by throwing back that large multitude, who had for considerable periods of time adopted that eastward position, than in frustrating their many brethren, who are now desirous of adopting the dress. The position of facing the Lord's Table and leading the people as the eastern and scriptural shepherd led his flock, was early and largely adopted upon what they considered sufficient grounds by numerous Churchmen in every direction ever since the Church revival, and so much so, indeed, that it had begun to be generally recognised as one of those uncontentious points as to which the votary of either position had the right to be unmolested, but not to molest. Practices of Mr. Mackonochie, which had nothing to do with the dry question of the priest's position, led the Judicial Committee to consider the signification of the rubric before the Prayer of Consecration with the result as contained in the judgment which Lord Cairns delivered in December, 1868.

" The rubric before the prayer of consecration then follows, and is in these words :—

" ' When the priest, standing before the table, hath so ordered the bread and wine that he may with the more readiness and decency break the bread before the people, and take the cup into his hands, he shall say the prayer of consecration, as follows.'

" Their lordships entertain no doubt on the construction of this rubric that the priest is intended to continue in one posture during the prayer and not to change from standing to kneeling or vice versâ; and it appears to them equally certain that the priest is intended to stand, and not to kneel. They think that the words ' standing before the table' apply to the whole sentence; and they think this is made more apparent by the consideration that acts are to be done by the priest before the people as the prayer proceeds (such as taking the paten and chalice into his hands, breaking the bread, and laying his hand on the various vessels) which could only be done in the attitude of standing."

This decision afforded much comfort to those who felt strongly in favour of the eastward position, and did not, as far as I am aware, give offence on the other side. I have endeavoured to sum up in 'My Hints towards Peace,' the grounds, for the decided convictions and keen feelings of those persons, lay as well as clerical, who attached value to that position, and I cannot do better than to repeat them here with only a few additions.

(1) That the usage of the Universal Church (exception being of course made of those Anglican priests who have from time to time taken another position) points to the celebrant standing at the broad side of the Lord's Table, as the minister and representative of the congregation, offering in their name and in his own the commemorative sacrifice.

(2) That the position of the priest in those old "Basilican" churches, in which he stands at the further side of the altar and faces the people, is no exception to the first proposition, inasmuch as in that case also he faces the broad side.

(3) That the later usage, observed by the English Church before the Reformation, and by those members of it since who have taken the west side, is not, as falsely alleged, an attitude of turning his back to the people, but one of facing the same way as the people, of whom the priest is the præses and representative.

(4) That the usage of the Eastern Churches (including the Armenians and the Separatist bodies), not to mention that of the Latin Churches in communion with Rome, of taking the west side, is also that of all the Protestant bodies which have preserved a liturgical framework of worship.

(5) That there is sufficient evidence of a continuous catena of clergymen in our own Church taking the west side from the Reformation down to our own day.

(6) That, in their opinion, the rubric inserted at the last revision under the influence of such theologians as Bishop Cosin, can only be literally read as signifying that the celebrant is to stand before the Lord's Table throughout the Prayer of Consecration, and that the passage of the judgment

in Martin v. Mackonochie, relating to this rubric, can only be taken to mean this. What Lord Cairns, the author of this judgment, said upon the question in the House of Lords, may reasonably be taken to mean as much.

(7) That the difficulties attaching to the history of the question during the Reformation century can be solved by considering the practice, practically obsolete in and after 1662, and which quite died out after not many more years, of the Lord's Table being placed at communion time lengthways down the chancel, so that the "north side" was really one of its broad sides, and standing at the north side was also standing before the table, while likewise this identical north side became the west one as soon as the table was turned round and put altarwise. Therefore even at the period which is held to be most opposed to the idea of the priest turning his back to the people, the idea of an end position had not yet taken root.

(8) That a remarkable evidence exists of the deep feeling which has, in our own time, grown up among English Churchmen regarding the position in the declaration made (in my own hearing) at the Ritual Commission by that eminently cautious, moderate, and conciliatory Primate, Archbishop Longley. A proposal having been made to alter the rubric so as to enforce the Prayer of Consecration being read at the north end, the Archbishop rose, and, while explaining his personal non-adoption of the west side, begged the Commission not to touch the question, as any attempt to prohibit the practice would produce "exasperation" among the clergy. In consequence of this emphatic appeal the question was never again raised in the Commission, either during his primacy or that of his successor.

The matter was not, however, allowed to slumber long, for his choice of the eastward position was one of the points objected to in Mr. Purchas, and the judges in that undefended case came to a decision adverse to the practice, and supported their conclusions by an argument of which the following are the salient passages.

"The north side being the proper place for the minister throughout the Communion office, and also while he is saying the prayer of consecration, the question remains, whether the words 'standing before the table' direct any temporary change of position in the minister before saying the prayer of consecration? This is not the most important, but it is the most difficult question. Our opinion is that of Wheatley, who interprets the rubric as sending the priest to the west side of the table to order the elements. This, however, would be needless if the elements were so placed on the table as that the priest could 'with readiness and decency' order them from the north side, as is often done."

"The learned judge in the court below, in considering the charge against the respondent, that he stood with his back to the people during the prayer of consecration, briefly observes, 'the question appears to me to have been settled by the Privy Council in the case of Martin v. Mackonochie.' The question before their lordships in that case was as to the posture, and not as to the position of the minister. The words of the judgment are, 'their lordships entertain no doubt on the construction of this rubric' (before the prayer of consecration) 'that the priest is intended to continue in one posture during the prayer, and not to change from standing to kneeling, or *vice versâ*; and it appears to them equally certain that the priest is intended to stand and not to kneel. They think that the words " standing before the table" apply to the whole sentence; and they think this is made more apparent by the consideration that acts are to be done by the priest before the people, as the prayer proceeds (such as taking the paten and chalice into his hands, breaking the bread, and laying his hand on the various vessels), which could only be done in the attitude of standing.' This passage refers to posture or attitude from beginning to end, and not to position with reference to the sides of the table. And it could not be construed to justify Mr. Purchas in standing with his back to the people, unless a material addition were made to it. The learned judge reads it as if it ran, 'they think that the words " standing before the table," apply to the whole sentence, and that before the table means between the table and the people on the west side.' But these last words are mere assumption. The question of position was not before their lordships; if it had been, no doubt the passage would have been conceived differently, and the question of position expressly settled."

"Upon the whole, then, their lordships think that the words of Archdeacon, afterwards Bishop, Cosin in A.D. 1687 express the state of the law, 'doth he [the minister] stand at the north side of the table, and perform all things there, but when he hath special cause to remove from it, as in reading and preaching upon the gospel, or in delivering the sacrament to the communicants, or other occasions of the like nature.' (Bishop Cosin's 'Correspondence,' Part I., p. 106. Surtees Society.) They think that the prayer of consecration is to be used at the north side of the table, so that the minister looks south, whether a broader or a narrower side of the table be towards the north."

The excitement which the judgment caused may be estimated by the fact that within a short time of its being pronounced, 4761 clergymen of many various schools and practices, including those who did and those who did not adopt the particular use, signed the following remonstrance.

"*To the Archbishops and Bishops of the Church of England.*"

"We, the undersigned clergy of the Church of England, hereby offer our solemn remonstrance against the decision of the Judicial Committee of the Privy Council, in the case of 'Hebbert v. Purchas.'

"Without referring to all the points involved in this judgment, we respectfully submit the following considerations touching the position of the minister during the prayer of consecration at the Holy Communion.

"1. That the rubrics affecting this particular question having been diversely observed ever since they were framed, the Judicial Committee has given to these rubrics a restrictive interpretation condemnatory of a usage which has continuously existed in the Church of England, and has for many years widely prevailed.

"2. That this decision is opposed to the comprehensive spirit of the Reformed Church of England, and thus tends to narrow the church to the dimensions of a sect.

"3. That this restriction will press very unfairly upon a large body of the clergy who have never attempted, by resort to law or otherwise, to abridge the liberty of those whose practice differs from their own.

"4. That the rigorous enforcement of a decision so painful as this is to the consciences of those whom it affects, might involve the gravest consequences to a large number of the clergy, and lead to results most disastrous to the Established Church.

"On these grounds, although many of us are not personally affected by the judgment, we earnestly trust that your lordships will abstain from acting upon this decision, and thus preserve the ancient liberty of the Church of England.

"*March* 8th, 1871."

Sir John Taylor Coleridge in his pamphlet on the judgment, from which I have already quoted as to the ornaments rubric, deals as follows with the topic of the priest's position.

"As to the place of standing at the consecration, my *feeling* is with them. It seems to me not desirable to make it essential or even important that the people should see the breaking of the bread or the taking the cup into the hands of the priest, and positively mischievous to encourage them in gazing on him, or watching him with critical eyes while so employed. I much prefer the *spirit* of the rubric of 1549, 1st Book of Edward VI., which says, 'These words before rehearsed are to be said turning still to the altar, without any elevation, or shewing the Sacrament to the people.' The use now enforced, I think, tends to deprive the most solemn rite of our religion of one of its most solemn particulars. Surely whatever school we belong to, and even if we consider the whole rite merely commemorative, it is a very solemn idea to conceive the priest at the head of his flock, and, as it were, a shepherd leading them on in heart and spirit, imploring for them, and with them, the greatest blessing which man is capable of receiving on earth; he alone uttering the prayer—they meanwhile kneeling all, and in deep silence listening, not gazing, rather with closed eyes,—and with their whole undistracted attention, joining in the prayer with one heart, and without sound until the united 'Amen' breaks from them at the close, and seals their union and assent.

"This is my *feeling*—and I see no word in the sober language of our rubric which interferes with it—but my *feeling* is of no importance in the argument, and I mention it only in candour, to show in what spirit I approach the argument."

The course of the debates in the Committee of the House of Lords upon the Public Worship Regulation Bill having brought this very sore subject under discussion during last June, Lord Cairns, as Lord Chancellor, offered these observations.

" As to the position of the minister in the Communion service during the time of consecration, that is a subject on which it will not be expected, nor would it be proper, that I should give any expression of opinion as to what the law on the subject may be. But I wish to call your lordships' attention to the position of the question. I think that there are in the Church of England a great number of persons, a large number of clergymen, who have no sympathy whatever with the ritualists, I use a familiar expression, or ritualism, who have no sympathy with those extravagances and those departures from the law that have been referred to in this House, and who yet feel themselves much distressed and disquieted by the present law on the subject of the position of the minister during the time of consecration. Upon that subject there have been two decisions more or less final by the Judicial Committee of the Privy Council. I do not desire to say one word as to the law on the question, but every one knows how extremely difficult it is for any person—for any layman, perhaps for any lawyer—to be satisfied that those two decisions are reconcileable with each other. In one of those cases no defence was made, and only one side was heard. Those decisions, I think, cannot be regarded as final. If we look at the past history of the Judicial Committee of the Privy Council, we shall be able to find that certainly there is at least one case of great importance in which a decision arrived at by the Judicial Committee was afterwards altered by the same tribunal. Suppose it should hereafter be decided by the final tribunal of the country that the proper position of the minister at the time of consecration is to stand in front of the people looking towards the east—remember that if it should be so decided, that decision will be compulsory upon every clergyman of the Church of England. Now, if that should turn out to be the law of the church, it is a law which would press heavily upon the consciences of a great many clergymen of the Church of England. But suppose the tribunal should decide that the proper position for the clergyman is to stand looking towards the south. There are said to be hundreds of clergymen whose habit it has been all their lives, before ritualism was thought of, certainly before it was developed, to stand in the other position. I ask your lordships to consider how a final declaration of the law to the effect that I have mentioned would bear upon the consciences of those clergymen. But suppose the Court of Ultimate Appeal should say the rubrics are not sufficiently clear to enable them to define the position, that they do not find materials in the rubric to make the obligation certain, and they therefore leave the question of the position of the minister during the time of consecration *in dubio;* then, after a long, difficult, and acrimonious litigation, you will have come to the very conclusion at which the proposal of the Right Rev. Prelate asks your lordships to arrive."

These were words spoken in a very grave and courteous assembly by a man in the most dignified and one of the most responsible offices which a layman can fill, on a question upon which he had judged and might have again to judge, and in the presence of other members of the same House, whose judgment he was at the time taking upon himself to criticise. When these circumstances are brought into account, the true value and full import of Lord Cairns' language can hardly be a mystery to any one who does not approach it with a pre-formed bias. With Lord Cairns' words sounding in our ears, and remembering that the Purchas judgment was *in personam* not *in rem,* and in an undefended suit, it will hardly be disrespectful to discuss the question as an open one.

As the first step in our investigation, it may be as well to take in order all the rubrics which are found in the actual Prayer Book, and in that of 1552, which in any way refer to the priest's position. The first is the initiatory one.

"The table at the Communion-time having a fair white linen cloth upon it, shall stand in the body of the church, or in the chancel, where Morning and Evening Prayer are appointed to be said. And the priest standing at the north side of the table shall say the LORD's Prayer with the Collect following, the people kneeling."

This is vulgarly assumed to be an order which is very easy to be understood, and I do not deny that it may be so; but there is only one way of understanding what the entire rubric

CHAP. V. RUBRIC AFTER OFFERTORY SENTENCES. 177

means, and that is to have a clear idea upon the words "north side." I shall adduce evidence to show that these words are very often greatly misunderstood. The rubric first appears in this shape in the book of 1552 with only the differences that "having" comes after "Table," that "*the* collect following" is "this," and that "the people kneeling" does not occur at all. "Turning to the people" which is found in our present rubric before the reading of the ten commandments, was an insertion of 1662. Surely this implies a recognition of previously turning *from* the people as present to the revisers of 1662, in such a manner as it was not to those of 1552, and which illustrates and is illustrated by the new rubric which they inserted before the Prayer of Consecration which is so vital an element in the present discussion.

There are also noteworthy variations as between 1552 and 1662 in the rubric or rubrics which occur between the offertory sentences and the prayer for the Church Militant. In the earlier book there is only one paragraph which has reference exclusively to the collection to be then made, and it runs thus.

"Then shall the Churchwardens, or some other by them appointed, gather the devotion of the people, and put the same into the poor men's box; and upon the offering days appointed, every man and woman shall pay to the Curate the due and accustomed offerings: after which done, the Priest shall say."

In 1662 the form is as follows:—

"Whilst these Sentences are in reading, the Deacons, Churchwardens, or other fit person appointed for that purpose, shall receive the alms for the poor, and other devotions of the people, in a decent basin; to be provided by the Parish for that purpose, and reverently bring it to the Priest, who shall humbly present and place it upon the holy Table.

"And when there is a Communion, the Priest shall then place upon the Table so much Bread and Wine, as he shall think sufficient. After which done, the Priest shall say."

In the first paragraph of these directions we see several variations, such as the seemly "basin" and the reverent presentation to the priest of the money, followed by its being offered on his part to the Almighty, substituted for the clumsy and irreverent device of the money being dropped into a box. These less reverent arrangements were, I should point out, taken literally from 1549. Another variation deserving of particular notice is the introduction in 1662 of the term "Holy Table," which cannot be found either in 1552 or in 1549.

So far as the first clause goes (which was all that the book of 1552 contained) the rubrics or rubric has nothing to do with the priest's position. But in 1662 the second clause, relative to the placing on the table of the elements, was added, which is an inferential order to the priest to turn to it in that action.

The three last words in the present rubric which precedes the absolution,

"Then shall the priest (or the bishop being present) stand up, and turning himself to the people, pronounce this absolution,"

are in 1552 simply "say thus." It is a fair inference that both in 1552 and in 1662 a "turning to the people" must follow a turning to the Lord's Table, in whichever direction that table in itself might lie.

In the rubric before the Prayer of Humble Access we now read,

"Then shall the priest, kneeling down at the LORD's table, say, in name of all them that shall receive the Communion, this prayer following."

"At the Lord's Table" is "at God's Board" in 1552.

Up to this point, as it will be observed, the chief differences between 1552 and 1662, have been in the rubrics before the Prayer for the Church Militant. We now, however, reach a very important change. In the book of 1552, the rubric which

CHAP. V.   PRAYER BOOKS OF 1549 AND 1552.   179

precedes the Prayer of Consecration, is in this short and unexplanatory form:

"Then the priest standing up shall say, as followeth."

These words in 1662 were changed to,

"When the Priest, standing before the Table, hath so ordered the Bread and Wine, that he may with the more readiness and decency break the Bread before the people, and take the Cup into his hands, he shall say the Prayer of Consecration, as followeth."

It is frequently assumed that there is a discrepancy between this rubric and the one at the commencement of the service; and so there may be if Lord Cairns interprets the former rightly, as I submit that he does. But the discrepancy, if any, is not of the nature commonly assumed, or rather, as I should put it, the discrepancy arises out of no conflict of words, but out of the eventful history of the thing with which the words deal.

Before advancing a single step further, I must direct particular attention to the seventh of the reasons which I offered for the priest's position being a question of high interest to many persons; and I must explain that in testing these rubrics, and in considering the whole question, I cannot deal with it as one which only has to do with the priest's position towards the Holy Table. It is equally and inextricably one of the position of that Holy Table towards the church itself in which it is standing, and to the congregation in whose behalf it is used. Unless the discussion is taken up with this clear view, and in the desire to face and understand the whole broad issue, it never can be brought to a satisfactory conclusion.

In order really to understand the question, we must put in evidence another document besides the Books of 1552 and 1662, namely that of 1549. The relations of the two Prayer Books of 1549 and of 1552 towards each other have, according to the bias of different writers, been represented either as those of modification or of contrariety. Much may, I believe, be said for either view, and the investigator who rather wishes to ascertain the absolute truth than to set up any preformed opinion, should be prepared to compare them under both lights. I shall in this spirit endeavour to work out what may be gathered from the comparison of the rubrics of the two versions of our Prayer Book upon the closely-allied questions of the position of the Lord's Table itself and of the minister towards that table.

The initiatory rubric of position stands in 1549 as follows:—
"The priest, standing humbly afore the midst of the Altar, shall say the Lord's Prayer with this collect." The Gloria in Excelsis is then said after these prayers, with only the intervention of the introit and versicles, for the Book of 1549 follows the unreformed rituals in assigning this early position in the office to the hymn. It is preceded by the rubric —" then the Priest standing at God's board shall begin." At the close of this canticle we read, "Then the Priest shall turn him to the people and say." After that there is no rubric of position till we meet the one before the Prayer of Consecration. "Then the Priest, turning him to the Altar, shall say or sing, plainly and distinctly, this Prayer following." The Prayer of Consecration of 1549 (embodying as it did the present prayer for the Church militant) did not, as in the later books, conclude with the words of Institution, for the "oblation" followed, of which a considerable portion is retained in our present book in the first of the two prayers after the reception. Between the words of institution and this part of the prayer the following rubric is inserted, "These words before rehearsed are to be said, turning still to the Altar, without any elevation, or shewing the Sacrament to the People."

We have, further on, these rubrics,—" Here the Priest shall turn him towards those that come to the Holy Communion, and shall say" (with a similar one before the absolution): and "Then shall the Priest, turning him to God's board, kneel down, and say, in the name of all them that shall receive the Communion, this Prayer following."

CHAP. V.   GOD'S BOARD—LORD'S TABLE—ALTAR.   181

As to the phraseology used it will be observed that "God's Board" is common to the books of 1549 and 1552, but that in the latter "Lord's Table" replaces the "Altar" of the other.

It will be at once seen that, waiving minor differences, the two points in which the rubrics of 1549 and 1552 differ are, that the former mentions an "Altar" without stating where it is to stand, and places the priest at its "midst," the latter introduces us to the "Lord's Table," which it places in the body of the church, or in the chancel, and that it orders the priest to stand at the north side of it. What I shall show is that the real difference between the two rubrics rests on the different handling of Altar and Lord's Table, and that relatively to the "Board"—whether "Altar" or "Table"—upon which the Holy Communion is celebrated, the position of the minister himself remains unaffected. In 1549 the old altars remained in their places, and were assumed to be available for the new rite. This state of things was displeasing to the Swiss reformers, who had then the upper hand in England, and the destruction of altars commenced even in the days when they were still the legal and formal ornaments of the church, that is, in the very period when the Book of 1549 was our statutory form of worship. So where we read "Altar" or "God's Board" in 1549, we read "Lord's Table" or "God's Board" in 1552, "Holy Table" having been introduced in 1662. As a decided and loyal son of the reformed Anglican Church, I make no scruple now, and always, of confessing my deepest regret at this omission of a scriptural term hallowed by the tradition of all Christendom from the earliest times, at the dictation of a few headstrong and unstable foreigners, who had, in their own ecclesiastical polity, already thrown over principles, forms, and practices, which the Church of England, in spite of their interference, has never from then till now been cajoled into abandoning. Happily, however, their policy could go no further than to omit from the rubrics the word "Altar;" what it signified, namely, the place at which the Church of

England rightly celebrated the Supper of the Lord, still remained, and names were still assigned to it expressive of the great sanctity environing all which appertains to Christ's own ordinance—" Lord's Table " or "God's Board," which remained from 1549; while "Holy Table," added in 1662, is, indeed, formally and absolutely the liturgical identical of "Altar,"—the two terms Ἱερα τραπέζα, "Holy Table," and Θυσιαστήριον, "Altar," being used indiscriminately in the most ancient Greek liturgies, and still being taken as equivalent all over the East. The fancy that Altar must mean Roman Catholic Altar, is simply a baseless prejudice, as the word was in full and accepted and undoubted use all over the Christian world for centuries before the growth of the Roman corruption; so that if Altar does imply distinctive Romanism, then distinctive Romanism is a much more ancient and authoritative matter than, as a sound Anglican, I should like to admit. I believe, indeed, that much of the prejudice which has grown up about the word arises from the ignorant confusion which exists between the Jewish and Christian Altars respectively on the one side, and the heathen altars on the other, among persons who are ignorant that the latter are always named Βῶμος (Bomos), and the former Θυσιαστήριον (Thusiasterion), two totally distinct words, and which are respectively represented in Latin by Ara and Altare.

There is another name very commonly applied to this " ornament of the church," " Communion Table," as to which the peculiarity is that, while it occurs both in the canons and in innumerable other documents of varying authority, it is not once found in the Prayer Book, and can hardly, therefore, I should submit, claim equal authority with those which are found there. Still, it would be affectation to deny that it has got incorporated into our ecclesiastical vocabulary, and I am well content that it should have done so, for it is an accurate description of a fact. Still it does not suggest the reverence attaching to " Lord's " or " Holy " Table, and in this respect also (in addition to the lower authority of the term to which the Prayer Book is a stranger) these appellations are certainly preferable. Particularly must I protest, therefore, against the policy of thrusting it forward as if it were the authoritative appellation in the reformed Church, in contrast to the unreformed "Altar," when, as I have shown, it is out of several names the one which happens to have the least authority. I must, most especially, protest (grateful as I am in other respects to that judgment) against the direct contrast which the Judges in "Liddell v. Westerton" make between the altar of 1549, and what they call the Communion Table of 1552, as if the latter book had substituted the one name for the other. This is simply not the fact, inasmuch as what 1552 provided was a "Lord's Table," a "God's Board," (the latter word also being found in 1549) and inasmuch as they were sitting to judge a case under 1662 which has enacted a "Holy Table," namely, that which in the Oriental liturgies, primitive and present, is the alternative name for "Altar."

Happily, however, no persistence of Calvin, Peter Martyr, or Alasco, was able to stamp out the name and the idea of an Altar from the minds and hearts of Englishmen and Englishwomen, and so long as every bridegroom who seeks the Church's blessing brings his bride to the "Altar," and not to the "Communion Table," we may despise and write 'failure' against the aggressive unrest of Swiss innovators which worked so unfortunately upon the weakness of the English Prelacy in 1552.

I cannot better sum up this digression on the name and meaning of "altar," than in the words of one of the canons made by the Convocation of Canterbury in 1640, which, although owing to the troubles unsanctioned and therefore invalid in the eyes of the Law Courts, still remain on record as the formal voice of the Church of England at an important epoch.

"That the standing of the Communion Table side-way under the east window of every chancell, or chappell, is in its own nature indifferent, neither commanded nor condemned by the Word of God either expressly or by immediate deduction, and therefore that no religion is to be placed therein, or scruple to be made thereon. And albeit at the time of reforming this Church from that grosse superstition of Popery, it was carefully provided that all meanes should be used to root out of the mindes of the people, both the inclination thereunto, and memory thereof, especially of the idolatry committed in the masse, for which cause all Popish altars were demolished; yet notwithstanding it was then ordered by the injunctions and advertisements of Queen *Elizabeth*, of blessed memory, that the Holy Tables should stand in the place where the altars stood, and accordingly have been continued in the Royall Chappels of three famous and pious princes, and in most cathedrall, and some parochiall churches, which doth sufficiently acquit the manner of placing the said tables from any illegality, or just suspition of Popish superstition or innovation. And therefore we judge it fit and convenient, that all churches and chappels do conform themselves in this particular to the example of the cathedral or mother churches, saving alwaies the generall liberty left to the bishop by law, during the time of administration of the Holy Communion. And we declare that this situation of the Holy Table doth not imply that it is, or ought to be, esteemed a true and proper altar, whereon Christ is again really sacrificed; but it is, and may be, called an altar by us, in that sense in which the Primitive Church called it an altar, and in no other."

In this connection, and in further evidence that the difference between the "Altar" of 1549 and the "Lord's Table" is (whatever the foreign innovators may have desired to make it) not fundamental, I may as well quote one of the passages of the Liddell *v.* Westerton judgment, in which that use of the name Communion Table has been made on which I have felt bound to comment. A decision may be quite sound, while the words in which it is clothed are not strictly accurate; but in this case the inaccuracy is more to be regretted, because the right terms would have so much strengthened the judges' own reasonings. Among the things which Mr. Westerton and Mr. Beal objected to in the Churches of St. Paul's and St. Barnabas' was a little side table (called *Credence*), in each, on which the unconsecrated elements were to stand, until, in the terms of the rubrics before the Prayer for the Church Militant, first introduced in 1662, the priest was to place them on the Holy Table. Though there had been ample precedent for it in the practice of some of our most weighty divines, the Credence found no favour in the lower Courts, but the Privy Council sanctioned it with these observations:—

"Now what is a Credence Table? it is simply a small side-table on which the bread and wine are placed before the consecration, having no connection with any superstitious usage of the Church of Rome. Their removal has been ordered on the ground that they are adjuncts to an altar; their Lordships cannot but think that they are more properly to be regarded as adjuncts to a Communion Table.

"The rubric directs that at a certain point in the course of the Communion Service (for this is, no doubt, the true meaning of the rubric) the minister shall place the bread and wine on the Communion Table; but where they are to be placed previously is nowhere stated. In practice they are usually placed on the Communion Table before the commencement of the service, but this certainly is not according to the order prescribed. Nothing seems to be less objectionable than a small side-table, from which they may be conveniently reached by the officiating minister, and at the proper time transferred to the Communion Table."

Two thoughts very naturally present themselves on this passage: one is, that the very line of reasoning which the judges adopt shows that, after all, Altar and Communion Table could not be such antagonistic terms, or the Credence could not so readily adapt itself to both. I fear that the canon of 1640 was hardly present to their minds when they penned the passage. The other one has reference to the whole ritual controversy. We here see a piece of church furniture, nowhere mentioned in any rubric, sanctioned on principles of common sense, in that very judgment which lays down the stern view of the ornaments rubric, which the Council in Martin v. Mackonochie made still more stern. Does not this instinctive and inevitable admission that omission cannot always mean prohibition on the part of those very Judges who are currently quoted as having laid down the contrary principle, apply as a ruling hint to further matters than the one single case of the Credence?

This digression on the Altar and the Credence has taken me away from the immediate question of the priest's position. But I am sure that it will not only help but tend to shorten the whole argument of my book. I must have met these points at some time, and I believe that what I have just said will make what is to follow upon my immediate topic more clear.

The situation then stood as follows, apart from questions of the material or fashion of the Table, which are not of consequence to the present point. The moderate reformers, represented by the Book of 1549, maintained a reformed "Altar" where the unreformed altar had stood. The more advanced reformers of 1552 converted the "Altar" into a "Lord's Table," and placed it, as we learn from contemporary evidence, lengthways in "the body of the Church" (*i.e.* nave) "or in the chancel," with its short ends east and west, and its broad sides north and south. This change of its position may at this moment be only partially visible in the actual words of the rubric, but the evidence that it took place, and that the compilers meant that it should take place, is one of the points on which history does not tell us two stories. Having done this, they had to place the minister, and here they showed themselves conservative. The points of the compass in the Table itself had been changed with placing the Table lengthways, so the "midst of the Altar" must necessarily have been either the north side looking south, or the south side looking north. Between these the former one was insisted on, probably from some lingering respect for the older customs, in which the north part of the Altar was the one assigned to the higher minister.

Thus explained, the difficulties attending the Prayer Book, as it was left in 1552, disappear. The Table was lengthways, the priest's position in its "midst," standing at the broad "north side," and looking south. The practical confusion, coming from so great a change all over England, we have every reason to believe was through the reign of Edward VI., enormous, and then came the episode of the restoration under Mary of the old rites. On Elizabeth's accession, as we have seen in the matter of the ornaments rubric, there was a certain ceremonial reaction from 1552. So an attempt was made at compromise to the position of the Holy Table, out of which has grown the confusion, from which, in some shape or other, the question has never fully succeeded in extricating itself.

The injunctions which the Queen issued in 1559, on coming to the throne, after (in strong contrast to the policy of the authorities between 1549 and 1552) forbidding the destruction of altars by private persons, and after ordering the retention of such as had not been pulled down, contain this passage:—

"And that the Holy Table in every church be decently made, and set in the place where the altar stood; and there commonly covered, as thereto belongeth, and as shall be appointed by the visitors; and so to stand, saving when the Communion of the Sacrament is to be distributed, at which time the same shall be so placed in good sort within the chancel, as whereby the minister may be more conveniently heard of the communicants in his prayer and ministration, and the communicants also more conveniently, and in more number, communicate with the said minister. And after the Communion done, from time to time the same Holy Table to be placed where it stood before."

It will be observed that this passage twice contains the term "Holy Table," which has so distinct a signification as a primitive synonym for Altar, but which did not come into the Prayer Book till 103 years after. The use of the expression can hardly have been accidental, but must have been a covert protest against the iconoclasm which had, in the last days of Edward, threatened to overwhelm all goodly forms. The movability also of the Table is by the injunction circumscribed—to "within the chancel," omitting "the body of the church." The compromise was essentially clumsy, based on no sound principle, and it broke down as soon as it was devised. The varieties of ritual to which it gave rise were even more salient than those which have disturbed public opinion in our own time. At one extremity stood the Queen's Chapel, in which there can be no doubt that the Altar ever maintained its position at the east end of the building. Canterbury Cathedral came next, with a combination nothing less than ludicrous of the higher and the puritan ceremonials, as we find in a description in Strype's 'Memorials of Parker' of the state of things there at the commencement of 1565 :—

"The Common Prayer daily through the year, though there be no Communion, is sung at the Communion Table, standing north and south, where the high altar stood. The minister, when there is no Communion, useth a surplice only, standing on the east side of the table, with his face toward the people.

"The Holy Communion is ministred ordinarily the first Sunday of every month through the year. At what time the table is set east and west. The priest which ministereth, the Pystoler and Gospeler, at that time wear copes."

Next came the churches in which attention was paid to the injunction, but in which no vestment was used, and lastly, those in which the Lord's Table never was placed altarwise. So matters dragged on through the reign of Elizabeth. The confusion in which the question was left may easily be fathomed by consulting the 82nd Canon, prescribing a "decent Communion Table in every church."

"Whereas we have no doubt, but that in all churches within the realm of England, convenient and decent tables are provided and placed for the celebration of the Holy Communion, we appoint, that the same tables shall from time to time be kept and repaired in sufficient and seemly manner, and covered, in time of divine service, with a carpet of silk or other decent stuff, thought meet by the ordinary of the place, if any question be made of it, and with a fair linen cloth at the time of the ministration, as becometh that table,

CHAP. V.   OBSCURITY OF EIGHTY-SECOND CANON.

and so stand, saving when the said Holy Communion is to be administered; at which time the same shall be placed in so good sort within the church or chancel, as thereby the minister may be more conveniently heard of the communicants in his prayer and ministration, and the communicants also more conveniently, and in more number, may communicate with the said minister; and that the Ten Commandments be set up on the east end of every church and chapel, where the people may best see and read the same, and other chosen sentences written upon the walls of the said churches and chapels, in places convenient; and, likewise, that a convenient seat be made for the minister to read service in. All these things to be done at the charge of the parish."

The canons are generally tolerably successful in making their meaning clear (always excepting the 24th, in its English form). In this case, however, the directions are notably, if not intentionally obscure. They are also, like the rubric which they follow, more puritanical than Elizabeth's injunction in allowing the alternative of "church" (*i. e.* nave) "or chancel." We do not get much clearer light when we turn to the Latin edition and read "quæque certo loco consistant, nisi cum Sacramentum erit administrandum." A sharp critic might suggest that the "certus locus" of a Communion Table would be the place of the Communion itself. It altogether reads like the conclusions of persons who are rather ashamed of themselves, and, in familiar phrase, hardly know "what to do with it."

The period of the canons was, in fact, the dawn of a different state of things in the English Church in regard to the Holy Table. In the plan of Bishop Andrewes' chapel, to which I have already referred, we see the commencement of a better reasoned out system of ceremonial, which the higher Churchmen of the seventeenth century adopted. I need not load these pages with the history of the movement, of which Laud was the conspicuous leader, to make the altarwise position of the Holy Table general at communion time, as well as other occasions, and to define its place by rails. However persons may differ as to the nature or the manner of this proceeding, there is no doubt as to the fact, and, with so much to say, I shall not, therefore, repeat the tale.

The movement only concerns me now in so far as it illustrates the question of the priest's position relatively to the Holy Table. It is obvious that, with the unaltered rubrics of 1552 still in force, the question must soon have forced itself into notice whether, after the permanent change of position in the altar, the now impossible "north side" was to be represented by that *west side*, which was, in fact, the actual north side turned round, or by the *north end*, which was nothing more than what had been the east end, similarly turned round. If the men, whose determination won for our churches the restoration of the Christian altar in its due place of honour, faltered and stammered upon this point we must not think unkindly of them. It was a daring fight on their part, and they paid for their attempt with poverty, exile, imprisonment, and even death, and in their own generation their endeavour was, to all human calculation, abortive; but yet, in the fulness of time, it revived, and even in the coldest and most apathetic days which our reformed Church has ever known, when its success would have seemed most impossible, it took root and has asserted itself as the unwritten but irreversible rule of the English Church.

No doubt the right position of the altar was, from a concurrence of circumstances, assumed as a naked proposition and at the expense of the position of the celebrant becoming a question of perplexing embarrassment; but from extraneous circumstances it was beyond the power of those who settled the one point to command the solution of the other.

My much honoured friend, the Bishop of Lincoln, in his recently-published 'Plea for Toleration by Law in certain Ritual Matters,' argues that the seventeenth-century ceremonialists adopted the north end as the place at which the celebrant ought to consecrate, and he adduces these reasons:—

"The Church of England in her rubric at the beginning of her office for the Holy Communion, recognizes *two* positions of the Com-

CHAP. V.   BISHOP OF LINCOLN ON PRIEST'S POSITION.   191

munion Table as equally lawful. The table may stand 'in the body of the church.' This is the first position which it specifies. And in this case it would stand long-wise, i.e., parallel to the north and south walls of the church.

"This was the position of the table in most parish churches during the seventeenth century, and at the last review; as appears from the Seventh Canon of the Convocation of 1640, Archbishop Laud's Convocation.

"In this case it is certain that the celebrant did not occupy an *eastward* position, but stood on the north side of the table with his face to the south.

"The second lawful position of the Holy Table was 'in the chancel,' at the east end; and there it stood cross-wise, i.e., from north to south.

"This was its position 'in most cathedral churches, and in some parochial churches,' as the same Canon declares; and has now become general.

"That in cathedrals the celebrant stood at the north end (called the *north side* in the rubric, which is purposely framed so as to suit both positions of the table) is clear from the testimony of the continued and uniform usage of all cathedral churches to the present times. In the case of a very few cathedrals the eastward position has been introduced within the last ten years. But I am speaking of the practice up to the beginning of the present century.

"The engraving which Laud's bitter enemy, William Prynne (who would gladly have convicted him of any practice regarded by Puritans as Papistical), published of the arrangement of the Archbishop's private chapel (London, 1644, p. 123), where the cushion for the celebrant (for a cushion there was) is placed at the *north end* of the table, leads to the same conclusion.

"This is further demonstrated by the well-known rubric of the Non-jurors (no favourers of Protestantism) in their Prayer Book, where the words '*before* the table,' are explained to mean 'the *north side* thereof.'"

I think from what I have adduced it is clear that the Bishop in this sketch joins together several epochs. 1. The epoch of 1552, which insisted on the table at Communion time (the only time surely when its position was of much moment to any reasonable person) standing lengthways. 2. The epoch of 1559, when Elizabeth's advisers endeavoured to compromise matters by ceremoniously setting up the table as an altar, and even saying portions of the altar service at it when there was no communion, merely to bring it down again when there was one. 3. Its restoration in the seventeenth century to the permanent altarwise position, if not, 4, also to the condition of things (to which I shall advert later) under the present rubrics. The Bishop also assumes that when the table stands longwise it is to be in the nave and when crosswise in the chancel, although Elizabeth's injunction assumes that it is never to leave the chancel, although it is alternatively to stand crosswise or longwise in that chancel. About the argument from the cushion in the chapel of which Prynne published the plan, I must note that it was strictly the plan, not of Laud's, but of Andrewes' chapel. Laud, indeed, obtained it for the purpose, which he carried out, of copying it in his own chapels; but it can only be taken as authoritative evidence on smaller points of detail in regard to Bishop Andrewes' practice. Premising this, I should say that the cushion which most unmistakably appears at the north end of Andrewes' altar with none to match it on the south, leads me to the directly contrary conclusion. The plan (to recapitulate) represents to us this cushion at the north end, and in the centre of the table two patens and a vessel for the water of admixture with the wine, with, save as I shall have to point out, appended letters referring to the description in the key. The chalice, which is also referred to under a letter in the key, does not, however, in fact, appear upon the plan. What does all this show? I should say that it showed that the north end was intended as the place of official dignity for the Bishop to kneel at, and in general to follow the bulk of the service (whether said by self or chaplain) with his book, which would rest upon the cushion, but that the centre was reserved for the consecration itself. Surely this inference stands to reason, for if Andrewes' practice had been to consecrate at the north end, he never would have hampered that particular part of the table with a cushion which would make the decent performance of the rite on his part so very difficult, nor would he have so emphatically shown the sacred vessels ranged exactly in the middle. It is somewhat curious that while in the key he employs letters, Greek or capital Roman, for reference to the other articles, Andrewes uses a cross to indicate the place of the vessel of admixture, and that this happens to stand in the exact centre of the Holy Table. I cannot help surmising that this exceptional use of the cross as a mark of reference in the key was intended as a sort of private note that that central point of the table was to be used as the place of consecration.

In answer, however, to the suggestion of the Bishop of Lincoln, which, as I have shown, stands on a somewhat insecure foundation, I can adduce positive evidence that the leaders of churchmanship in the seventeenth century, not indeed universally nor in the least degree compulsorily, brought their work of securing the altarwise position of the Lord's Table to a consistent conclusion by taking the same position towards it in its restored place which in the former one was the "north side," namely, the new west side. In fact, not to have done so, would have been in setting right one innovation to have made themselves guilty of another. The longwise position of the Lord's Table was an innovation upon the practice of all Christian antiquity, but at all events the minister who took the north side of one so placed, ruled himself towards it as every priest before him, from the earliest days of authentic evidence, had done towards the Altar at which he officiated, that is to say, he stood in the midst of it facing its broad side. The priest who should stand at the end of the Holy Table now restored to its ancient position, would rule himself towards it as no priest had ever done towards any Altar, except in England, and at some uncertain date later than 1559 and (I have personally little doubt) than 1600.

In proof, however, of my assertion, I must again call up Peter Smart, from whom we learn that,

"Dr. Cosin did officiate at the said altar, with his face towards the east, and back toward the people, at the time of the administration of the Holy Communion."

The often quoted excuse which Bishop Wren in serious and well-founded alarm for his life (which was saved), and his liberty (which he lost), made to the Parliament for consecrating at the west side, that he took that place because he was so short, can hardly be treated by a fair advocate for the north end as very valuable evidence. It proves how perilous the bishop felt his situation to be (as to which the results showed that he was not mistaken) when he had to fall back upon arguments of that class, but it equally proves that he could not deny the fact, and had therefore to look about for some secondary reason which might be materially tenable wherewith to parry the charge. Those who never have been in terror of their lives under similar circumstances, may no doubt find it easy to be indignant at one who was standing in jeopardy of execution, and who did in fact suffer eighteen years' very severe imprisonment for a circumstantial plea of "not guilty." The author of the article on the "Ritual of the English Church" in the 'Quarterly Review' for October, 1874, seems to look upon this plea of Wren as a very conclusive argument against the west side. "Wren had actually consecrated with his back to the people; he too is anxious not to be misunderstood." No doubt he is; but what he is most anxious for is not to be beheaded. Laud's parallel plea that he took the west side to allow the priest the freer use of his hands, which seems to the reviewer to be equally conclusive as his view, is if possible an even more unstable prop. Laud like Wren was in peril of his life, but unlike Wren did not save it. So he also looked for some plea which should be materially true but yet as little compromising as possible. He found it in the incontrovertible fact that a celebrant standing at the broad side had freer use of his hands than if he were remanded to the narrow end. Those who are familiar with Laud's theological position will easily perceive that when he made this statement in a very solemn manner, and accompanied by an appeal to Almighty God that he knew of "no other intention," he implied that any imputation drawn from it that he thereby intended to imply some doctrine contrary to that of the Church of England, and in particular symbolising any error of Rome was a calumny. The use of his hands was free when he stood at the west side, it was not free when he stood at the north end, particularly if the table, as in Andrewes' chapel, was at that place encumbered by a cushion. At the same time Laud felt that wherever he might be standing, he was equally celebrating with the same honest Anglican intention. Feeling this, and at the same time answering, an aged prisoner, to a capital charge, he justified his proceeding before his judges on the material reason for the action; particularly because (as I shall show further on) he had specific grounds for urging this plea.

I wonder that the learned reviewer when on this subject had not in the course of his reading lighted on an incident in Wren's episcopal career which I must now proceed to notice. There is direct evidence of the practice of Wren (a man whom, as it will be recollected, Clarendon especially commends for his knowledge of ancient liturgies), under circumstances which reveal the real opinions of the prelate. Just after his consecration as Bishop of Hereford in 1634 he was called upon to consecrate a church under exceptional circumstances. The old monastic church of Abbey Dore in Herefordshire, which had fallen into ruins, was at that time restored by a very zealous Churchman, the Viscount Scudamore, and Wren prepared the form of consecration. At the time fixed, however, he was detained in town by his duties as Clerk of the Closet, and, therefore, delegated the consecration to Dr. Field, Bishop of St. David's, so that, as it happened, the ceremonial which I shall quote had the sanction of two bishops, besides which Lord Scudamore is known to have been a friend of Laud. The form of the consecration of Abbey Dore church exists in two manuscripts preserved in the British Museum and at Lambeth, and the former one has during the present year been published with copious notes by Mr. Fuller Russell, consequently the judges in the Purchas case had not the advantage of being able to refer to it. The narrative which is very circumstantial is written in the present tense, and may either be a draft of the intended ceremony or a record of what took place, but in either case it is authoritative. It mostly takes the shape of a formally recited service with explanatory rubrics. The rubric before the Prayer of Consecration runs thus :

"Then the bishop standeth up and setteth ready in his hand the bread and wine with the paten and chalice, but first washeth his fingers with the end of the napkin besprinkled with water. Then layeth he the bread in the paten, and poureth of the wine into the chalice, and a little water into it, and *standing with his face to the table, about the midst of it,* he saith the Collect of Consecration."*

I must note that the "Table" here mentioned was the ancient altar slab which Lord Scudamore had recovered and set up again on short pillars at the east end of the church, where it is still standing. So that when Bishop Field, acting for Bishop Wren, faced the table at Abbey Dore " about the midst of it," he was looking eastward. One example like this is worth a bushel of conjectures. This was no deed done in a corner, but an occasion when the men who acted had the means and the will to do what they believed to be most right. The church had been restored by a munificent nobleman of whose sympathies Wren was sure, and Wren accordingly availed himself of the occasion to set out his ideal of the truest and most decent ritual. Besides, if the Abbey Dore form had never been published or had been lost in manuscript, persons

---

* The italics are my own.

would have argued that such a thing as bishops of that age consecrating eastward could not have been, there was no real evidence for it; but that the notion was on the face of it absurd. This isolated but unanswerable evidence has appeared, and he would be a bold disputant who should argue that it must be a unique case, or that there was anything in it to show that it did not embody the ritual which the same school of men practised in other cases, and by practising approved. In fault of proof to the contrary, I am much more disposed to believe that the practice in Queen Elizabeth's chapel resembled that of Wren, than that it conformed to the austere prescriptions of 1552.

The Bishop of Chester has just published a curious volume of 'Fragmentary Illustrations of the History of the Book of Common Prayer,' comprising the service which Bishop Sanderson compiled out of the Prayer Book during the Commonwealth, when it was unsafe to use the actual book, and also notes on the revision of the Prayer Book, which Wren after his long captivity prepared in 1661 as one of the committee of eight bishops appointed by the Convocation of Canterbury. In these, Wren proposes, in lieu of the existing first rubric, to read, "And the priest standing at the north of the table the people all kneeling, shall begin to say the Lord's Prayer." He also offers a consecration rubric different from the one which was ultimately adopted and which I shall quote further on.

This suggestion of Wren, an old man of seventy-six, broken by the sufferings of eighteen years' harsh imprisonment, upon charges of which, as we have seen, his standing before the table was not the least conspicuous, might seem in contradiction to his practice twenty-seven years before, when he was in the vigour of mature life. But I believe the incident may be better explained in another manner, which does not seem to have occurred to the Bishop of Chester, who in his prefatory matter merely says, " Standing at the 'north of the table' is directed p. 74 and recognised pp. 75 and 81." This would appear almost to marshal Wren in 1661 as a witness for the southward position during the Prayer of Consecration, while it left him equally willing to compromise for the north end at the earlier part of the service. Wren's proposed rubric before the Prayer of Consecration, to which the Bishop of Chester calls attention, is, "Then the priest standing before the table shall so order and set the bread and the wine that, while he is pronouncing the following collect, he may readily take the bread and break it, and also take the cup to pour into it (if he pour it not before) and then he shall say." When Wren wrote these two rubrics, I believe he was living again his life of twenty-four years previously, when he had an important share in revising the Scotch Prayer Book of 1637, which although drawn up by bishops of that country was in substance the reflex of the then churchmanship of England. In the rubrics of this book a compromise was attempted by way of keeping the northern position of the celebrant towards the altar at the commencement of the communion service, but of leaving him free to consecrate eastwards. Accordingly in the initiatory rubric the relative position of the "Presbyter" was thus adjusted:—

"The Holy Table, having at the communion time a carpet, and a fair white linen cloth upon it, with other decent furniture, meet for the high mysteries there to be celebrated, shall stand at the uppermost part of the chancel or church, where the presbyter, standing at the north side or end thereof, shall say the Lord's Prayer, with this collect following for due preparation."

But the rubric before the Prayer of Consecration stood, "Then the presbyter standing up shall say the Prayer of Consecration as followeth, but then during the time of Consecration he shall stand at such a part of the Holy Table, where he may with the more care and decency use both his hands." This points at, without daring directly to enforce, the eastward position, while its practical reasoning would commend itself to the man who could make his own height a consideration in the case. These two rubrics taken together show the arrangement which the ritualists of that time would have closed with—inconsistent as it would have been alike with the history of the question and with natural congruity—namely, the recognition of the north *end* in substitution for the north *side* at the beginning of the service, but the assumption of the position "in the midst of the Altar" (to which the north *side* of the misplaced table really corresponded) at the Consecration. It is fair to say that this policy is consistent with the Abbey Dore rubric, and, as I have argued, seems also to be pointed at in Andrewes' cushion. Certainly when we compare the Scotch rubrics of 1637 and Wren's proposed rubrics of 1661 together, their remarkable similarity both of prescript and of reason for the prescript is at once apparent. At the same time the peculiarity of Wren's phraseology in using "pour" as an intransitive verb without an accusative may be noticed. It will be owned that these two sets of rubrics—the Scotch revised by Wren, and Wren's own proposed form—correspond together, while neither of them corresponds with the English rubrics of any of our Prayer Books either in intention or in wording. If we admit this, the consequence follows that Wren wished in 1661 to carry out the views of 1634 and 1637, not that he had receded from them. The wording of these Scotch rubrics is an additional proof, if one were needed, that Laud and Wren (the English bishops most responsible for them) did in their pleas before their judges, neither attempt to "throw over" the eastward position so far as they themselves had dared to legalise it, nor screen themselves by unworthy pretexts. The framers of the Scotch book had for reasons of policy not ordered, but only recommended, the position which they personally preferred, and had based their recommendation on material considerations. It was reasonable that when the two English prelates who had been directly involved in the transaction were put upon their trial in reference to the whole question, of which these rubrics in the Scotch book were a part, they should adopt a line of defence consistent with those recommendations. The legal position in fact of Laud and his school on the question seems on a fair examination of evidence to have been this. Personally they preferred the eastward position, they thought it the right one, and they practised it when they could. They did not, however, feel strong enough, with only the rubrics of 1552 as their appeal, to enforce it, as they did the altarwise position of the table. Having, however, an exceptional opportunity in the Scotch book, of recasting the rubrics of the communion office, they ventured to recommend the position at the most important point, the Prayer of Consecration; but founded the recommendation only upon material reasons, and balanced it by giving up the eastward position for the earlier part of the service. When upon their trial they rested their defence on what they had legally and officially done, and did not indulge men who were thirsting for their blood with a revelation of their innermost preferences. The use of "collect" both in the Abbey Dore rubric and in Wren's of 1661, as the description of the Prayer of Consecration, is also a peculiarity which deserves notice, while it is a further evidence that Wren's thoughts still ran in the old groove. It is an obvious inaccuracy, for "collect" means a short, collected-up, prayer, and though our actual Consecration Prayer is shorter than that of any ancient liturgy or than that of 1549, yet "collect" is just what it is not. I cannot quit this subject without expressing pleasure at having, I believe, cleared up a point which the Bishop of Chester seems to have left in some obscurity, for all who care for the consistency of public men would prefer to believe that Wren in his old age had adhered to the views of his vigorous middle life. As things, however, fell out at the revision, a form of rubric due to Cosin and introducing the words "before the table" was prepared. I am, however, forestalling a later stage of the inquiry.

There were, unfortunately, divided counsels among churchmen in the earlier part of the seventeenth century and some of them thought it quite sufficient to have made good the altarwise position of the table. Among them the versatile and voluminous Peter Heylin was prominent, and an opportunity came unfortunately to hand for him to show his perverse ingenuity. Archbishop Williams, then Bishop of Lincoln, in 1627 fell foul of the Vicar of Grantham, who had put his table altarwise, and Heylin flew to the relief. Nothing was pleasanter either to him or to Williams than a sharp fight of pamphleteering, and they carried on the war with a will on both sides, Heylin's tracts bearing titles like 'A Coal from an Altar,' 'Antidotum Lincolnense,' &c.; and Williams', 'The Holy Table, name, and thing.' The peculiarity of the controversy was, that Heylin contrived to draw wrong conclusions from right premisses, and Williams right conclusions from wrong premisses. Heylin was anxious to secure the altarwise position of the table, but the rubrics puzzled him, so he argued that "side" meant "end," and that the priest ought to stand at the north end. Williams, whose object was to keep the table standing lengthways in the body of the church, or the chancel, argued that "side" could not mean "end," and that, therefore, the lengthways position was the only logical one. I rate Heylin's sophisms at very little beside the practice of Andrewes, Wren, and Cosin. It is nevertheless certain that his unfortunate intervention has done much to darken and perplex the question, while the cautious policy which his superiors felt bound to follow in the matter was reason enough why they should leave him to fight the battle in his own way, and persuade whom he might that when a "side" was spoken of an "end" was meant.

A witness, who is not less trustworthy, because very hostile, appears in the clever Scotch minister, Robert Bayley, who met the revival of the Prayer Book with his 'Parallel or Brief Comparison of the Liturgy with the Mass Book,' published in the critical year 1661. My quotations are long, but the evidence is so conclusive that I do not scruple to make them, particularly as it is almost the first quotation on which I have ventured from the voluminous literature of the Puritans. He says of our prelates:—

"But now while to their consecration [they] will add a clause of the minister's posture in this act, commanding him during the time of consecration to leave the former stance he was enjoined in the first rubricks to keep at the north end of the table, to come to such a part of the table where he may with more ease and decency use both his hands, the world will not get them cleared of a vile and wicked purpose. The Papists will have their consecration kept altogether close from the ears of the people, for many reasons . . . . The reformed church counts the secret murmuration of their canon and words of consecration a very vile and wicked practice against nature, reason, and all antiquity; so that we must take it in very evil part to be brought towards it by our Book; for when our table is brought to the east end of the quire, so near the wall as it can stand, and the minister brought from the end of it to the broadside, with his face to the east, and his back to the people, what he speaks may be Hebrew, for them; he may speak so low as he will, or what he will, for were his face to the people and his voice never so extended, yet so great is the distance he could not be heard; but now, being set in the furthest distance that is possible, and being commanded not only to turn his shoulder, as he was by his north stance in all the former action, but his very back by his new change of place, and not being enjoined to extend his voice as somewhere he is, what can we conceive but it is their plain mind to have the consecration made in that silence which the Romish rubrick in this place enjoins? . . . . This injunction we are directed to keep, while we are not only enjoined to go so far from the people as the remotest wall and table will permit, but to use such a posture that our back must be turned to them, that so our speech may be directed to the elements alone, and that in what language you please; and no ways to the people from whom we have gone away, and on whom we have turned our back. . . . . We reprove in the Papists their folly to course from one nook of their altar to the other, from the north to the south, from the right horn to the left, from the end to the midst, and from it to the end again; for these mysterious reasons we may read in the Rationalists. What other thing does our rubrick import, bidding us leave our north-standing, where we were in our preface, and come to another part of the altar during the time of consecration, that when it is ended we may return again to the north end? Also that the end of our coming to another place in the consecration is the more case to use both our hands, what use here of both hands is possible, but that which the Romish rubricks at this place do enjoin,—the multiplication of crosses, whiles with the right, whiles with the left hand, whiles with both the arms extended so far as they may be? This could not be done if we stood at the north end of the table, for then the east wall of the church would hinder us to extend our left arm, and so to make the image of Christ's extension on the cross perfectly. The Papists, to recompense the want which the people have in their ear by the priest's silence, and turning his back upon them during the time of consecration (as our book speaks), they think meet to fill their eyes with dumb shows, not only to set up the crucifix on the altar, on the pillars, on the tapestry, on the east glass window, where it may be most conspicuous to the eye, but chiefly to cause the priest at the altar to make a world of crosses and gestures, all which must have a deep spiritual sense. Will not the present rubrick give us leave to entertain our people with the same shows? The crucifixes are already set upon the altar, on the tapestry, on the walls, on the glass windows, in fair and large figures. The lawfulness of crossing, not only in baptism, but in the supper and anywhere, is avowed, as in the self-conviction is shewn; what other bar is left us to receive all the crossings that are in the mass, but the sole pleasure of our prelates, who, when they will, may practise that which they maintain, and force us to the particular use of those things which they have already put in our book in general terms?"

Bayley's inferences as to the intended introduction of the multiplied crossings of the missal are of course the fruit of his own unchecked imagination; but the whole tenor of his declamation shows that it was well understood in 1661 that the High Church party of that day were men who believed in the eastward position, and who had practised it before the temporary downfall of the Church. It is in evidence of this fact that I quote him, and I must in addition remind my readers of two facts. 1. At the date when he wrote, the actual rubric before the Prayer of Consecration was not yet in existence, although the question was agitating men's minds, so that all which he says refers to practices under the far different rulings of 1552, and is direct evidence upon the estimate which their adversaries had of the opinions of the men who were called in at that time to reconsider the Prayer Book. 2. Among the men against whom he is inveighing are Cosin and Wren, whom we actually find proposing competing solutions of the question both favourable to the eastward position. In particular, Bayley distinctly refutes the argument of Dean Howson at the Chester Conference, alleging Laud and the Scotch Office to show "that the northward position should be observed through the whole service."

I have now cleared the way up to the present rubric before the Prayer of Consecration. The meaning of that rubric is most abundantly clear: the Martin v. Mackonochie judgment, Sir John T. Coleridge and Lord Cairns, have told it. My object, therefore, is merely to show how it came into the Prayer Book in company with other rubrics, which, if the table is to stand altarwise, can with difficulty be reconciled with it. The answer, I believe, is, that the authors of the rubric of 1662 gave up, or would not attempt, the task of reconciling the whole series of rubrics; they embodied what they wanted and inserted it into their own new rubric, and then they left the clergy either to reconcile the older rubrics (which, from reasons of expediency, they did not dare to handle) with the new one by reading those in the spirit and not the letter, namely by interpreting the now impossible "north side" as the possible west side—or to close with the somewhat clumsy Scotch Prayer Book compromise, and while beginning at the north to work round at the Consecration to the west—or even (as Heylin had counselled them) boldly to take "side" to mean "end," and stick to the northern position all through. This policy was characteristic of the bold and practical Cosin, and contrasted remarkably with the more scholastic but feebler counsels of Wren. It must not be forgotten that these revisers went to the question, after their attention had at the Savoy Conference been called to the desirability of the minister turning to the people in praying, which they answered in these terms:—

"The minister's turning to the people is not most convenient throughout the whole ministration. When he speaks to them, as in lessons, absolution and benedictions, it is convenient that he turn to them. When he speaks for them to God, it is fit that they should all turn another way, as the ancient church ever did; the reasons of which you may see. Aug. lib. ii. *de Ser. Dom. in monte.*"

These words do not especially refer to the Eucharist, but they establish a principle of action. The Quarterly Reviewer thinks that he has made a great point by the discovery in the facsimile, published at the instance of the Ritual Commission, of the Prayer Book, upon which the revisers of 1662 had worked with their manuscript alterations, that "part" had been inserted for "side" and then erased. I look upon this (which I believe I was myself the first to perceive when the newly recovered volume was shown to some of our body) as only showing that the revisers were determined to do something to weaken the bad tradition of the north end, and had not quite decided what to do. "North part" might of course consistently mean the more northern portion of the west side.

We must never forget, in estimating the conduct of churchmen in 1662, that the internal differences of the Church at that moment of material success for that body were really more marked than we have, at this distance of time, any adequate idea of, looking back, as we do, at things through a diminishing glass. Prynne, for instance, Laud's foe (now a reconciled royalist), was still at work, and wrote a bitter treatise against the ceremonial of the Church, after the Restoration, in which he railed, for pages, against the surplice. These difficulties, I fully believe, would furnish a very ample justification to the restorers of liturgical order for—as in the case of the ornaments rubric, so in that of the position—appearing to us to have been reformers in purpose more than reformers in deed, satisfied with leaving on record sound views for a future generation to deal with. As I have already shown in connection with that rubric, they could not have anticipated how the misconduct of Charles and James, and the advent of William, would have successively marred the development of genuine Anglican principles. Even in this matter of the position of the Holy Table, it is, I believe, a mistake to suppose that, with the Restoration, the altarwise position at once became universal. It may have been so in more cultivated places, but no doubt the old disorders still prevailed in rustic churches. We learn, indeed, incidentally, that even in a place which was already growing into importance, Liverpool, the Holy Table stood lengthways till 1687, by a notice in the diary of Bishop Cartwright, of Chester, published by the Camden Society in 1842, that on visiting Liverpool in that year he ordered it to be placed altarwise. Indeed the necessary presence in the Established Church of that great multitude who, without any very strong convictions, conform to the existing order of things, whatever it may be, must have had a lowering influence on the prevalent Church feeling considering the customs and teaching to which they had been habituated between 1640 and 1660. In fact the movement, which might have been successful in 1689 for lowering the tone of the Prayer Book, proves the prevalence of this more lax churchmanship. If High Churchmen had been in complete possession of the field in 1662, latitudinarianism would hardly have been so powerful in twenty-seven years, and, in fact, of the Restoration Bishops one (Dr. Reynolds, of Norwich) was a reconciled Nonconformist.

Cosin was always believed, and is now known to have had, although as Bishop of Durham a member of another Convocation, a very powerful influence over the more confidential deliberations on the question as before the Convocation of Canterbury. He had, in fact, been sent to London as delegate of the Northern Convocation. As Wren's suggestions for revision have just been published, so a short time before those of Cosin have also been put forth by the Surtees Society. The late Mr. Baskerville Walton has also contributed important facts in his valuable 'Rubrical Determination of the Celebrant's Position,' to which

I beg to refer all who desire fuller satisfaction on the subject matter of this Chapter, although it was published before the additional lights of the Abbey Dore Consecration and of Wren's suggestions had been thrown upon the question. Mr. Walton gives from the original at Durham a photograph of Cosin's own manuscript draft, full of additions and of erasures, of the rubric written into a Prayer Book, from which it seems that his first idea was to draw a rubric like the Scotch, but, as he worked on, other considerations presented themselves to his mind, until it ultimately attained its present shape. The words "standing before the Table" happen to head the whole note, being introduced over a caret above the beginning "when the priest." Before I part with Cosin, to whom I have had so often to refer, I may as well point out the very extraordinary attempt which the Judicial Committee, in Hebbert *v.* Purchas, make to enlist him on their side. If the reader will refer back to the quotations which I made from their judgment in the beginning of this chapter, they will find the passage. By a very odd misprint, the date of the Visitation articles of Cosin is put at 1687— fifteen years after his death—instead of at 1627. I have already pointed out that as Visitation articles must deal with the conventional minimum of worship, their value as to the maximum is not so great; therefore that which Cosin might inquire about as a young Archdeacon in 1627, need not be what, as Bishop of Durham and a man of the highest influence in the Church, he might desire to establish in 1661.

But here occurs one of the most remarkable incidents of this very remarkable judgment. The passage of Cosin's Visitation articles, which the Judicial Committee with so much pomp extracts from a then very recently published volume, are extracted from the manuscript draft of those articles. We also possess the articles in their final and complete form as published, and in them *this passage does not occur.* So if the incident means anything, what it implies is that Cosin, on second thoughts, decided, from whatever reason, not to make the inquiry. I cannot say then that this reference to Cosin has much strengthened the argument of the Judicial Committee, nor made me inclined to agree with its decision. One of the most common arguments of the popular kind which has been brought to show that the rubric in question cannot be intended to mean that the priest is to stand before the people, is the assumed difficulty in his being able, if so placed, to break the bread " before the people." Those who urge this imagine that " before the people " means so that every one can see him do it. I am quite unable to follow this interpretation. " Before " means " in front of "—" in the presence of." Any one would translate

" Ne pueros coram populo Medea trucidet "

" Let not Medea kill her children *before the people ;*" but no one, I should think, would thence infer that it laid down that Medea was to take any particular position in regard to them upon the stage, as, for instance, on the left side, looking across it. A relation of mine, a clergyman of the old school, who has always taken and acted on " before the table " in its natural sense, was not long since arguing with his curate upon its meaning, and said he would put the question to a practical test. He rang the bell, and ordered the servant, without giving her any reason, to stand before the sideboard. The girl turned round and faced its broad side.

Besides there may be another meaning of a more technical kind attached to the direction to break the bread before the people. As the rubric is new, so also is the direction in the Consecration Prayer following for the priest to break the bread in the act of consecrating. To " break the bread before the people," may mean, " make that *public* fraction of the bread, which is by the following Prayer of Consecration for the first time ordered." With a new order like this, a particular instruction might have been needed. This meaning is the more probable from the collocation of words. It exactly suits " break the bread before the people and take the cup." The popular meaning of the words would have required "break the bread, and take the cup, before the people."

In truth, I have sometimes been led to think that the excessive jealousy with which some excellent persons cling to the necessity of seeing the priest perform the act of breaking the bread has something in it akin to the importance which Roman Catholics attach to seeing the elevation of the Host at the analogous passage of their consecration service. In both cases it is an excessive desire to have ocular cognisance of the element of bread at the moment of its consecration.

I can hardly bring myself to treat with patience the charge sometimes brought against the eastward position as being an act of turning his back to the people by the priest. It is turning his back, as the good shepherd turns his back to the sheep whom, by Oriental custom, he is leading—as the officer turns his back to the soldiers whose march he is directing—as the parent turns his back to his children whom he is guiding. A clergyman under examination before the Ritual Commission put it well when he said, "I object altogether to take to myself the opprobrious expression which has been used, of turning my back to the people. I look in the same direction that my people do; I look eastward." So it is, the priest at the altar is the spokesman of his flock; he is offering up, in his and their names, the highest of devotions, and it is but meet that he and they should turn alike in prayer to that East from which the Sun of Righteousness uprose.

Whatever may be its advantages or disadvantages, the north end position is a purely local one, and I believe, for the reasons which I have adduced, that in the sense of its being an "end" position, it is one so exceedingly modern as to be actually posterior not only to 1552, but even to 1600, and is, in fact, the growth of the movement for placing the table altarwise, without any further provision being made for the place of the minister's position. The north-side position was the position of standing before an altar placed in a novel and unprecedented

P

way. The tradition of the Universal Church in every age has been that God's priest should plead the great sacrifice of Christ in front of the Holy Table. East and West are at one upon that. So, too, in all Protestant bodies which preserve liturgical worship, the minister stands before the Altar when he offers the prayers of the Altar, as well as at the Communion itself. I have specific proofs of this, but it is needless to press what every one knows.

At the same time I should think it exceedingly wrong to force the eastward position on any clergyman who prefers and believes in the one at the north end. In return, I ask that the liberty of those who take the west side, and of the communicant members of their flocks to whose religious feelings this posture is most congruous, should not be infringed. The Church is wide enough for both, and the best compromise, I believe, will be to let each party follow its own way.

The Bishop of St. Andrews, in a letter which he has done me the honour of addressing to me, proposes the compromise of taking the rubrics as they are, reading "north side" as "north end," and only allowing the eastward position at the Prayer of Consecration. I do not think this would satisfy any party. The present rubrics are obviously inconsistent, and it would be labour lost to crystallise them into a system. His brother, the Bishop of Lincoln, proposes the wider compromise of equally tolerating the three uses of the west side, the north end, and the old basilican usage of the priest standing in the midst of the altar, but on the other side and looking across it to the people. This settlement, I believe, would be widely acceptable. It is right that a usage so venerable as that of the basilican form of celebration should be recognised, together with the others. At the same time I doubt how far it would be likely to be acted on. It would be so great an innovation on all existing customs, that any clergyman must be very sure of the confidence of his congregation before he attempts it. Besides it could only be carried out either in new churches or in churches very much altered; for the constructional relations of the altar to the east wall and to all the arrangements of the sanctuary as well as its own appointments would have to be recast.

If I have written strongly on this question of the priest's position, it is because I feel very deeply upon it, more deeply than upon any other question of controverted ceremonial; and I believe that vast numbers, both of clergy and of laity, are animated by the same strong sense of its importance, and would equally feel any restriction in this respect of their Christian liberty. If the authorities, in whose hands the ultimate solution of all such questions lies, were to refuse and to prohibit a distinctive Eucharistic dress, I should regard their decision as a mistake, a misfortune, and a loss; but I should wait in patience for days, in which reason might have the advantage of prejudice. But if, at the highest moment of Christian worship—when God's priest most impressively pleads Christ's sacrifice in Christ's own words, in Christ's own ordinance—loyal and peaceable children of the Church of England were to be forbidden to unite themselves with that priest in the great act, according to the order in which the Holy Catholic Church has, from the first, been wont to show forth the Lord's death, while thoroughly acknowledging that the efficacy of the sacrament was no way affected, I should in my inmost soul feel that there was a great wrong done.

CHAPTER VI.

Furniture of altar — Credence Table — Immovable stone altar prohibited in the St. Sepulchre's case, but solid wooden altar with stone or marble slab legal — St. John's chapel, Westminster Abbey — Frontals varying according to season legalised by judgment in Liddell v. Westerton — Altar crosses legalised by the Liddell v. Westerton judgment as explained by the second judgment in Beal v. Liddell — Crucifixes in Lutheran and "Evangelical" churches abroad — Potsdam and Berlin, Berchtesgaden and Salzburg — Against present English feeling, but not Popish — Lighted candles enjoined by Edward VI. — Candlesticks and candles on the altar in cathedrals and chapels before the revival — Candles forbidden by Dr. Lushington, allowed by Sir R. Phillimore, forbidden by Mackonochie judgment — Disallowed by Ritual Commission — Its unfounded distinction between cathedrals and parish churches. —Ambiguous use of phrase "sufficient evidence" — Fuller — Dr. Donne's sermon on Candlemas Day — The symbolism of the lights defended from the teaching of that day — Our Lord "a light to lighten the Gentiles" — Cosin's notes — Archbishop Sancroft — Appeal to common sense, do lighted or unlighted candles best typify that Christ is the very true light?—We have got candles and candlesticks, and may light them on dark days, frivolous to impose restrictions on lighting them according to the teaching of the injunction — Only pleading for the two lights according to injunction—No more than two used in old English Church — Constitution of Archbishop Walter — Abroad use even of two candles appears not to have been universal — Perkins' Tournay Pontifical — Numerous candles modern Roman use — Greater beauty of more simple altar with two lights — Altar nosegays lawful — Ceremonial compensation of present age — Mixed chalice — Reasons for valuing the rite — Forbidden by Purchas judgment — Judges mistaken in supposing that private mixture not in Eastern Church — Supported by First Prayer Book, Andrewes, Overall, Laud, Wren, Sir W. Palmer — Impolicy of crushing it out — Question of leavened or unleavened bread stands on a quite different footing — East used leavened, West unleavened bread — Dispute whether Last Supper was Passover or not — Wafers ordered by Elizabeth and Parker — In Elizabeth's and Andrewes' chapels — Defended by Hooker, sanctioned in Andrewes' Notes to Prayer Book — Their revival dissuaded — Incense differs from other rites — Practice of almost every religion true or false — Altar of incense commanded to Moses for all generations — At altar of incense Gabriel appears to Zacharias — Frankincense offered by the wise men — Incense in

CHAP. VI.   IMMOVABLE STONE ALTAR FORBIDDEN.   213

the Apocalypse — Naturally adopted in Christian Church — Not in Prayer Book, but supported by Andrewes, Herbert, Cosin, Sancroft — Censing of persons and things forbidden by Sir R. Phillimore — Not to be regretted — Custom deteriorated by Roman ceremonialists — Censing of persons and things differs from offering incense to God — If revived, must be so by authority, and as such offering.

THE object of the present Chapter will be to review the ornaments of the Holy Table, Lord's Table, or Altar. I have already described its necessary adjunct, the Credence Table. The immovability and material of the Holy Table formed the subject of the first of the ceremonial lawsuits which have marked the present reign. An immovable stone altar, which had been placed in St. Sepulchre's Church, Cambridge, during its restoration, was objected to by the then incumbent, sustained by the Diocesan Court of Ely, and prohibited in the Arches Court, in 1845, by Sir Herbert Jenner Fust. No appeal was taken to the Judicial Committee. The question was again raised in regard to the Knightsbridge churches, and was disposed of in the same way. These judgments have, however, been in practice held to admit of any amount of solidity in the Altar itself, and of stone or marble being employed for its slab, if only it is not constructively fastened down to the floor. The altar in the rebuilt chapel of St. John's College, Cambridge, is a massive wood frame, richly carved and bearing a marble slab, so is the new altar in Westminster Abbey, which has scriptural scenes, the Crucifixion in the centre, sculptured round the wooden substructure.

The canon, as we have seen, orders the Lord's Table to be covered with a "carpet of silk or some other decent stuff," and pious persons, since the recent revival of Christian art, began the practice of indicating the successive Christian seasons by altar cloths or frontals of the respective colours which in the unreformed rites were held to symbolise those times of joy or mourning, and of varying richness, according to the importance of the occasions. This custom appeared to them to be not only a plain case of omission not carrying prohibition, but to be actually pointed out and vindicated by the prevalent use of the black altar-cloth and hangings during Lent. It was clear to them, that as the carpet must be of some colour, it need not always be of the same colour. This practice was, however, displeasing to Mr. Westerton and Mr. Beal, and formed part of their indictment against the Knightsbridge churches. Their objection was sustained by Dr. Lushington and Sir John Dodson. When the case, however, came before the Privy Council, that tribunal overruled the narrow decisions of the Courts below, and asserted the legality of the varying frontals in these terms:—

"Next, as to the embroidered cloths, it is said that the canon orders a covering of silk, or of some other proper material, but that it does not mention, and therefore, by implication, excludes more than one covering. Their Lordships are unable to adopt this construction. An order that a table shall always be covered with a cloth surely does not imply that it shall always be covered with the same cloth, or with a cloth of the same colour or texture. The object of this canon seems to be to secure a cloth of a sufficiently handsome description, not to guard against too much splendour. In practice, as was justly observed at the Bar, black cloths are in many churches used during Lent, and on the death of the sovereign, and some other occasions; and there seems nothing objectionable in the practice. Whether the cloths so used are suitable or not, is a matter to be left to the discretion of the Ordinary. In this case their Lordships do not see any sufficient reason for interference; and they must, therefore, advise the reversal of the sentence as to the cloths used for the covering of the Lord's Table during the time of divine service, both with respect to St. Paul's and to St. Barnabas."

The Holy Table thus vested with its frontal proportionate in colour and in richness to the season, covered but not concealed at the time of communion with a white linen cloth, and provided with the attendant Credence, is ready in all essentials for the celebration of the Holy Mysteries. But there are other ornaments belonging to it alike seemly and lawful, although to be by no means forced upon unwilling congregations. The

Privy Council has, as we shall see, sanctioned the long narrow ledge, called a superaltar, which is wont to be placed on the Altar to carry those ornaments, unless, indeed, they be detached from the table altogether, so as structurally to belong to the fabric itself. Of these ornaments the most important and central one is the movable altar cross, of wood, in the plainest churches, and of metal, when possible. The legality of this ornament has been established by two successive lawsuits, namely, by the original judgment in the case of the Knightsbridge churches, followed by a supplementary one, in which Mr. Beal endeavoured to show non-compliance with its rulings on the part of St. Barnabas, which came before a Committee of the Council presided over by Lord Justice Knight Bruce. The decision allowing the cross on the chancel screen of St. Barnabas legalised crosses in general as pious decorations of the church. But there was a cross in each of these churches existing under circumstances which demanded separate consideration; each had such an altar cross as I have described, but in both cases the cross had been screwed on to the table, so as to become a fixture. The Court entertained strong opinions upon the necessity of the table in itself being movable, and also possessing a level surface capable of being covered by the communion cloth, which in their opinion would not have been the case if the presence of a projecting fixture intervened. Accordingly, while accepting the crosses simply as crosses, for the reasons which had led them to sanction the screen cross, they say of the one attached to the table at St. Paul's:—

"Next with respect to the wooden cross attached to the Communion Table at St. Paul's. Their Lordships have already declared their opinion that the Communion Table intended by the canon was a table in the ordinary sense of the word; flat and movable, capable of being covered with a cloth, at which, or around which, the communicants might be placed in order to partake of the Lord's Supper. And the question is, whether the existence of a cross attached to the table is consistent either with the spirit or with the letter of those regulations. Their Lordships are clearly of opinion that it is not; and they must recommend that upon this point also the decree complained of should be affirmed."

The case of St. Barnabas was complicated by the Altar itself being, in the opinion of the Court, inadmissible, as being made of stone and structurally immovable; so in this case both the Altar and the cross, as they then existed, were condemned. In consequence of this judgment, the cross at St. Paul's was made movable, and no litigation has from that day ensued in respect of it. At St. Barnabas also the present Altar was substituted for that which had been censured, and the cross, which had been screwed to the former one, was placed upon a ledge immediately over the Holy Table. This did not satisfy the former prosecutor, Mr. Beal, and he again went to law against the authorities of the church for alleged disobedience of the former judgment in this and one or two other matters.

The case came before the Judicial Committee, and judgment was passed in June, 1860, by a Court composed of Lord Justice Knight Bruce (who drew the report), Lord Justice Turner, Sir Edward Ryan, Sir J. T. Coleridge, and Archbishop Longley (then of York). The question of the cross was decided as follows:—

"Now, there was formerly a cross which stood upon the stone table, and was, in a sense at least, affixed to it; which was objected to, and, as it appears, properly objected to. The stone table has been altogether removed, and with it the cross; but the cross has been placed in another part of the church or chapel, not in any sense upon the table which has been substituted for the stone table, nor in any sense in communication, or contact, or connection with it. It remains in the church as an ornament of the church, and their Lordships think (if the word may respectfully be applied to such a subject) not an unusual or improper ornament; in no sense remaining there so as to disobey or conflict with the order contained in this monition.

"Their Lordships, therefore, think that that part of the monition which directs the structure of stone to be removed, together with the cross on or near the same, has been obeyed.

"It then directs that there shall be provided, 'instead thereof, a flat movable table of wood.' That has been done. It is stated, however, with truth, that upon this table there is placed, and in general stands, a movable ledge of wood for the purpose of holding candlesticks and vessels: at least, that is the purpose for which it is used. It is, as I have said, not fixed to the table. If remaining there when the cloth is to be placed upon the table for the purpose of the administration of the Lord's Supper, as it would interfere with that, it is accordingly removed, and the cloth is placed upon the table, and then the ledge replaced.

"It is not shown, and their Lordships think it ought not to be inferred, that there is anything superstitious (if the term may be used), or anything improper, in the addition of that ledge. But, even if there were, their Lordships are not satisfied that it is within the terms of this monition, or that the monition in any sense or respect extends to it."

This decision legalises, as plainly as language can do, the movable altar cross, when not "affixed to" the Holy Table, and at all events when upon a ledge over it, while it goes on to give reasons why the movable ledge should be accounted lawful. A question having been lately raised as to a cross, so situated, by one who had participated in the original Liddell *v.* Westerton judgment, strong and almost direct evidence was produced to show that the very learned and universally respected Sir John Patteson had informed an inquirer that in concurring in that judgment he had implied the legality of the movable cross.

In our adoption of this ornament of the movable altar cross, we fall below the ritual standard of the Lutheran Churches of Germany and Scandinavia, and of the so-called "Evangelical" Church of Prussia, which was, in the reign of the last King but one of Prussia, established by an amalgamation of the former Lutheran, or "Protestant," and Calvinist, or "Reformed," Churches of that kingdom. In all these bodies the centre of worship is a solid altar, with a crucifix and two candles, which are lighted during service time. My readers will recollect the ritual described in the account of a Norwegian Sunday, which I quoted in my fourth chapter; and those who happened to take up the 'Graphic' of September 19th of this year, may have noticed a wood-cut of the Confirmation of the eldest son of the Prince Imperial of Germany, in the Royal "Frieden" Church of Potsdam, before an altar garnished with crucifix and lighted candles. Some years ago, indeed, this ceremonial of the Evangelical Church of Prussia was rather amusingly brought under the ken of members of that party in the Church of England who also call themselves Evangelical, with not quite an identical use of language. The late King of Prussia, near the close of his active reign, gave an hospitable reception to the cosmopolitan body, styled the Evangelical Alliance, in Berlin, and assigned a church in that city as the place of meeting for its committee. The result was, that the paper which in England represented in 1857 as now the party in our Church which has most sympathies with that Alliance, gave utterance to feelings of surprise and disgust at the committee of so very Protestant a body having to deliberate in the presence of an altar furnished with crucifix and candles. We are not aware whether any similar remonstrances were made at Berlin. They would probably have caused much astonishment there, to the minds of those to whom they were addressed.

These two are instances of the custom in the Prussian Established Church. The Lutherans in Southern Germany adhere to the same practice. I do not refer to the elaborate ornaments and ritual still preserved in the unchanged mediæval churches of Nuremberg. This may be fairly considered as an antiquarian peculiarity of that most curious place, and it would, therefore, be hardly fair to quote it as a specimen of Lutheran ceremonial in general; but I can give instances from churches of that persuasion, standing in places where the Roman Catholic religion is the dominant faith, and where, accordingly, it might be supposed that Protestants would be most chary of any accidental resemblance with the rites of that Church. The 'Guardian' of September 9th, 1874, contains an account of the Lutheran Sunday service at Berchtesgaden, in the Bavarian Highlands, as it was performed on the 30th of August, by a minister in a "black gown with sleeves and bands." " The Communion Table was covered with a white cloth; on it were a book, and two tall candlesticks with lighted candles. Raised considerably above the table stood a crucifix. The table was surrounded with flowers and evergreens." The service included the Epistle and Gospel and the Apostles' Creed, and was, in fact, the reflex of our own truncated Communion Service. At it "all the prayers of the minister were said with his back to the people, and his face to the Communion Table." Personally I was never more struck with the incongruity of a north-end celebration than when I happened to attend the English service, in the autumn of 1871, at Salzburg, a city not many miles from Berchtesgaden, although in the Austrian Empire. A recently built Lutheran Church was at that time lent to the English visitors for their worship, and the chaplain duly celebrated (in a very reverent way, let me say) at the north end of a large and solid marble altar, surmounted with a tall gilt crucifix and candles, which were not lighted for the English service. The discrepancy between the action and its surroundings was, to myself at least, a very convincing argument against the propriety of that position, as embodying the mind of the Church of England in regard to the Holy Communion. No worshipper, I should imagine, felt, up to the moment of the Consecration, that there was any thing which jarred against his religious feelings in the familiar words of the service being read at that stately Communion Table. There were those, I dare say, who felt that if its ornaments told any lesson, it was that the rite to be performed was one which showed forth the Lord's Death, till He came, to worshippers pledged not to be ashamed of the Cross of Christ. To those who were possessed with such feelings, it was something like a shock to see the celebrant, at the most solemn moment of the worship, creep round as if he were a stranger and an interloper, and only venture to occupy one poor corner of all the structure, like a man who hardly felt that he had a right to be there at all, or to make any use of so reverent a presentment of the Lord's Table.

I well know that while we gladly accept the representations of the Crucifixion at the east ends of our churches, in pictures or painted windows, and in carved reredoses, or, as at Westminster Abbey, upon the front of the Holy Table itself, yet that any attempt to add the movable crucifix to the ornaments of our parish churches would be sure to occasion much distress, and, in all probability, to create public disturbance. I do not attempt to analyse this difference of feeling. It exists, and while it does so, it ought to be respected by every rule of charity and every counsel of prudence. If, however, it should at any time happen that popular feeling in England were to change with regard to the public use of the crucifix, I do not think that the most timid need fear the inroads of Popery from the adoption of a rite which is the legal and obligatory custom of that Church of which the German Emperor is the most exalted, and Prince Bismarck the most powerful, member.

My readers will not have failed to notice that the foreign Protestant examples which I have just been adducing, include, as ornaments of the altar, lighted candles as well as the central crucifix. The present legal position of these candles in the Church of England is the somewhat peculiar one of a partial lawfulness. It is at all times legal to place the candlesticks and candles upon the Lord's Table, but the latter may only be lighted when needful for the purpose of giving light, or, in short, when any of the other lights in the Church are also used. The direct Reformational authority for such candles is found in the 3rd Injunction of Edward VI., issued in 1547, in the following terms:

Chap. VI. TWO LIGHTS BY EDWARD VI.'S INJUNCTION. 221

" And shall suffer from henceforth no torches nor candles, tapers or images of wax, to be set before any image or picture, but only two lights upon the High Altar, before the Sacrament, which, for the signification that Christ is the very true light of the world, they shall suffer to remain still."

Candlesticks with unlighted candles were, accordingly, a frequent ornament in such places as cathedrals and Royal and college chapels, even before the ceremonial revival. But, after that date, in compliance with the Injunction of Edward VI., the lighting of the candles was introduced into various churches, including those at Knightsbridge; in regard to which it was forbidden by Dr. Lushington in the first instance, while he sanctioned the candles and candlesticks in themselves. There was no appeal from this portion of his judgment, for the defendants, at the time, were well content to have secured the candles themselves. However, the practice of lighting the candles at the Holy Communion, even when the day happened not to be a dark one, was continued in various Churches, and formed a portion of the charges brought by Mr. Martin against Mr. Mackonochie. Sir Robert Phillimore, in his judgment as Dean of Arches emphatically sanctioned them, saying that

"they were ordered by injunctions having statutable authority, which injunctions had not been directly repealed; that they were Primitive and Catholic in their origin, Evangelical in their proper symbolism, purged from all superstition and novelty by the very terms of the injunction which ordered their retention in the Church; and that, therefore, it was lawful to place them on the Holy Table during the time of the Holy Communion 'for the signification that Christ is the very true light of the world.'"

The Judicial Committee, however, reversed this decision, for reasons of which the following is the most important portion:

" The lighted candles are clearly not 'ornaments' within the words of the rubric, for they are not prescribed by the authority of Parliament therein mentioned, namely, the First Prayer Book; nor is the injunction of 1547 the authority of Parliament within the meaning of the rubric. They are not subsidiary to the service, for they do not aid or facilitate—much less are they necessary to—the service; nor can a separate and independent ornament, previously in use, be said to be consistent with a rubric which is silent as to it, and which by necessary implication abolishes what it does not retain.

"It was strongly pressed by the respondent's counsel that the use of lighted candles up to the time of the issue of the First Prayer Book was clearly legal; that the lighted candles were in use in the second year of Edward VI.; and that there was nothing in the Prayer Book of that year making it unlawful to continue them. All this may be conceded, but it is in reality beside the question. The rubric of our Prayer Book might have said: those ornaments shall be retained which were lawful, or which were in use in the second year of Edward VI.; and the argument as to actual use at the time, and as to the weight of the injunction of 1547, might in that case have been material. But the rubric, speaking in 1661, more than one hundred years subsequently, has, for reasons which it is not the province of a judicial tribunal to criticise, defined the class of ornaments to be retained by a reference, not to what was in use *de facto*, or to what was lawful in 1549, but to what was in the Church by authority of Parliament in that year; and in the Parliamentary authority which this committee has held, and which their Lordships hold, to be indicated by these words, the ornaments in question are not found to be included.

"Their Lordships have not referred to the usage as to lights during the last 300 years, but they are of opinion that the very general disuse of lights after the Reformation (whatever exceptional cases to the contrary might be produced), contrasted with their normal and prescribed use previously, affords a very strong contemporaneous and continuous exposition of the law upon the subject.

"Their Lordships will, therefore, humbly advise Her Majesty that the charge as to lights also has been sustained, and that the respondent should be admonished for the future to abstain from the use of them, as pleaded in these articles."

In the meanwhile the question had come before the Ritual Commission, and in its Second Report, which is undated, but was issued in the summer of 1868, the following passage is found:—

" 4. The use of lighted candles at the celebration of the Holy Communion has been introduced into certain churches within a period of about the last twenty-five years. It is true that there have been candlesticks with candles on the Lord's Table during a long period in many cathedral and collegiate churches and chapels, and also in the chapels of some colleges, and of some royal and episcopal residences; but the instances that have been adduced to prove that candles have been lighted, as accessions to the Holy Communion, are few and much contested.

" 5. With regard to parish churches, whatever evidence there may be as to candlesticks with candles being on the Lord's Table, no sufficient evidence has been adduced before us to prove that at any time during the last three centuries lighted candles have been used in any of these churches as accessories to the celebration of the Holy Communion until within about the last twenty-five years."

In company with some of my colleagues, I declined to sign this report, as well on account of these allegations, as of the general scope of its recommendations. In itself this passage insinuates a difference between cathedral and parish churches, which, I believe, is contrary to fact. The inference to be drawn from the division of the question into what was the practice in "cathedral and collegiate churches and chapels," and in "parish churches," would be, that one ritual naturally belonged to one class of places of worship, and another to the other. The true condition of matters, both legally and practically, is, as we contended, that the only real difference is, that cathedrals, and similar churches, are intended as models of worship to the diocese, and are, therefore, bound to a more strict exhibition of the ceremonial than other places whose means and opportunities are so much inferior, and whose responsibilities are so much less, but that these, on their part, are equally bound in theory to conform, according to their ability, to the prescription.

By drawing this distinction the Commission, while grudgingly compelled to own that some "few" instances of lighted candles had been found in the superior class of church, which it asserted to be "much contested," rather cleverly enabled itself to assert that in parish churches "no sufficient evidence" of the practice could be found. Plausible as the assertion sounds, its whole value is neutralised by there being no reliable test to show what is meant by "sufficient evidence." If it means to say that documents were not adduced stating in absolute language that "on such a day candles were placed on the Holy Table of such a church, and those candles were lighted," then I grant that it might be sustained. But if it means that "lights" have not been mentioned in reference to our churches since the Reformation in terms which, according to the ordinary value of language, and in compliance with the recognised rules of common sense would lead to the inference that they must have been lighted, then I submit that the Commission indulged in statements of so elastic a nature as to be only convincing when they tally with preformed impressions.

We must clear our own minds as to what we are discussing. It is not the presence of lights generally on or about the Holy Table, but of two upon it, signifying that Christ is the "very true light of the world." Two, rather than one light (which would have been apparently as symbolical) were, no doubt, selected, not only in consonance with more general ancient practice, and from the greater symmetry of the arrangement, but also because a significance had been piously attached to the number as exemplifying our Lord's Two Natures, which ratifies the especial value which we of the Church of England ought to attach to two, rather than to any larger number, of candles upon the Altar. That stout old representative of national prepossessions, Fuller, speaking of Edward VI.th's Injunctions, gives vent to the feelings about these lights, which a strong English Churchman of decidedly anti-Roman bias might entertain.

"They reduced candles, formerly *sans* number in churches, to two upon the High Altar, before the Sacrament; these being termed lights, showing they were not *lumina cæca*, but burning."

From similar reasons to those which lead me to refrain from recapitulating the evidence for the use of copes in the cathedrals of the sixteenth and seventeenth centuries, I shall not marshal the instances which I have before me of the employment of lighted candles in the royal and episcopal chapels and the cathedrals of the same period. The Ritual Commission, by the confession extorted from it that there were a "few" instances of the usage which met its arbitrary test of "sufficient evidence," has, in fact, surrendered the question, as far as it affects these, the model places of worship. How common it was in them only incidentally crops out by casual evidence. I happen to possess a bad old picture of the interior of Westminster Abbey of, I suppose, the beginning of the last century, and in it candles are burning upon the altar. With regard to the more general practice I shall first adduce a man of an original genius, Dr. Donne, who, as all know, was for some time Dean of St. Paul's, and who, while preaching in the reign of James I., says:

"I would not be understood to condemn all use of candles by day, in divine service, nor all churches that have or do use them; for so I might condemn even the Primitive Church in her pure and innocent estate. And therefore, that which Lactantius, almost three hundred years after Christ, says of those lights, and that which Tertullian, almost a hundred years before Lactantius, says in reprehension thereof, must necessarily be understood of the abuse and imitation of the Gentiles therein; for, that the thing itself was in use before either of these times, I think admits little question."

This sermon was preached on the Feast of "the Presentation of Christ in the Temple, commonly called the Purification of St. Mary the Virgin," and, still more familiarly, Candlemas Day, from the custom prevalent upon it of illuminating the churches with many candles. The first inference which might be drawn from the fact of this having been the occasion of Donne's sermon, would probably be that it is hardly a case in point, because there would be a reason for lighting candles upon Candlemas Day which did not exist at any other time of the whole year. The second thought would be that Candlemas Day happens to be the one anniversary of the whole year which is the most appropriate for the declaration of the whole mind of the Church of England upon this practice of an emblematic and honorific lighting of lights on the Lord's Table. The reason for the lights at all, according to the Injunction of Edward VI., is that "Christ is the very true light of the world." But what is the Feast of the Presentation of Christ in the Temple, but the great day on which the voice of inspiration declared Him " to be a light to lighten the Gentiles, and to be the glory of thy people Israel?" Thus does this harmless and beautiful rite of lights on His own Holy Table for ever present our Redeemer to us in His Temple as the light which has led us Gentiles to the fold of His people Israel.

We find upon the question of altar lights, as upon other matters, that Cosin, in his notes, speaks with a force and a directness which admits of no doubt as to his meaning, and in this case it will be seen that the illustration which he adduces from the practice of Lord Burghley is very suggestive of there having been various other instances which happen not to have been recorded simply by the accidents of history. I have already made the quotation, but it will save trouble to repeat it :—

"Amongst other ornaments of the Church also then in use in the second year of Edward VI., there were two lights appointed by the injunctions (which the Parliament had authorised him to make, and whereof otherwhiles they make mention, as acknowledging them to be binding) to be set upon the High Altar, as a significant ceremony of the light which Christ's Gospel brought into the world ; and this at the same time when all other lights and tapers superstitiously set before images were by the very same injunctions, with many other abused ceremonies and superstitions, taken away. These lights were (by virtue of the present rubric referring to what was the use in the second of Edward VI.) afterwards continued in all the Queen's chapels during her whole reign; and so are they in all the King's, and in many cathedral churches, besides the chapels of divers noblemen, bishops, and colleges, to this day. It was well known that the Lord Treasurer Burleigh (who was no friend to superstition or Popery) used them constantly in his chapel, with other ornaments of fronts, palls, and books upon the altar. The like did Bishop Andrews, who was a man who knew well what he did, and as free from Popish superstition as any in the kingdom besides. In the latter end of King Edward's time they used them in Scotland itself, as appears from Calvin's Epistle to Knox, and his fellow-reformers there, anno 1554 (Ep. 206), where he takes exception against them for following the custom of England. To this head we refer the organ, the font, the altar, the communion table, and pulpit, with the coverings and ornaments of them all; together with the paten, chalice, and corporas, which were all in use in the second of Edward VI., by the authority of the Acts of Parliament then made."

The special references to the use of the lights which Cosin adduces are taken from the cathedrals and chapels which the Ritual Commission chose to treat as a class apart. But, unlike that body, Cosin reasons from the known practice in the places which were always intended as models of ceremonial, and in which the utmost care had been bestowed upon the performance of Divine worship, up to what he considered was the general ritual law of the Church. He would, I believe, have been very much surprised and puzzled if he had been told that in a later generation a body of experts, discussing this very matter, had on purpose put on one side the precedents derived from our highest normal type of worship in order to be able to assert that there was "no sufficient evidence" to justify them in recognising this particular rite.

I must, however, request my readers to look back to the passage which I gave at page 109 of my fourth Chapter from Cosin's familiar account of the service, as habitually performed in parish churches, which Nicholls has offered in a translation from the Latin, and in which, in naming the white cloth, the Bible, the Prayer Book, the chalice and paten, as its usual furniture, he adds that "two wax candles are to be set on" the Lord's Table. If they will then compare this notice with those more formal statements of the same writer which I have just been quoting, they will be compelled to own that Cosin, in that description, must have intended to imply that the candles so used in the ordinary parochial worship were or ought to be lighted. He would hardly have paraded the *lumina cæca* in such terms. As I have pointed out, the whole phraseology of this description, the things which it mentions and the things which it omits, clearly prove that it was written as a familiar description of a usual English Sunday service for the use of persons (no doubt foreigners) who knew nothing of it, but desired information, not upon our ritual law, but about what we actually did. There exists too of the date of 1685—a form for dedicating certain ornaments of the Church, drawn up by Archbishop Sancroft, which I shall further on have to quote in a connection which may surprise some of my readers. In it stands a solemn form of words for dedicating the candlesticks. This in itself is not proof that they were intended for the ceremonious burning of candles; but it is not very probable that Sancroft would have used so particular a form over a mere article of utilitarian furniture.

These are the grounds on which I base my plea that, whatever may be the actual law on the matter—a nice point, all must own—the permission of lighted candles at Holy Communion in churches where the congregations like it, would be a concession alike gracious, politic, and charitable. My appeal rests upon the grave declarations of men in former days, both learned and able, who very well knew what they intended, and were very capable of expressing their meaning in unambiguous language. They are speaking, by common consent, of one out of two things,—one or other of which is certainly now the law—either of lights upon the Holy Table, *lighted* to signify that "Christ is the very true light of the world," or of lights on the Holy Table *unlighted* to signify that "Christ is the very true light of the world." Let me then for a moment pass by the wire-drawn distinctions of lawyers, and appeal to the manly sense and good feeling of Englishmen. We have already got and we use in innumerable instances the material thing. The candlesticks and the candles upon the Holy Table have been ruled to be the custom of our Church, and no man nor Court can now deprive us of them. Even the power of lighting the candles is in the celebrant's hands according to the flexible and unprovable wants of his own eyesight. He may use his licence foolishly, but I do not think that Lord Penzance would patiently waste his life in gauging the darkness of many miscellaneous chancels. Is it not, then, merely vexatious and harsh—is it not (respect for those whose policy I am criticising restrains me from using other words than frivolous and unwise) to check persons who believe that they are complying with the Church's mind by using these lights for the object for which they were made, and which, as these Churchmen have learned from their English fathers in the faith, at Christ's own Ordinance significantly show forth "the truth as it is in Jesus?"

I have been pleading for the use of the two lights on the altar, which the Church of England has so decidedly recognised, and to which she has specifically attached a pious signification, but for nothing more. I am well aware that for this rite primitive usage cannot be alleged. At the time, however, when these lights were allowed and others ordered to be taken away, I believe that nothing in this respect was subtracted from the ornaments of the English altar. The two lights on the altar were the old English use, or rather they were that use in its most ample form. The Constitution of Archbishop Walter, of the year 1332, is well known, in which he orders that "Tempore quo missarum solemnia peraguntur, accendentur duæ candelæ, vel ad minus una;" and this Constitution appears to be repeated from one of Oxford of 1222, which is identical except in concluding "vel ad minus una cum lampade," which would seem to show that less was demanded in 1332 than in 1222. Abroad (even down to a very late period of the Middle Ages) the use of two lights, or even of one, seems to have been far from having obtained as a universal custom. This circumstance was brought before me in a very direct manner last year. I was examining the manuscripts which were to be disposed of at the famous Perkins sale, when my attention was attracted by a very beautiful Pontifical, written and illuminated for a Bishop of Tournay, who flourished in the third quarter of the fifteenth century. It is full of very elaborate illuminations of pontifical rites, including in each the representation of an altar—and of an altar, too, as prepared for the administration of the Bishop. Yet out of all these altars only two carry any candle, and in each case it is only a single one. It happens that the illumination figured in the catalogue of the library is one of these two. I have since looked at other manuscripts and have noted also in them the absence of altar candles. Modern Roman use orders behind the altar not two, but many lights; and this recent and alien practice has, I am sorry to say, its Anglican imitators. I cannot (while fully believing that these votaries of exuberant ceremonial have lapsed into the practice without considering its bearings) regard the question as immaterial, for those who follow it let go their hold of English tradition, of all legal sanction which they can claim for their use of altar lights, and of the pious meaning for which those lights have been retained amongst us. The pretext that such lights may not be upon the altar itself, but upon a superaltar or superaltars behind, is no defence, for they are intended to group with, and belong to, the altar; to be, in short, according to the plain meaning of language, altar lights.

The symmetrical simplicity of the stately cross, flanked by the two conspicuous candlesticks, and perhaps the two modest nosegays between, is more consonant with the canons of true taste, and therefore more beautiful and reverential than the crowd of candles, tall and short, or the confused apparition of many-branched candelabra, with which some persons delight, in spiritless imitation of very modern foreign usage, to heap their altars. It may also be without difficulty conceded that for those who appeal to the injunctions of Edward VI. for the sanction of their proceedings to do the specific thing which those injunctions directly prohibit, is action which can hardly be qualified as prudent or defensible policy.

I have already noticed that the decoration of the altar with nosegays is a practice which even the promoters of the Purchas suit were willing to leave as sanctioned by the judgment of the Court of Arches. I may point out to those who feel most deeply the value of the symbolical teaching of the lighted candles, that in the odour and beauty of these lately-accepted ornaments of the Holy Table resides a treasure of emblematic meaning. In them we offer to the Lord's honour the lily and the rose of Sharon, joined to the passion-flower of the new world. Yet we have no evidence that this rite of altar flowers, any more than the altar cross, was known to Donne, or Cosin, or Sancroft. Thus, in the long life of the Christian Church, things new and old are wont to mingle, and later generations can show their compensations for gifts in which they seem to have fallen below their fathers' standard. We may in our time suffer the trial of being roughly called to account for honouring the Lord's Table with rites which the great nursing fathers of the young and still struggling reformed English Church supported at their own personal loss of means, and liberty and life; but at least we owe to them the chancel and the altar in its own place, and following up this gain we can plead, as they could not, how frequently that same English Church can now prepare herself to show forth the Lord's death at cross-crowned altars, in parish chancels resonant with the sacred song of white-robed choirs. The men in those days who denounced the cope, were also prepared, when they had the opportunity, to tear up the surplice. In our day the surplice is by all parties recognised as the vesture of the English ministry, and the table before which that surplice is worn, stands, without contradiction, altar-wise.

I am totally unable to realise the mental or moral contexture of the persons who imagined they were doing God service, or showing kindness to their fellow-creatures, when they dragged before the law courts the custom which many clergymen observed of mixing a little water with the wine which was to be consecrated. The custom may or may not have been strictly within the letter of the actual rubrics. But it was absolutely unostentatious. The material results which it could have produced would be absolutely inappreciable by the communicants—or, if they were not so, so much the worse for the frame of mind in which those critics were communicating. The motives which led to the practice were of a peculiarly sacred and delicate character, not less than the belief that the celebrant—while following pious counsels of his own, and the all but universal usage of the whole, Church—was also showing forth the Lord's death in the same cup which He distributed at His own institution of the Holy Communion, as well as recalling the blood mingled with water which flowed from the wounded side. This was the rite which it pleased certain persons, in their zeal for the scriptural purity of our religion, to disturb. Shall we say of them, "Blessed are the peacemakers"? Sir Robert Phillimore, sitting in judgment in the Purchas case, allowed the rite, if performed unostentatiously in the vestry. The Judicial Committee overruled even this permission, while they coupled their prohibition with an assertion which they would find exceedingly difficult to establish, that the private mixture "has not prevailed at all," either "in the East" or "in the West." The fact remains, that it is the rule of the Eastern Church for the deacon to mix the cup privately in the "diaconicon," or vestry. As to the mixture in itself, they call it, with a very daring use of language, "the exceptional direction and practice of Bishop Andrewes."

The rite is ordered in the first Prayer Book in these words:

CHAP. VI.   ANDREWES ON MIXED CHALICE.   233

"And putting the wine into the chalice, or else in some fair or convenient cup, prepared for that use (if the chalice will not serve), putting thereto a little pure and clean water; and setting both the bread and the wine upon the Altar." This direction disappeared in 1552, and has never been restored. But that those who were best able to judge of the mind of the Church did not conceive that this omission was any prohibition may be gathered from sufficient evidence. Bishop Andrewes' not "exceptional" directions on the subject, contained in Nicholls' 'Additional Notes,' are :—

"Here the Priest having made Adoration, poureth water upon the napkin ready for that purpose, and cleaneth his hands: mystice respiciens illud Psalmi, 'Lavabo in innocentiâ manus meas, et sic introibo ad Altare Dei ut annunciem vocem εὐχαριστίας.' Moraliter et decorè, uti cum magnatibus accubituri sumus. Posteà Panes è canistro in Patinam ponit. Dein Vinum è Doliolo, ad instar sanguinis erumpentis in calicem haurit. Tum Aquam è Triconali Scypho immiscet. Postremò omnibus ritè, et quam fieri potest, decentissimè atque aptissimè compositis, stans pergit et peragit. In rariore solennitate hîc l'ergit Episcopus et consecrat."

Bishop Andrewes' form of consecrating a church is an even more authoritative expression of his views than this note, and in it the following rubric occurs :—

"Cæteris rebus ordine gestis, demum Episcopus sacram Mensam redit (sacellanis utrisque ad aliquantulum recedentibus), lotisque manibus, pane fracto, vino in calicem effuso, et aquâ admistâ, stans ait. . . . . Cum vinum, quod prius effuderat, non sufficeret, Episcopus de novo in calicem ex poculo quod in Sacrâ Mensâ stabat effundit, admistâque aquâ, recitat clara verba illa consecratoria."

We are also told, upon the authority of Wheatley, that the mixture was continued in the Chapel Royal all the time that Andrewes was dean of it; and Overall, in Nicholls' 'Notes,' says: "Our Church forbids it not for ought I know, and they that think fit may use it, as some most eminent do it at this day."

We also know very well that Bishop Andrewes was not content with inculcating this rite in rubrics, or enforcing it at the Chapel Royal, but that he also made it his own practice, as is already shown by the plan of his chapel, in which the cross, which is placed in the direct centre of his Altar—possibly, as I have ventured to suggest, indicating by a sort of private mark the spot of consecration—is in the accompanying explanation defined as "the Tricanale, being a round ball with screw cover, whereout issue three pipes, and is for the water of mixture." We also know that Laud copied this chapel and its furniture, and indeed the plan itself survives from having been seized among his papers and published by Prynne, as a document valuable towards the Archbishop's condemnation. It is also on record that Laud, when rector of All-Hallows, Barking, in London, introduced the practice of the mixture; so that the authority of this Primate must be added to that of Andrewes.

We have next the direct authority of Wren, whose rubric at the consecration of Abbey Dore church will bear repetition:—

"Then the Bishop standeth up, and setteth ready to his hand the Bread and Wine with the paten and chalice, but first washeth his fingers with the end of the napkin besprinkled with water. Then layeth he the Bread on the paten, and poureth of the Wine into the chalice, and a little water into it; and standing with his face to the Table, about the midst of it, he saith the Collect of Consecration."

Previously to this, as I should have noted, the admixture had been one of the uses in Prince Charles's Chapel at Madrid. I pass over the opinions and practice of the Nonjurors on this point, decided as they were and supported by learned argument; for I have laid down the rule not to avail myself of the assistance of that body, deeply read in liturgical lore as it was, lest their separation from the great body of the Church of England should be retorted upon me as a fact which vitiated the value of their testimony.

In the 'Origines Liturgicæ' of that most cautious of the

first leaders of the Oxford movement, Sir William Palmer, the following passage occurs in reference to the mixed chalice:—

"In after ages we find no canons made to enforce the use of water, for it was an established custom. Certainly none can be more canonical and more conformable to the practice of the Primitive Church. In the English Church it has never been forbidden or prohibited; for the rubrick which enjoins the priest to place bread and wine on the table, does not prohibit him from mingling water with that wine."

No one, of course, can regard the rite of the mixed chalice as essential, but it is, as we have seen, a custom of the most venerable antiquity, carrying with it teachings of a peculiarly sacred character, and consonant with the views and practice of some of our most honoured prelates and writers, and one which can by no possibility jar against the feelings of any worshipper. If the powers of the new Ecclesiastical Judge should be invoked to crush it out, I think that a most unwise and needless policy of tormenting tender consciences will have been set on foot by those whose office should rather be to comfort than to scourge.

The question of leavened or unleavened bread stands on an entirely different footing from that of the mixed chalice. Neither form of the sacramental bread has been a Catholic usage, for the East has as tenaciously stuck to the leavened as the West to the unleavened loaf, while their respective views have been supported by a difference of opinion, into which I forbear to enter, as to whether the Last Supper was or was not the Passover, and whether, therefore, leavened or unleavened bread was used at it. As a point also of practical policy the feelings and prepossessions—prejudices, if my reader pleases, but still prejudices which ought to be respected—of individual worshippers may be very painfully engaged in the presence or absence of the sacramental bread in the form in which they are accustomed to have it administered. There can be no doubt that at the commencement of the reformed order of things in England the rule was to use round and unleavened loaves, called wafers, although of a thicker substance than those which had served in pre-reformational times. The rubric of the first Prayer Book on the subject runs as follows:—

"For avoiding of all matters and occasion of dissension, it is meet that the bread prepared for the Communion be made, through all this realm, after one sort and fashion; that is to say, unleavened, and round, as it was afore, but without all manner of print, and something more larger and thicker than it was, so that it may be aptly divided into divers pieces: and every one shall be divided into two pieces, at the least, or more, by the discretion of the minister, and so distributed. And men must not think less to be received in part than in the whole, but in each of them the whole body of our Saviour Jesus Christ."

At the restoration of the reformed order, under Elizabeth in 1559, a similar provision was repeated in this injunction:—

"Item. Where also it was in the time of King Edward VI. used to have the sacramental bread of common fine bread, it is ordered for the more reverence to be given to those Holy Mysteries, being the Sacrament of the Body and Blood of our Saviour Jesus Christ, that the said sacramental bread be made and formed plain, without any figure thereupon, of the same fineness and fashion round, though somewhat bigger in compass and thickness, as the usual bread and wafer heretofore named singing cakes, which served for the use of the private mass."

and subsequently confirmed in Archbishop Parker's Visitation Articles:—

"And whether they do use to minister the Holy Communion in wafer bread, according to the Queen Majesty's injunctions?"

On this action of Parker, Strype makes these remarks:—

"There was now in the churches of the kingdom great variety used in the sacramental bread, as to the form of it. As in some (and they the most) the form of it was round, wafer-like; in some the form was otherwise, as ordinary bread; though the wafer-form of the bread to be used in the Communion had been before agreed upon, upon good deliberation between the Archbishop and the Bishop of London; yet this order about the bread would not prevail to bring in an uniformity therein. The tidings of this variety came new to the court, and gave great offence. . . . . As there was this stir at this time about the form of the bread, so there was, not long before, as great about the kind of it, whether wafer-bread, or loaf, or common bread. The archbishop had appointed it to be wafer-bread; and so he enjoined it in his injunctions to his clergy. And it was generally so used, though some would rather make use of the loaf-bread, which did not please the archbishop."

I need hardly add that wafer bread was used in Elizabeth's Chapel, in which, on Easter day, 1593, it was, as we are told, "waffer bread of some thicker substaunce." It was also the practice in the chapel of Bishop Andrewes. Hooker defends it by the analogy of Geneva, asking whether those in that place have not

"the old Popish custom of administering the Blessed Sacrament of the Holy Eucharist with wafer cakes? These things the godly there can digest. Wherefore should not the godly here learn to do the like, both in them and in the rest of the like nature?"

In the Notes to the Prayer Book, by Bishop Andrewes, which I have already had occasion to quote, the following passage is found:—

"Lectâ confessione Nicenâ, the Priest adores, then he removes the bason from the back of the altar to the forepart. The Bishop ascends with treble adoration, and lastly kneels down at the altar.

"Into his hands the Priest from a by-standing table on the south-side reaches first the wafer-bread, in a canister close covered and lined with linen. 2ndly. The wine in a barrel on a cradle with four feet. These the Bishop offers in the name of the whole congregation upon the altar.

"Then he offers into the bason for himself, and after him the whole congregation, and so betake themselves to their proper and convenient place of kneeling. Bishops and Priests only within the septum, deacons at the door, the laiety without, the Priest (meanwhile) reading the peculiar sentences for the Offertory. 'Solis ministerio sacro deditis ad Altare ingredi et communicare licet, Conc. Laod. can. 19.'"

I could multiply evidence on the bread, but I think I have said enough to show that the use of unleavened bread was, during the first portion of the Reformation century the rule of our Church, and during the remainder of it a recognised custom. But recent experience has shown that it is a practice about which worshippers are very apt to be susceptible; and I should certainly counsel exceeding circumspection in its revival, especially since its condemnation under the Purchas judgment may be alleged against it, while no one can contend that it is in any way essential.

The last specific rite on which I feel that I am bound to speak is one which differs from any which has hitherto engaged my attention. They have all been religious practices growing out of the Christian dispensation. This one, while of very extensive prevalence all over the Christian Church from the earliest ages, has also been a pious custom of almost every religion, true or false, of which the world's history bears record. I refer to the use of incense, which was ceremoniously burned in Egypt, in Greece, and in Rome, as it now is by the votaries of the false religions of the far East. To Moses in the Holy Mount the Lord commanded that he should "make an altar to burn incense upon"—"and Aaron shall burn thereon sweet incense every morning; when he dresseth the lamps he shall burn incense upon it. And when Aaron lighted the lamps at even, he shall burn incense upon it, a perpetual incense before the Lord throughout your generations." And so with many backslidings, and sad intervals of idolatry, of ruin, and of captivity, did Aaron and his successors, in the Tabernacle, in the Temple of Solomon, and in the Temple of Zorobabel, till after many generations, to the priest Zacharias, as he was executing his priest's office before God, and "his lot was to burn incense when he went into the Temple of the Lord," was the Angel Gabriel sent "standing on the right hand of the altar of incense," with the glad news of the dawn of the dayspring from on high. Frankincense accordingly was one of the offerings which, under divine guidance, the wise men laid down at the Redeemer's cradle in Bethlehem. In that vision of heavenly worship the Revelation of St. John, the "four beasts and four and twenty elders fell down before the Lord, having every one of them harps, and golden vials full of odours, which are the prayers of the saints;" and at the opening of the seventh seal "another angel came and stood at the altar, having a golden censer; and there was given unto him much incense, that he should offer it with the prayers of all saints upon the golden altar which was before the throne. And the smoke of the incense which came with the prayers of the saints, ascended up before God out of the angel's hand." Can we wonder that the Church of God, all shivered and rent as it was by the pride and sin of man, hating and fighting with itself in its sundered portions, should yet unite in the pious offering of incense at the Holy Sacrament? No mention is made of incense in the Prayer Book of 1549, nor, I need hardly add, in those which followed. Still, notices from time to time are found during the Reformation century to show that those who cared for the dignity of worship conceived that the use of incense was still permissible. In the curious accounts of Elizabeth's Chapel, "ships" and "arks," that is, vessels for frankincense, are mentioned. Among the furniture of Bishop Andrewes's Chapel we find "A Triquetral censer, wherein the clerk putteth frankincense at the reading of the first lesson," and "The Navicula, like the keel of a boat with a half-cover, and a foot, out of which the frankincense is poured." George Herbert directs the country parson to have his church "at great festivals strewed and stuck with boughs, and perfumed with incense." It is fair to say that this does not necessarily imply that it should be burned during service time. In Peterhouse Chapel, as we learn from 'Canterbury's Doom' during the Mastership of Cosin, "there was on the altar a pot, which they usually called the incense pot," and we are also told of "a little boat out of which the frankincense is poured, which Dr. Cosin had made use of in Peter House Chapel when he burned incense." But, considering the lateness of the date, perhaps the most remarkable recognition of the use of incense in the Church of England is that which was afforded by Archbishop Sancroft in 1685. The then Lord Digby, having made an offering of communion plate to Coleshill Church, where the well-known divine Kettlewell was curate, Archbishop Sancroft himself went there and conducted a service, combining the offering of the plate on the part of the donor and its consecration by himself according to a form which he drew up. From this form I extract the consecutive portions containing the consecration of candlesticks, to which I have already referred in the earlier pages of this chapter, and also of a censer:—

"When there are candlesticks presented, while the bishop receiveth them and placeth them upon the altar the chaplains say as before :—

"'Thy word is a lantern unto my feet, and a light unto my paths.

"'For in Thee is the fountain of life; and in Thy light shall we see light.'

"So likewise when a censer is presented and received, they say:—

"'While the king sitteth at his table, my spikenard sendeth forth the smell thereof.

"'Let my prayer be set forth before Thee as the incense; and let the lifting up of my hands be as the evening sacrifice.'"

It does not appear that a censer formed part of the gift of plate to Coleshill Church, but its absence there makes it, perhaps, more remarkable that Sancroft should have thought necessary to provide in his general order of consecration for a censer being given. I do not quote the instances of incense being burned during coronation processions, for in those cases it was used as an adjunct of a state pomp.

Its ceremonious use for "censing persons and things" was declared illegal by Sir Robert Phillimore in the case of Mr. Purchas, and this is not to be regretted. "Censing persons and things," which Mr. Purchas did, is very different from offering incense to God, as the Lord commanded Aaron by the mouth of Moses, as Zacharias did in the Gospel, and as the angels are revealed to us doing in the Apocalypse. I am no advocate for the Roman practice of censing, and very much deprecate and regret any attempts which may have been made to revive it among us. I equally deprecate, in the existing state of general feeling, any attempt to revive the use of incense on the private responsibility of any clergyman. Unfortunately the outward aspect of the unreformed rite of incense, after the multiplied manipulations of a long series of mediæval ceremonialists, is such as materially to obscure the pious significance of its original institution; and in a more direct view of the question, it is one which, with the perpetual unrest of its swinging censers, is peculiarly liable to irritate staid and undemonstrative English worshippers. I can hardly, therefore, say how deeply I regret that where incense has been revived among us, it has been so in minute subservience to precedents, which a wider perception of things as they are would have shown to be not only inapplicable, but absolutely to be avoided. Indeed it is not uncharitable to describe the use of incense in the unreformed rites in its ceremonious repetition of censings of the altar in various places, of the ministers of every grade, of the book, and of the congregation themselves, as in fact a lowering of that which was in its origin a direct act of worship—a solemn offering to God Himself of incense, as the revealed symbol of prayer—down to little more than a complicated lustration (a sort of emblematic washing) of the apparatus of worship, animate and inanimate, and even of the worshippers themselves. It would be difficult to defend such a use of incense consistently with the principles which underlie the Anglican rule of worship; and if the hearts of our congregations should be turned again to desire to honour their Maker with that offering of a sweet savour which He Himself ordained for His ancient people, which He Himself accepted in His cradle, and He Himself revealed in Apocalyptic vision, the custom should be set up, not at the will of single clergymen, but upon the authority of the Church itself, and under regulations framed in disregard of the burdensome and man-serving minutiæ of mediæval ritual—regulations which should recall that Altar of incense, which God, in His good providence, chose for the spot at which His angel announced to the offering priest the glad tidings of great peace, the birth of the forerunner of Christ the King.

(243)

CHAPTER VII.

Ideal of an Anglican communion — Distinctive simplicity — Capacity of highest beauty — "Statuesque"—Growth of complicated unreformed rites — Benedictine order — No distractions, minds concentrated on worship — Our office and mediæval like in main features of Eucharist for the Church at both dates the same — Literal and uncritical use of Sarum ritual a snare more than a help— Minute changes of posture unmeaning to us — Ceremonious reading of Gospel — Two particulars in which I hope our service may never be altered — Audible reading — Communicants at principal celebration — Retirement of non-communicants not to be compulsory — Classes specially attracted by ritualism — In rich services they find those forms of beauty of which they have glimpses, but cannot otherwise gratify — Souls risked by sweeping away system — Not to be supposed they are specially attracted by illegal peculiarities — General beauty, lightsomeness, and warmth — Attraction of hearty hymnody — Take ultra-ritualism at its worst — Is it worst evil of the times? — Condition of spiritual things about us — Apathy, false doctrine, scepticism, superstition, gross vice — Prelates as peers of Parliament can pass this by, and pronounce harshest censures on those brethren who believe highest Christian truths and devote their lives to the ministry — Do they expect by this to advance Christ's kingdom or strengthen the Establishment? — Conduct of policemen not natural action of spiritual fathers — Ritualistic excess no reason to refuse reasonable claims — Position and distinctive dress — We want peace, but not peace which means worse war — Treaty must be based on self-respect and principle — Balance of dress and position by giving up Athanasian Creed and Communion service emphatically rejected — Compromise must be within service itself — Dress and position alternative; gown, railsfuls, evening communions permissible.

I HAVE now gone through all the specific practices of which I think it necessary to speak. All through the examination I have had present to my mind the ideal of a distinctive Anglican Communion as differing from other and older rites in its simplicity, but as capable of the highest degree of solemnity and beauty as any earthly thing can compass. Nothing is so difficult as to draw out in words the lineaments of an ideal. I may, however, say that I believe the characteristic distinction of our Communion Office can best be described by an adjective, which has so often been the resource of art critics at a loss for a telling epithet, that I should doubt about using it if it did not happen to be the word which most conveniently embodies my meaning. Our most dignified celebrations—those in which the celebrant is assisted by the Gospeller and Epistler, where the service is chorally rendered and which correspond with the High Mass of other Communions—appear to me to be conspicuously "statuesque." The position which the three ministers at the beginning assume, the celebrant in the centre, the Gospeller to his left, and the Epistler rather lower down to his right, are those which they ought generally to retain, except at the offertory or when they turn to the people for Commandments, Epistle, Gospel, and exhortations, while they must totally abandon their stationary attitude at the distribution of the elements, in which they ought to take their part. Any further shifting and changes would, I must submit, be upon a natural and dispassionate reading of our formularies unreal, and hardly consistent with the spirit of our Communion Office; for they would be motions, for which it would be difficult to adduce corresponding words, or trains of thought which it was necessary to symbolise.

In the unreformed office it is otherwise, for round the ceremonial of High Mass, in the course of many generations, has grown up a vast accretion of minute observances. Some of them are the fruit of pious simplicity, and others of wire-spun ingenuity; but they are, as a whole, too complicated and artificial for beauty or dignity, and little calculated to promote edification in a reading and critical age, or among persons who have not been brought up in their familiarity. The case could not be otherwise when the performance of the divine office had been for century after century the special inheritance all over Western Europe of numerous and teeming religious corporations of men, many of them endowed with the highest intellectual gifts, but by the then conditions of the world, by their own tastes, and by the responsibilities of their vows, concentrated on one work, easy in their circumstances according to the ideas of their times as members of the great Benedictine Society, but individually forced to discipline and restricted living in virtue of their allegiance to the rule of their founder. For them existed neither printing nor newspapers, nor the avocations of family life—no travelling, except afoot or upon the pad's or the mule's back. For them the perpetual service of the altar was not merely their duty to God, but, so to speak, their duty to man also, in another sense from what it is to the clergyman, who, by a word which has now unluckily received a limited signification is a "curate," that is a man having the cure of others' souls. Undoubtedly the Benedictine did, to a certain extent, fulfil a curate's duties. But his first and greatest human obligation to perpetual worship was one of mutual contract. He enjoyed his position of monk with its advantages and liabilities, on the condition of his executing his duties in Church, not in behalf of a parish, and with consideration for the secular wants of his flock, but in co-ordination with his brother monks, whose days and duties were identical with his own. All monks, of course, were not priests, but a large proportion were, and every member of the corporation was a "religious." With men so placed, the ordinary considerations even of time (to take the most practical view of the matter) did not exist. The higher, so to speak, the High Mass could be made, the more satisfactorily would the day be filled up, while that laudable spirit of competition, without which men deteriorate into fossils, prompted house to rival house in the grandeur and the intricacies of its religious appointments. I have spoken of "monks," because the members of the great Benedictine Order, were, I believe, the principal agents, during the earlier middle ages, in building up the mediæval Mass, but of course what I have been saying applies, in due proportion, to the less strict religious corporations of canons who were equally, though not monks, bound to long and high observances.

From such causes, working through many centuries of civil violence and secular ignorance, grew up in its luxurious redundance of bewildering ceremonial the Mass of Sarum, York, or Hereford, each, I may in passing notice, named from a cathedral church served by canons: such, too, was the origin of that of Rome. Those offices and ours have in common the great features of the Christian Eucharist, for that Church of the Middle Ages and our own are the same English branch of the one Church Catholic. But when we come to details, the ritual of Sarum, no less than that of Rome, would be as much a snare as a help to the priest who desired to act out his present English celebration with all due honour, and who went to it for literal and uncritical guidance. Indeed, the existence alongside of High Mass (of which I need hardly say I have been exclusively speaking) of the Low Mass, in which the same order of words is presented in so different a form, may be taken as evidence that the spirit of the English Communion Office would hardly be embodied in the literal form of pre-reformational ritual; for in proportion as the existing office was intended to be less complex than the High Mass, so was it also intended to be more deliberate and comprehensible than the Low Mass. In fact, the monastic origin of the complications of High Mass has made the co-existence, for the working world, of Low Mass a necessity. But the English ceremonialist, who might be tempted to regret his inability to act out the intricate symbolism of the one, would, if he reflected, find his consolation in being spared the temptation of hurrying through the service with the inaudible rapidity which is not deemed irreverent in a Low Mass. I may, in illustration of my train of thought, take one or two particulars. At various points of the missal service the deacon places himself immediately behind the priest and the subdeacon behind the deacon, so that all three stand in a row, while the deacon's duty is from time to time to hold up the celebrant's vestment. These changes of posture have their reason in the office to which they belong, and whether they are or are not graceful in themselves, on which opinions may differ, they can plead a motive for their use in correspondence with the whole substance and spirit of that of which they are component parts. But if they are imported into our simple liturgy they become merely arbitrary posturings which irritate the unlearned by their strangeness, and thinking men by their incongruity. Again, the stately ceremonial which accompanies the reading of the Gospel in the unreformed rite—the procession, the torches, the upraised cross, the censings, the book ceremoniously held up for the deacon's use—may all be defended by those to whom the ceremony is familiar as implying the supreme honour due to God's Holy Word. But the whole rite is too long, too ornamental, too complicated, and as it were too solid, to be defensible, if adopted upon the private judgment of any particular incumbent as his rendering of eleven words of our actual rubrics —" Then shall be read the Gospel (the people all standing up)." If, in the fulness of time, the Church of England were to see its way to a greater ceremoniousness in the reading of the Holy Gospel, it would, no doubt, take due order for the purpose. Already, as I have seen at Ely, Gospeller and Epistler have gone down from the altar to read their respective portions of Scripture at the screen gates to the congregation in the nave. In the meanwhile it is the counsel of prudence, not less than of towardness, for single clergymen not to provoke angry recriminations by startling innovations, adventured upon their own unsupported responsibility.

There are two particulars in which I trust that our own Communion service may never abandon its actual peculiarities. I hope the custom of an inaudible recitation of the prayers, and especially of that of Consecration, owned even by candid Romanists to be an innovation upon primitive practice, may never creep in. I also hope that the great communion of the laity may never be divorced from the highest celebrations. I cannot conceive a spectacle more cheering to the Christian's heart—

more calculated to remind him of the lost fervour of primitive days—than that glorious crowd of hundreds of devout communicants streaming up to the altar of some well-cared for church at the great celebration on Christmas or Easter Day. It would be, I believe, a blow to the reviving spirit of national piety, if these persons were to be told that they must, of necessity, approach the bread of life on such a day either early or not at all—that the Holy Communion, in its highest aspect of song and ceremonial, at Christmas, Easter, or Whitsuntide, need not be a communion, but ought to be a spectacle, and that they were there not to partake but to assist. The statuesque beauty of the well-ordered pose may be for the time being lost as the clergy move up and down with the sacred elements—the rhythmical progress of the Mass may be wanting—but what are these externals to the great reality? At the same time I am far from wishing to run into an opposite extreme and say that all who did not intend to communicate should therefore depart. The *Missa Catechumenorum* was a portion of ancient discipline when all hung on together; but now that the Church has generally abandoned that discipline I do not see why she should be so tenacious of one fragment. To substitute gazing for communicating is an error dangerous to the soul's health, and should on all accounts be discouraged. But why, when the habitual communicant is for any reason unable to communicate, but at the same time desires to mingle his prayers with those of his brethren and the Church at the Confession and Prayer of humble access—to raise the song of praise at the *Ter Sanctus* and the *Gloria in Excelsis*, and humbly to meditate on the mystery of Christ's death while His minister is showing it forth —why, I say, when he desires all this, he should be expelled from the Church, I never could understand.

One feature about the ritualistic movement, so called, is absolutely certain in London, and I conclude also in other large towns, namely, that it has, with a peculiar fascination, taken possession of a class of society which has hitherto been painfully inapproachable by the influences of religion. It is a class which I can best describe as the one which, without sharing in the easy circumstances of the so-called upper and upper middle classes, has the disadvantage of being, by the stern laws of conventionality, compelled to burden itself with the characteristic dress of those classes—clerks, dressmakers, the young men and women employed in the wholesale establishments, and so on. Any one who is acquainted with the social condition of our large towns is aware how large an amount of the population is included under this description. After all, these persons have souls to save, as much as any working-man or any member of either House of Parliament. It has been discovered as if by accident, as rich lodes of ore are struck by a casual blow of the pickaxe, that these persons are impressionable by an æsthetic worship, as they are not by more simple religious forms. This is not to be wondered at; their technical training, and the persons and objects with which in their business they are brought into contact, give them glimpses of beauty and ideas of refinement, which they cannot follow out or gratify with their own resources. But if they see the free and loving Church of God as the "Queen in a vesture of gold, wrought about with divers colours," opening her arms to them and to all, without distinction of person, their souls are naturally melted to the influences of divine grace. How many souls may he not risk who sweeps away the system in which these men and women find spiritual peace? I do not believe that the unwise or illegal peculiarities of ultra-ritualism are what has attracted them. They are people who have neither the learning nor the taste to draw antiquarian distinctions. What is "Sarum use" to them but an unconned lore? How are they concerned with the difference of vestment or cope, of alb or surplice? What has attracted them is the general beauty, lightsomeness, and warmth, of the higher ceremonial. For their sakes let these be sacred in the hands of our bishops and our judges. For their sakes equally let those who are especially responsible for their spiritual condition, those who have opened out to them this higher worship, take care lest in obstinately clinging to some peculiarity, they make forfeit of all the treasure of which they are but trustees for the sake of their flocks.

The abundant and hearty hymnody introduced at various parts of the service is one of the things which most attracts the persons of whom I have been speaking to their favourite churches. I trust that it may never be interfered with; for, although it is not strictly rubrical, it edifies many, and can harm none. I should not have thought it necessary to express this hope, had not that grave and venerable man Lord Hatherley, whom all love and respect, even when they cannot agree with him, adduced irregular hymn-singing as his chief charge against ritualism, in a speech during the debates on the Public Worship Bill. No doubt it startled him, because he was not expecting it, and could not find it in the rubrics. But I appeal from the judge to the man, and I ask him what good could come of checking a practice which in no way contravenes the doctrine of the Church, which only affects its discipline on an external point, and which is a source of so much religious comfort to many whom it has hitherto been a hard task to bring at all to church.

After all, let us take ultra-ritualism at its worst. Let us stamp its often defective appreciation of the temper of the times with the most condemnatory brand of impolicy, let us most sharply rebuke its deviations from the spirit and the code of the English Church, but then let us ask ourselves is it the worst evil of the times? Is it a festering sore, or is it the vicious excess of God's wonderful revival of religious life in our Church, a revival which by the law of human progress could not have gone so far without developing an extreme phase? Let us as men and as Christians look at the condition of spiritual things about us. Let us first inquire among Churchmen, and ask whether it is the ritualists who keep their churches closed from Sunday to Sunday? Is it the ritualists who evacuate Christ's own sacraments of any especial grace? Is it the ritualists who, in their zeal for preaching, too often neglect the ministration of God's Holy Word to the sick in mind and body? Is it the ritualists who inflate the sovereign virtue of faith until they place themselves upon the slippery pinnacle of Antinomianism? Is it the ritualists who, in their zeal for private judgment, deprave the inspiration of the Holy Scriptures, and use language suspiciously doubtful of the divinity of our Blessed Lord and Saviour? Is it the ritualists who struggle to engraft the fanaticism of spiritualism upon the mysteries of the Gospel? Are there, or are there not, such men as I have described in the ministry of our Church, and do they or do they not belong to the ritualistic fraternity? Outside of the Church is there no cold, despairing materialism in much honour in the high places of science? Has the mocking genius of Voltaire ceased to inspire the guides of public opinion? Are not our millions corroded with the canker of a suspicious, self-sufficient, uninquiring, negation of belief? When there is a recoil from this hopeless condition, is it not too often into some wild form of grotesque unblessed superstition? Beyond the labyrinth of scepticism, or the abyss of mere atheism, is there not a hell of gross unbridled vice yawning at our feet? Yet those upon whose shoulders the chief responsibility of Christ's Church in this realm rests can pass by these things, and employ that secular position which, as peers of Parliament, they may possess, for the harshest censures upon their younger brethren in the ministry, who, whatever may be their aberrations of opinion or of practice, hold fast to their unwavering faith in the Ever Blessed Trinity, and in Christ's atoning mediation; who are instant in season and out of season, in sickness and in health, in their ministrations of God's Holy Word and sacraments, and their unsparing temporal help in church, and at the noisome bed-side of the indigent sufferer; who are ever planning, discreetly or indiscreetly, but with the single end of God's glory and the comfort of His people, new schemes and fresh societies of Christian help. Nor were these censures limited even to those delinquents. We all remember the passage in that speech introducing a recent Act which appealed to popular indignation against a northern clergyman, who dared to do what Wren and Cosin had done before, and stand before the Holy Table; who dared to do what, later on in the same debates, the Lord Chancellor plainly intimated was, in his reading of the rubric, that which he was very well justified in doing. Put the insubordination of that clergyman, one who has in his time done good service to the Church of England, at the worst, and then say if his misdeed was so gross as to entitle him to be the one minister of all the Church of England singled out for individual and direct reprobation by the Primate of that Church in an age of 'Essays and Reviews,' of a trial at Healaugh and a trial at Natal? These things evoked no archiepiscopal legislation; but Dr. Dykes cannot believe that the words "'standing before the table' apply to the whole sentence" without inspiring a "Public Worship Regulation Bill."

I am genuinely pained at having to write this, from the deep respect and much gratitude for many personal kindnesses which I feel for the exalted dignitary on whose policy I am compelled to comment. But, in the national controversy which he has raised, public men must be openly discussed according to their public words and actions. I must, therefore, ask, do the rulers of our Israel really believe that by such policy they are advancing the cause of Christ's kingdom on earth? Do they dream that they are strengthening the cords of that Church Establishment in England, which never will be sustained by magisterial Acts of Parliament or manifold prosecutions, but will, by God's grace, flourish so long as it continues to embrace and foster the zeal for Christ's sake of Christ's own ministers, variously working according to their several gifts to meet the manifold spiritual wants of differing congregations?

In face of present trials of faith many men, who have no sympathies with the developments of ritualism, are sick at heart when they see the heaviest hand of episcopal severity let drop upon men who are guilty of nothing more than ceremonial variations, some of them variations of the most moderate kind, and known and practised before ritualism, so called, was heard of. This may be the conduct of active policemen, but it is not the natural action of Fathers in God. It is not, however, even the characteristic of a good police to direct all its severity against one side, nor does the consciousness of this peculiarity mitigate the wide distress. It is no answer to the protests of Churchmen to appeal to ritualistic excesses. The Ritualists may be foolish or they may be wrong—foolish and wrong to any extent. But their folly or their misdeeds can be no reason why, when pious, thoughtful, and loyal sons of the Church of England rise on every side to say that they are convinced that the Church of England, by its latest solemn pronouncement, and in conformity with the venerable usage of Christ's Universal Church, has said that it is meet right and congruous with the principles of our Reformation that the priest should stand before the Holy Table at the Communion and wear a dress distinctive of that sacred rite—that then they should be met by a refusal based on the deeds or words of men for whom they are not responsible. They feel that this is evasion, not argument. If we ask for bread and our fathers give us stones, let them, at least, not upbraid us with the surfeitings of other men.

If, however, they do condescend to offer us relief, let them be careful not to do so in the spirit of relieving officers dealing with clamorous paupers. We desire peace, but not that peace at all price which means later and worse war. The treaty must on both sides be based on principle and self-respect, and no trafficking of faith and morals for ceremonial actions can be entertained. Any ignoble suggestion to balance dress and position at a sacrifice of the public confession of the eternal truths of the Catholic Faith, and the denouncing of God's anger and vengeance against sinners, has only to be thrown out to be emphatically rejected, more emphatically rejected because those who dangle the bait had themselves so lately professed to have settled the Athanasian trouble.

If there is to be a compromise, and I think there ought to be a compromise, it must lie within the four corners of the question, and deal on both sides with the ceremonies of the Holy Communion. A compromise framed according to the strict requirements of even justice would be one which gave an equal allowance to the opposing customs upon which the minds of Churchmen are at this time conspicuously divided. It would be an arrangement which placed vestment or surplice, west side or north end, upon a footing of impartial toleration. But I go much further than that in my ideas of concession. Many persons think the change of the surplice for the gown during the Communion service a purposeless complication. The practice at the reception of the Holy Communion of saying the words of administration to a whole railful and not to each communicant, is a direct contravention of the rubric, and it is also by many Christians held materially to weaken the intended moral effect of that holy rite by not recalling directly and personally to each penitent and believing soul that sacrifice upon the Cross which Christ made for him—that one single person, born eighteen hundred years after the Passion—as completely, specifically, fully, and consciously, as for the whole vast multitude of all mankind in every age. The practice of celebrating the Holy Communion in the evening—a practice for which there is not a word of sanction in the Prayer Book or in the immemorial usage of our own or of any other Church—is exceedingly painful to many pious Christians, in thought of the irreverence which must attend so holy an action, coming after the toil, the heat, the distractions of spirit, the eating and drinking of an English day, not to mention the still deeper offence which it gives to those who consider the pious practice of fasting communion to be an obligation of binding force. Yet these practices are all of them dear to many people. Let them, then, enjoy their customs at the churches where they are acceptable, on their own responsibility; but let them, in return, leave in peace persons who only desire to follow, for their own edification, "every·established doctrine or laudable practice of the Church of England, or indeed of the whole Catholick Church of Christ."

ALBEMARLE STREET, LONDON,
April, 1874.

MR. MURRAY'S

GENERAL LIST OF WORKS.

ALBERT (THE) MEMORIAL. A Descriptive and Illustrated Account of the National Monument erected to the PRINCE CONSORT at Kensington. Illustrated by Engravings of its Architecture, Decorations, Sculptured Groups, Statues, Mosaics, Metalwork, &c. With Descriptive Text. By DOYNE C. BELL. With 24 Plates. Folio. 12*l*. 12*s*.

——— (PRINCE) SPEECHES AND ADDRESSES ON PUBLIC Occasions; with an Introduction, giving some outline of his Character. With Portrait. 8vo. 10*s*. 6*d*.; or *Popular Edition*, fcap. 8vo. 1*s*.

ABBOTT'S (REV. J.) Memoirs of a Church of England Missionary in the North American Colonies. Post 8vo. 2*s*.

ABERCROMBIE'S (JOHN) Enquiries concerning the Intellectual Powers and the Investigation of Truth. 19th *Edition*. Fcap. 8vo. 3*s*. 6*d*.

——— Philosophy of the Moral Feelings. 14th *Edition*. Fcap. 8vo. 2*s*. 6*d*.

ACLAND'S (REV. CHARLES) Popular Account of the Manners and Customs of India. Post 8vo. 2*s*.

ÆSOP'S FABLES. A New Version. With Historical Preface. By Rev. THOMAS JAMES. With 100 Woodcuts, by TENNIEL and WOLF. 64*th Thousand*. Post 8vo. 2*s*. 6*d*.

AGRICULTURAL (ROYAL) JOURNAL. (*Published half yearly.*)

AIDS TO FAITH: a Series of Theological Essays. 8vo. 9*s*.

CONTENTS.

Miracles	DEAN MANSEL.
Evidences of Christianity	BISHOP OF KILLALOE.
Prophecy & Mosaic Record of Creation	Dr. MCCAUL.
Ideology and Subscription	Canon COOK.
The Pentateuch	Canon RAWLINSON.
Inspiration	BISHOP OF WINCHESTER.
Death of Christ	ARCHBISHOP OF YORK.
Scripture and its Interpretation	BISHOP OF GLOUCESTER AND BRISTOL.

AMBER-WITCH (THE). A most interesting Trial for Witchcraft. Translated by LADY DUFF GORDON. Post 8vo. 2*s*.

ARMY LIST (THE). *Published Monthly by Authority.*

ARTHUR'S (LITTLE) History of England. By LADY CALLCOTT. *New Edition, continued to* 1872. Woodcuts. Fcap. 8vo. 2*s*. 6*d*.

AUSTIN'S (JOHN) LECTURES ON GENERAL JURISPRUDENCE; or, the Philosophy of Positive Law. 5th *Edition*. Edited by ROBERT CAMPBELL. 2 Vols. 8vo. 32*s*.

——— (SARAH) Fragments from German Prose Writers. With Biographical Notes. Post 8vo. 10*s*.

B

2 LIST OF WORKS

ADMIRALTY PUBLICATIONS; Issued by direction of the Lords Commissioners of the Admiralty:—
 A MANUAL OF SCIENTIFIC ENQUIRY, for the Use of Travellers. Edited by Sir JOHN F. HERSCHEL and ROBERT MAIN, M.A. *Fourth Edition.* Woodcuts. Post 8vo. 3*s.* 6*d.*
 GREENWICH ASTRONOMICAL OBSERVATIONS 1841 to 1846, and 1847 to 1871. Royal 4to. 20*s.* each.
 MAGNETICAL AND METEOROLOGICAL OBSERVATIONS. 1840 to 1847. Royal 4to. 20*s.* each.
 APPENDICES TO OBSERVATIONS.
  1837. Logarithms of Sines and Cosines in Time. 3*s.*
  1842. Catalogue of 1439 Stars, from Observations made in 1836 to 1841. 4*s.*
  1845. Longitude of Valentia (Chronometrical). 3*s.*
  1847. Description of Altazimuth. 3*s.*
   Twelve Years' Catalogue of Stars, from Observations made in 1836 to 1847. 4*s.*
   Description of Photographic Apparatus. 2*s.*
  1851. Maskelyne's Ledger of Stars. 3*s.*
  1852. I. Description of the Transit Circle. 3*s.*
  1853. Refraction Tables. 3*s.*
  1854. Description of the Zenith Tube. 3*s.*
   Six Years' Catalogue of Stars, from Observations. 1848 to 1853. 4*s.*
  1862. Seven Years' Catalogue of Stars, from Observations. 1854 to 1860. 10*s.*
   Plan of Ground Buildings. 3*s.*
   Longitude of Valentia (Galvanic). 2*s.*
  1864. Moon's Semid. from Occultations. 2*s.*
   Planetary Observations, 1831 to 1835. 2*s.*
  1868. Corrections of Elements of Jupiter and Saturn. 2*s.*
   Second Seven Years' Catalogue of 2760 Stars for 1861 to 1867. 4*s.*
   Description of the Great Equatorial. 3*s.*
  1856. Descriptive Chronograph. 3*s.*
  1860. Reduction of Deep Thermometer Observations. 2*s.*
  1871. History and Description of Water Telescope. 3*s.*
  Cape of Good Hope Observations (Star Ledgers). 1856 to 1863. 2*s.*
  ———————— 1856. 5*s.*
  ———————— Astronomical Results. 1857 to 1858. 5*s.*
  Report on Teneriffe Astronomical Experiment. 1856. 5*s.*
  Paramatta Catalogue of 7385 Stars. 1822 to 1826. 4*s.*
 ASTRONOMICAL RESULTS. 1847 to 1871. 4to. 3*s.* each.
 MAGNETICAL AND METEOROLOGICAL RESULTS. 1847 to 1871. 4to. 3*s.* each.
 REDUCTION OF THE OBSERVATIONS OF PLANETS. 1750 to 1830. Royal 4to. 20*s.* each.
 ———————————— LUNAR OBSERVATIONS. 1750 to 1830. 2 Vols. Royal 4to. 20*s.* each.
 ———————————— 1831 to 1851. 4to. 10*s.* each.
 BERNOULLI'S SEXCENTENARY TABLE. 1779. 4to. 5*s.*
 BESSEL'S AUXILIARY TABLES FOR HIS METHOD OF CLEARING LUNAR DISTANCES. 8vo. 2*s.*
 ENCKE'S BERLINER JAHRBUCH, for 1830. *Berlin,* 1828. 8vo. 9*s.*
 HANSEN'S TABLES DE LA LUNE. 4to. 20*s.*
 LAX'S TABLES FOR FINDING THE LATITUDE AND LONGITUDE. 1821. 8vo. 10*s.*

ADMIRALTY PUBLICATIONS—*continued.*

LUNAR OBSERVATIONS at GREENWICH. 1783 to 1819. Compared with the Tables, 1821. 4to. 7s. 6d.

MACLEAR ON LACAILLE'S ARC OF MERIDIAN. 2 Vols. 20s. each.

MAYER'S DISTANCES of the MOON'S CENTRE from the PLANETS. 1822, 3s.; 1823, 4s. 6d. 1824 to 1835. 8vo. 4s. each.

——— TABULÆ MOTUUM SOLIS ET LUNÆ. 1770. 5s.

——— ASTRONOMICAL OBSERVATIONS MADE AT GOTTINGEN, from 1756 to 1761. 1826. Folio. 7s. 6d.

NAUTICAL ALMANACS, from 1767 to 1877. 2s. 6d. each.

——————————— SELECTIONS FROM, up to 1812. 8vo. 5s. 1834-54. 5s.

——————————— SUPPLEMENTS, 1828 to 1833, 1837 and 1838. 2s. each.

——————————— TABLE requisite to be used with the N.A. 1781. 8vo. 5s.

SABINE'S PENDULUM EXPERIMENTS to DETERMINE THE FIGURE OF THE EARTH. 1825. 4to. 40s.

SHEPHERD'S TABLES for CORRECTING LUNAR DISTANCES. 1772. Royal 4to. 21s.

——— TABLES, GENERAL, of the MOON'S DISTANCE from the SUN, and 10 STARS. 1787. Folio. 5s. 6d.

TAYLOR'S SEXAGESIMAL TABLE. 1780. 4to. 15s.

——— TABLES OF LOGARITHMS. 4to. 60s.

TIARK'S ASTRONOMICAL OBSERVATIONS for the LONGITUDE of MADEIRA. 1822. 4to. 5s.

——— CHRONOMETRICAL OBSERVATIONS for DIFFERENCES of LONGITUDE between DOVER, PORTSMOUTH, and FALMOUTH. 1823. 4to. 5s.

VENUS and JUPITER: OBSERVATIONS of, compared with the TABLES. *London,* 1822. 4to. 2s.

WALES' AND BAYLY'S ASTRONOMICAL OBSERVATIONS. 1777. 4to. 21s.

——— REDUCTION OF ASTRONOMICAL OBSERVATIONS MADE IN THE SOUTHERN HEMISPHERE. 1764—1771. 1788. 4to. 10s. 6d.

BARBAULD'S (MRS.) Hymns in Prose for Children. With 112 Illustrations. Crown 8vo. 5s.; or *Fine Paper,* 7s. 6d.

BARROW'S (SIR JOHN) Autobiographical Memoir, from Early Life to Advanced Age. Portrait. 8vo. 16s.

——— (JOHN) Life, Exploits, and Voyages of Sir Francis Drake. Post 8vo. 2s.

BARRY'S (SIR CHARLES) Life and Works. By CANON BARRY. *Second Edition.* With Portrait and Illustrations. Medium 8vo. 15s.

BATES' (H. W.) Records of a Naturalist on the River Amazon during eleven years of Adventure and Travel. *Third Edition.* Illustrations. Post 8vo. 7s. 6d.

BEAUCLERK'S (LADY DIANA) Summer and Winter in Norway. *Third Edition.* With Illustrations. Small 8vo. 6s.

BELCHER'S (LADY) Account of the Mutineers of the 'Bounty,' and their Descendants; with their Settlements in Pitcairn and Norfolk Islands. With Illustrations. Post 8vo. 12s.

B 2

LIST OF WORKS

BELL'S (Sir Chas.) Familiar Letters. Portrait. Post 8vo. 12s.

BELT'S (Thos.) Naturalist in Nicaragua, including a Residence at the Gold Mines of Chontales; with Journeys in the Savannahs and Forests; and Observations on Animals and Plants. Illustrations. Post 8vo. 12s.

BERTRAM'S (Jas. G.) Harvest of the Sea: an Account of British Food Fishes, including sketches of Fisheries and Fisher Folk. *Third Edition.* With 50 Illustrations. 8vo. 9s.

BIBLE COMMENTARY. Explanatory and Critical. With a Revision of the Translation. By BISHOPS and CLERGY of the ANGLICAN CHURCH. Edited by F. C. Cook, M.A., Canon of Exeter. Medium 8vo. Vol. I., 30s. Vols. II. and III., 36s. Vol. IV., 24s.

Vol. I.
- Genesis .... Bishop of Ely.
- Exodus .... Canon Cook; Rev. Sam. Clark.
- Leviticus .... Rev. Samuel Clark.
- Numbers .... Canon Espin; Rev. J. F. Thrupp.

Vols. II. and III.
- Deuteronomy .... } Canon Espin.
- Joshua .... }
- Judges, Ruth, Samuel. Bishop of Bath and Wells.
- Kings, Chronicles, Ezra, Nehemiah, Esther } Canon Rawlinson.

Vol. IV.
- Job .... Canon Cook.
- Psalms .... { Dean of Wells, Canon Cook; Rev. C. I. Elliott.
- Proverbs .... Rev. E. H. Plumptre.
- Ecclesiastes .... Rev. W. T. Bullock.
- Song of Solomon .... Rev. T. Kingsbury.

BICKMORE'S (A. S.) Travels in the Eastern Archipelago, 1865-6; a Popular Description of the Islands, with their Natural History, Geography, Manners and Customs of the People, &c. With Maps and Illustrations. 8vo. 21s.

BIRCH'S (Samuel) History of Ancient Pottery and Porcelain: Egyptian, Assyrian, Greek, Roman, and Etruscan. *Second Edition.* With Coloured Plates and 200 Illustrations. Medium 8vo. 42s.

BISSET'S (Andrew) History of the Commonwealth of England, from the Death of Charles I. to the Expulsion of the Long Parliament by Cromwell. Chiefly from the MSS. in the State Paper Office. 2 vols. 8vo. 30s.

BLUNT'S (Rev. J. J.) Undesigned Coincidences in the Writings of the Old and New Testament, an Argument of their Veracity: containing the Books of Moses, Historical and Prophetical Scriptures, and the Gospels and Acts. *Eleventh Edition.* Post 8vo. 6s.

———— History of the Church in the First Three Centuries. *Fifth Edition.* Post 8vo. 6s.

———— Parish Priest; His Duties, Acquirements and Obligations. *Sixth Edition.* Post 8vo. 6s.

———— Lectures on the Right Use of the Early Fathers. *Third Edition.* 8vo. 9s.

———— University Sermons. *Second Edition.* Post 8vo. 6s.

———— Plain Sermons. *Sixth Edition.* 2 vols. Post 8vo. 12s.

———— Essays on various subjects. 8vo. 12s.

BLOMFIELD'S (Bishop) Memoir, with Selections from his Correspondence. By his Son. *Second Edition.* Portrait, post 8vo. 12s.

BOSWELL'S (JAMES) Life of Samuel Johnson, LL.D. Including the Tour to the Hebrides. By Mr. CROKER. A new Library Edition. Edited by ALEXANDER NAPIER, M.A. Portraits. 4 vols. 8vo. *In Preparation.*

BRACE'S (C. L.) Manual of Ethnology; or the Races of the Old World. Post 8vo. 6s.

BOOK OF COMMON PRAYER. Illustrated with Coloured Borders, Initial Letters, and Woodcuts. 8vo. 18s.

BORROW'S (GEORGE) Bible in Spain; or the Journeys, Adventures, and Imprisonments of an Englishman in an Attempt to circulate the Scriptures in the Peninsula. Post 8vo. 5s.

———— Zincali, or the Gypsies of Spain; their Manners, Customs, Religion, and Language. With Portrait. Post 8vo. 5s.

———— Lavengro ; The Scholar—The Gypsy—and the Priest. Post 8vo. 5s.

———— Romany Rye—a Sequel to "Lavengro." Post 8vo. 5s.

———— WILD WALES: its People, Language, and Scenery. Post 8vo. 5s.

———— Romano Lavo-Lil ; Word-Book of the Romany, or English Gypsy Language; with Specimens of their Poetry, and an account of certain Gypsyries. Post 8vo. 10s. 6d.

BRAY'S (MRS.) Life of Thomas Stothard, R.A. With Portrait and 60 Woodcuts. 4to. 21s.

———— Revolt of the Protestants in the Cevennes. With some Account of the Huguenots in the Seventeenth Century. Post 8vo. 10s. 6d.

BRITISH ASSOCIATION REPORTS. 8vo.

York and Oxford, 1831-32, 13s. 6d.
Cambridge, 1833, 12s.
Edinburgh, 1834, 15s.
Dublin, 1835, 13s. 6d.
Bristol, 1836, 12s.
Liverpool, 1837, 16s. 6d.
Newcastle, 1838, 15s.
Birmingham, 1839, 13s. 6d.
Glasgow, 1840, 15s.
Plymouth, 1841, 13s. 6d.
Manchester, 1842, 10s. 6d.
Cork, 1843, 12s.
York, 1844, 20s.
Cambridge, 1845, 12s.
Southampton, 1846, 15s.
Oxford, 1847, 18s.
Swansea, 1848, 9s.
Birmingham, 1849, 10s.
Edinburgh, 1850, 15s.
Ipswich, 1851, 16s. 6d.
Belfast, 1852, 15s.
Hull, 1853, 10s. 6d.
Liverpool, 1854, 18s.
Glasgow, 1855, 15s.
Cheltenham, 1856, 18s.
Dublin, 1857, 15s.
Leeds, 1858, 20s.
Aberdeen, 1859, 15s.
Oxford, 1860, 25s.
Manchester, 1861, 15s.
Cambridge, 1862, 20s.
Newcastle, 1863, 25s.
Bath, 1864, 18s.
Birmingham, 1865, 25s.
Nottingham, 1866, 24s.
Dundee, 1867, 26s.
Norwich, 1868, 25s.
Exeter, 1869, 22s.
Liverpool, 1870, 18s.
Edinburgh, 1871, 16s.
Brighton, 1872, 24s.

BROUGHTON'S (LORD) Journey through Albania, Turkey in Europe and Asia, to Constantinople. Illustrations. 2 Vols. 8vo. 30s.

———— Visits to Italy. 2 Vols. Post 8vo. 18s.

BROWNLOW'S (LADY) Reminiscences of a Septuagenarian. From the year 1802 to 1815. *Third Edition.* Post 8vo. 7s. 6d.

BURGON'S (REV. J. W.) Christian Gentleman ; or, Memoir of Patrick Fraser Tytler. *Second Edition.* Post 8vo. 9s.

———— Letters from Rome. Post 8vo. 12s.

BURN'S (COL.) Dictionary of Naval and Military Technical Terms, English and French—French and English. *Fourth Edition.* Crown 8vo. 15s.

BURROW'S (MONTAGU) Constitutional Progress. A Series of Lectures delivered before the University of Oxford. 2nd Edition. Post 8vo. 5s.

BUXTON'S (CHARLES) Memoirs of Sir Thomas Fowell Buxton, Bart. With Selections from his Correspondence. Portrait. 8vo. 16s. Popular Edition. Fcap. 8vo. 5s.

——— Notes of Thought. With Biographical Sketch. By Rev. LLEWELLYN DAVIES. With Portrait. Crown 8vo. 10s. 6d.

BURCKHARDT'S (DR. JACOB) Cicerone; or Art Guide to Painting in Italy. Edited by REV. DR. A. VON ZAHN, and Translated from the German by MRS. A. CLOUGH. Post 8vo. 6s.

BYRON'S (LORD) Life, Letters, and Journals. By THOMAS MOORE. Cabinet Edition. Plates. 6 Vols. Fcap. 8vo. 18s.

——— ——— and Poetical Works. Popular Edition. Portraits. 2 vols. Royal 8vo. 15s.

——— Poetical Works. Library Edition. Portrait. 6 Vols. 8vo. 45s.

——— ——— Cabinet Edition. Plates. 10 Vols. 12mo. 30s.

——— ——— Pocket Edition. 8 Vols. 24mo. 21s.

——— ——— Popular Edition. Plates. Royal 8vo. 9s.

——— ——— Pearl Edition. Crown 8vo. 2s. 6d.

——— ——— Childe Harold. With 80 Engravings. Crown 8vo. 12s.

——— ——— ——— 16mo. 2s. 6d.

——— ——— ——— Vignettes. 16mo. 1s.

——— ——— ——— Portrait. 16mo. 6d.

——— ——— Tales and Poems. 24mo. 2s. 6d.

——— ——— Miscellaneous. 2 Vols. 24mo. 5s.

——— ——— Dramas and Plays. 2 Vols. 24mo. 5s.

——— ——— Don Juan and Beppo. 2 Vols. 24mo. 5s.

——— ——— Beauties. Portrait. Fcap. 8vo. 3s. 6d.

BURR'S (G. D.) Instructions in Practical Surveying, Topographical Plan Drawing, and on sketching ground without Instruments. Fourth Edition. Woodcuts. Post 8vo. 6s.

BUTTMAN'S LEXILOGUS; a Critical Examination of the Meaning of numerous Greek Words, chiefly in Homer and Hesiod. By Rev. J. R. FISHLAKE. Fifth Edition. 8vo. 12s.

——— IRREGULAR GREEK VERBS. With all the Tenses extant—their Formation, Meaning, and Usage, with Notes, by Rev. J. R. FISHLAKE. Fifth Edition. Post 8vo. 6s.

CALLCOTT'S (LADY) Little Arthur's History of England. New Edition, brought down to 1872. With Woodcuts. Fcap. 8vo. 2s. 6d.

CARNARVON'S (LORD) Portugal, Gallicia, and the Basque Provinces. Third Edition. Post 8vo. 3s. 6d.

——— Reminiscences of Athens and the Morea. With Map. Crown 8vo. 7s. 6d.

——— Recollections of the Druses of Lebanon. With Notes on their Religion. Third Edition. Post 8vo. 5s. 6d.

CASTLEREAGH (THE) DESPATCHES, from the commencement of the official career of Viscount Castlereagh to the close of his life. 12 Vols. 8vo. 14s. each.

CAMPBELL'S (LORD) Lord Chancellors and Keepers of the
Great Seal of England. From the Earliest Times to the Death of Lord
Eldon in 1838. *Fifth Edition.* 10 Vols. Crown 8vo. 6s. each.

———— Chief Justices of England. From the Norman
Conquest to the Death of Lord Tenterden. *Third Edition.* 4 Vols.
Crown 8vo. 6s. each.

———— Lords Lyndhurst and Brougham. 8vo. 16s.

———— Shakspeare's Legal Acquirements. 8vo. 5s. 6d.

———— Lord Bacon. Fcap. 8vo. 2s. 6d.

———— (SIR NEIL) Account of Napoleon at Fontainebleau
and Elba. Being a Journal of Occurrences and Notes of his Conversations, &c. Portrait. 8vo. 15s.

———— (GEORGE) India as it may be: an Outline of a
proposed Government and Policy. 8vo.

———— (THOS.) Essay on English Poetry. With Short
Lives of the British Poets. Post 8vo. 3s. 6d.

CATHCART'S (SIR GEORGE) Commentaries on the War in Russia
and Germany, 1812-13. Plans. 8vo. 14s.

CAVALCASELLE AND CROWE'S History of Painting in
Italy, from the 2nd to the 16th Century. With Illustrations. 5 Vols.
8vo. 21s. each.

———— Early Flemish Painters, their Lives and
Works. Illustrations. Post 8vo. 10s. 6d.; or Large Paper, 8vo. 15s.

CHILD'S (G. CHAPLIN, M.D.) Benedicite; or, Song of the Three
Children; being Illustrations of the Power, Beneficence, and Design
manifested by the Creator in his works. 10th Thousand. Post 8vo. 6s.

CHISHOLM'S (Mrs.) Perils of the Polar Seas; Stories of Arctic
Adventure for Children. Illustrations. Post 8vo. 6s.

CHURTON'S (ARCHDEACON) Gongora. An Historical Essay on the
Age of Philip III. and IV. of Spain. With Translations. Portrait.
2 Vols. Small 8vo. 12s.

———— New Testament. Edited with a Plain Practical
Commentary for the use of Families and General Readers. With 100
Panoramic and other Views, from Sketches and Photographs made on
the Spot. 2 vols. 8vo. 21s.

CICERO'S LIFE AND TIMES. His Character as a Statesman,
Orator, and Friend, with a Selection from his Correspondence and Orations. By WILLIAM FORSYTH, M.P. *Third Edition.* With Illustrations. 8vo. 10s. 6d.

CLARK'S (SIR JAMES) Memoir of Dr. John Conolly. Comprising
a Sketch of the Treatment of the Insane in Europe and America. With
Portrait. Post 8vo. 10s. 6d.

CLIVE'S (LORD) Life. By REV. G. R. GLEIG. Post 8vo. 3s. 6d.

CLODE'S (C. M.) Military Forces of the Crown; their Administration and Government. 2 Vols. 8vo. 21s. each.

———— Administration of Justice under Military and Martial
Law, as applicable to the Army, Navy, Marine, and Auxiliary Forces.
2nd Edition. 8vo. 12s.

COLCHESTER (THE) PAPERS. The Diary and Correspondence
of Charles Abbott, Lord Colchester, Speaker of the House of Commons,
1802-1817. Portrait. 3 Vols. 8vo. 42s.

LIST OF WORKS

CHURCH (The) & THE AGE. Essays on the Principles and Present Position of the Anglican Church. 2 vols. 8vo. 26s. Contents:—

Vol. I.
Anglican Principles.—Dean Hook.
Modern Religious Thought.—Bishop of Gloucester and Bristol.
State, Church, and Synods.—Rev. Dr. Irons.
Religious Use of Taste.—Rev. R. St. John Tyrwhitt.
Place of the Laity.—Professor Burrows.
Parish Priest.—Rev. Walsham How.
Divines of 16th and 17th Centuries. —Rev. A. W. Haddan.
Liturgies and Ritual, Rev. M. F. Sadler.
Church & Education.—Canon Barry.
Indian Missions.— Sir Bartle Frere.
Church and the People.—Rev. W. D. Maclagan.
Conciliation and Comprehension.— Rev. Dr. Weir.

Vol. II.
Church and Pauperism.—Earl Nelson.
American Church.—Bishop of Western New York.
Church and Science. — Prebendary Clark.
Ecclesiastical Law.—Isambard Brunel.
Church & National Education.— Canon Norris.
Church and Universities.—John G. Talbot.
Toleration.—Dean Cowie.
Eastern Church and Anglican Communion.—Rev. Geo. Williams.
A Disestablished Church.—Dean of Cashel.
Christian Tradition.—Rev. Dr. Irons.
Dogma.—Rev. Dr. Weir.
Parochial Councils. — Archdeacon Chapman.

COLERIDGE'S (SAMUEL TAYLOR) Table-Talk. Portrait. 12mo. 3s. 6d.

COLLINGWOOD'S (CUTHBERT) Rambles of a Naturalist on the Shores and Waters of the China Sea. Being Observations in Natural History during a Voyage to China, &c. With Illustrations. 8vo. 16s.

COLONIAL LIBRARY. [See Home and Colonial Library.]

COOK'S (Canon) Sermons Preached at Lincoln's Inn. 8vo. 9s.

COOKERY (MODERN DOMESTIC). Founded on Principles of Economy and Practical Knowledge, and adapted for Private Families. By a Lady. Woodcuts. Fcap. 8vo. 5s.

COOPER'S (T. T.) Travels of a Pioneer of Commerce on an Overland Journey from China towards India. Illustrations. 8vo. 16s.

CORNWALLIS (The) Papers and Correspondence during the American War,—Administrations in India,—Union with Ireland, and Peace of Amiens. *Second Edition.* 3 Vols. 8vo. 63s.

COWPER'S (Countess) Diary while Lady of the Bedchamber to Caroline Princess of Wales, 1714—20. Edited by Hon. SPENCER COWPER. *Second Edition.* Portrait. 8vo. 10s. 6d.

CRABBE'S (Rev. George) Life and Poetical Works. With Illustrations. Royal 8vo. 7s.

CROKER'S (J. W.) Progressive Geography for Children. *Fifth Edition.* 18mo. 1s. 6d.

———— Stories for Children, Selected from the History of England. *Fifteenth Edition.* Woodcuts. 16mo. 2s. 6d.

———— Boswell's Life of Johnson. Including the Tour to the Hebrides. *Library Edition.* Portraits. 4 vols. 8vo. *In Preparation.*

———— Essays on the Early Period of the French Revolution. 8vo. 15s.

———— Historical Essay on the Guillotine. Fcap. 8vo. 1s.

CUMMING'S (R. Gordon) Five Years of a Hunter's Life in the Far Interior of South Africa. *Sixth Edition.* Woodcuts. Post 8vo. 6s.

CROWE'S and CAVALCASELLE'S Lives of the Early Flemish Painters. Woodcuts. Post 8vo, 10s. 6d.; or Large Paper, 8vo, 15s.

—————— History of Painting in Italy, from 2nd to 16th Century. Derived from Researches into the Works of Art in that Country. With 100 Illustrations. 5 Vols. 8vo. 21s. each.

CUNYNGHAME'S (Sir Arthur) Travels in the Eastern Caucasus, on the Caspian, and Black Seas, in Daghestan and the Frontiers of Persia and Turkey. With Map and Illustrations. 8vo. 18s.

CURTIUS' (Professor) Student's Greek Grammar, for the Upper Forms. Edited by Dr. Wm. Smith. *Third Edition.* Post 8vo. 6s.

—————— Elucidations of the above Grammar. Translated by Evelyn Abbot. Post 8vo. 7s. 6d.

—————— Smaller Greek Grammar for the Middle and Lower Forms. Abridged from the larger work. 12mo. 3s. 6d.

—————— Accidence of the Greek Language. Extracted from the above work. 12mo. 2s. 6d.

—————— Principles of Greek Etymology. Translated by A. S. Wilkins, M.A., and E. B. England, B.A. 8vo. *Nearly Ready.*

CURZON'S (Hon. Robert) Armenia and Erzeroum. A Year on the Frontiers of Russia, Turkey, and Persia. *Third Edition.* Woodcuts. Post 8vo. 7s. 6d.

—————— Visits to the Monasteries of the Levant. *Fifth Edition.* Illustrations. Post 8vo. 7s. 6d.

CUST'S (General) Lives of the Warriors of the 17th Century—The Thirty Years' War. 2 Vols. 16s. Civil Wars of France and England. 2 Vols. 16s. Commanders of Fleets and Armies before the Enemy. 2 Vols. 18s.

—————— Annals of the Wars—18th & 19th Century, 1700—1815. With Maps. 9 Vols. Post 8vo. 5s. each.

DAVIS'S (Nathan) Ruined Cities of Numidia and Carthaginia. Illustrations. 8vo. 16s.

DAVY'S (Sir Humphry) Consolations in Travel; or, Last Days of a Philosopher. *Seventh Edition.* Woodcuts. Fcap. 8vo. 3s 6d.

—————— Salmonia; or, Days of Fly Fishing. *Fifth Edition.* Woodcuts. Fcap. 8vo. 3s. 6d.

DARWIN'S (Charles) Journal of Researches into the Natural History of the Countries visited during a Voyage round the World. *Eleventh Thousand.* Post 8vo. 9s.

—————— Origin of Species by Means of Natural Selection; or, the Preservation of Favoured Races in the Struggle for Life. *Sixth Edition.* Post 8vo. 7s. 6d.

—————— Variation of Animals and Plants under Domestication. With Illustrations. 2 Vols. 8vo. 28s.

—————— Descent of Man, and on Selection in Relation to Sex. With Illustrations. 2 Vols. Crown 8vo. 24s.

—————— Expressions of the Emotions in Man and Animals. With Illustrations. Crown 8vo. 12s.

—————— Fertilization of Orchids through Insect Agency, and as to the good of Intercrossing. Woodcuts. Post 8vo. 9s.

—————— Fact and Argument for Darwin. By Fritz Muller. With numerous Illustrations and Additions by the Author. Translated from the German by W. S. Dallas. Woodcuts. Post 8vo. 6s.

DELEPIERRE'S (Octave) History of Flemish Literature. 8vo. 9s.
—————— Historic Difficulties & Contested Events. Post 8vo. 6s.
DENISON'S (E. B.) Life of Bishop Lonsdale. With Selections from his Writings. With Portrait. Crown 8vo. 10s. 6d.
DERBY'S (Earl of) Iliad of Homer rendered into English Blank Verse. 7th Edition. 2 Vols. Post 8vo. 10s.
DE ROS'S (Lord) Memorials of the Tower of London. Second Edition. With Illustrations. Crown 8vo. 12s.
—————— Young Officer's Companion; or, Essays on Military Duties and Qualities: with Examples and Illustrations from History. Post 8vo. 9s.
DEUTSCH'S (Emanuel) Talmud, Islam, The Targums and other Literary Remains. 8vo. 12s.
DOG-BREAKING; the Most Expeditious, Certain, and Easy Method, whether great excellence or only mediocrity be required. With a Few Hints for those who Love the Dog and the Gun. By Lieut.-Gen. Hutchinson. *Fifth Edition*. With 40 Woodcuts. Crown 8vo. 9s.
DOMESTIC MODERN COOKERY. Founded on Principles of Economy and Practical Knowledge, and adapted for Private Families. Woodcuts. Fcap. 8vo. 5s.
DOUGLAS'S (Sir Howard) Life and Adventures. Portrait. 8vo. 15s.
—————— Theory and Practice of Gunnery. Plates. 8vo. 21s.
—————— Construction of Bridges and the Passage of Rivers, in Military Operations. Plates. 8vo. 21s.
—————— (Wm.) Horse-Shoeing; As it Is, and As it Should be. Illustrations. Post 8vo. 7s. 6d.
DRAKE'S (Sir Francis) Life, Voyages, and Exploits, by Sea and Land. By John Barrow. *Third Edition*. Post 8vo. 2s.
DRINKWATER'S (John) History of the Siege of Gibraltar, 1779-1783. With a Description and Account of that Garrison from the Earliest Periods. Post 8vo. 2s.
DUCANGE'S MEDIÆVAL LATIN-ENGLISH DICTIONARY. Translated by Rev. E. A. Dayman, M.A. Small 4to. (*In preparation*.)
DU CHAILLU'S (Paul B.) EQUATORIAL AFRICA, with Accounts of the Gorilla, the Nest-building Ape, Chimpanzee, Crocodile, &c. Illustrations. 8vo. 21s.
—————— Journey to Ashango Land; and Further Penetration into Equatorial Africa. Illustrations. 8vo. 21s.
DUFFERIN'S (Lord) Letters from High Latitudes; an Account of a Yacht Voyage to Iceland, Jan Mayen, and Spitzbergen. *Fifth Edition*. Woodcuts. Post 8vo. 7s. 6d.
DUNCAN'S (Major) History of the Royal Artillery. Compiled from the Original Records. *Second Edition*. With Portraits. 2 Vols. 8vo. 30s.
DYER'S (Thos. H.) History of Modern Europe, from the taking of Constantinople by the Turks to the close of the War in the Crimea. With Index. 4 Vols. 8vo. 42s.
EASTLAKE'S (Sir Charles) Contributions to the Literature of the Fine Arts. With Memoir of the Author, and Selections from his Correspondence. By Lady Eastlake. 2 Vols. 8vo. 24s.
EDWARDS' (W. H.) Voyage up the River Amazons, including a Visit to Para. Post 8vo. 2s.

ELDON'S (LORD) Public and Private Life, with Selections from his Correspondence and Diaries. By HORACE TWISS. *Third Edition.* Portrait. 2 Vols. Post 8vo. 21s.

ELGIN'S (LORD) Letters and Journals. Edited by THEODORE WALROND. With Preface by Dean Stanley. *Second Edition.* 8vo. 14s.

ELLESMERE'S (LORD) Two Sieges of Vienna by the Turks. Translated from the German. Post 8vo. 2s.

ELLIS'S (W.) Madagascar, including a Journey to the Capital, with notices of Natural History and the People. Woodcuts. 8vo. 16s.

—————— Madagascar Revisited. Setting forth the Persecutions and Heroic Sufferings of the Native Christians. Illustrations. 8vo. 16s.

—————— Memoir. By HIS SON. With his Character and Work. By REV. HENRY ALLON, D.D. Portrait. 8vo. 10s. 6d.

—————— (ROBINSON) Poems and Fragments of Catullus. 16mo. 5s.

ELPHINSTONE'S (HON. MOUNTSTUART) History of India—the Hindoo and Mahomedan Periods. *Sixth Edition.* Map. 8vo. 18s.

—————— (H. W.) Patterns for Turning; Comprising Elliptical and other Figures cut on the Lathe without the use of any Ornamental Chuck. With 70 Illustrations. Small 4to. 15s.

ENGEL'S (CARL) Music of the Most Ancient Nations; particularly of the Assyrians, Egyptians, and Hebrews; with Special Reference to the Discoveries in Western Asia and in Egypt. *Second Edition.* With 100 Illustrations. 8vo. 10s. 6d.

ENGLAND. See CALLCOTT, CROKER, HUME, MARKHAM, SMITH, and STANHOPE.

ENGLISHWOMAN IN AMERICA. Post 8vo. 10s. 6d.

ESSAYS ON CATHEDRALS. With an Introduction. By DEAN HOWSON. 8vo. 12s.

CONTENTS.

Recollections of a Dean.—Bishop of Carlisle.
Cathedral Canons and their Work.—Canon Norris.
Cathedrals in Ireland, Past and Future.—Dean of Cashel.
Cathedrals in their Missionary Aspect.—A. J. B. Beresford Hope.
Cathedral Foundations in Relation to Religious Thought.—Canon Westcott.
Cathedral Churches of the Old Foundation.—Edward A. Freeman.
Welsh Cathedrals.—Canon Perowne.
Education of Choristers.—Sir F. Gore Ouseley.
Cathedral Schools.—Canon Durham.
Cathedral Reform.—Chancellor Massingberd.
Relation of the Chapter to the Bishop. Chancellor Benson.
Architecture of the Cathedral Churches.—Canon Venables.

ETHNOLOGICAL SOCIETY'S TRANSACTIONS. Vols. I. to VI. 8vo.

ELZE'S (KARL) Life of Lord Byron. With a Critical Essay on his Place in Literature. Translated from the German, and Edited with Notes. With Original Portrait and Facsimile. 8vo. 16s.

FAMILY RECEIPT-BOOK. A Collection of a Thousand Valuable and Useful Receipts. Fcap. 8vo. 5s. 6d.

FARRAR'S (A. S.) Critical History of Free Thought in reference to the Christian Religion. 8vo. 16s.

—————— (F. W.) Origin of Language, based on Modern Researches. Fcap. 8vo. 5s.

FERGUSSON'S (James) History of Architecture in all Countries from the Earliest Times. Vols.I.and II. With 1200 Illustrations. 8vo.
—————— Modern Styles of Architecture. With 330 Illustrations. Medium 8vo. 31s. 6d.
—————— Rude Stone Monuments in all Countries; their Age and Uses. With 230 Illustrations. Medium 8vo. 24s.
—————— Holy Sepulchre and the Temple at Jerusalem. Woodcuts. 8vo. 7s. 6d.

FLEMING'S (Professor) Student's Manual of Moral Philosophy. With Quotations and References. Post 8vo. 7s. 6d.

FLOWER GARDEN. By Rev. Thos. James. Fcap. 8vo. 1s.

FONNEREAU'S (T. G.) Diary of a Dutiful Son. 16mo. 4s. 6d.

FORD'S (Richard) Gatherings from Spain. Post 8vo. 3s. 6d.

FORSYTH'S (William) Life and Times of Cicero. With Selections from his Correspondence and Orations. *Third Edition*. Illustrations. 8vo. 10s. 6d.
—————— Hortensius; an Historical Essay on the Office and Duties of an Advocate. *Second Edition*. 8vo.
—————— History of Ancient Manuscripts. Post 8vo. 2s. 6d.
—————— Novels and Novelists of the 18th Century, in Illustration of the Manners and Morals of the Age. Post 8vo. 10s. 6d.

FORTUNE'S (Robert) Narrative of Two Visits to the Tea Countries of China, 1843-52. *Third Edition*. Woodcuts. 2 Vols. Post 8vo. 18s.

FOSS' (Edward) Biographia Juridica, or Biographical Dictionary of the Judges of England, from the Conquest to the Present Time, 1066-1870. (800 pp.) Medium 8vo. 21s.
—————— Tabulæ Curiales; or, Tables of the Superior Courts of Westminster Hall. Showing the Judges who sat in them from 1066 to 1864. 8vo. 10s. 6d.

FRANCE. *** See Markham, Smith, Students.

FRENCH (The) in Algiers; The Soldier of the Foreign Legion— and the Prisoners of Abd-el-Kadir. Translated by Lady Duff Gordon. Post 8vo. 2s.

FRERE'S (Sir Bartle) Indian Missions. *Third Edition*. Small 8vo. 2s. 6d.
—————— Eastern Africa as a field for Missionary Labour. With Map. Crown 8vo. 5s.
—————— Bengal Famine. How it will be Met and How to Prevent Future Famines in India. With Maps. Crown 8vo. 5s.
—————— (M.) Old Deccan Days; or Fairy Legends Current in Southern India. With Notes, by Sir Bartle Frere. With Illustrations. Fcap. 8vo. 6s.

GALTON'S (Francis) Art of Travel; or, Hints on the Shifts and Contrivances available in Wild Countries. *Fifth Edition*. Woodcuts. Post 8vo. 7s. 6d.

GEOGRAPHICAL SOCIETY'S JOURNAL. (*Published Yearly*.)

GEORGE'S (Ernest) Mosel; a Series of Twenty Etchings, with Descriptive Letterpress. Imperial 4to. 42s.

GERMANY (History of). See Markham.

GIBBON'S (Edward) History of the Decline and Fall of the Roman Empire. Edited by Milman and Guizot. *A New Edition*. Edited, with Notes, by Dr. Wm. Smith. Maps. 8 Vols. 8vo. 60s.
—————— (The Student's Gibbon); Being an Epitome of the above work, incorporating the Researches of Recent Commentators. By Dr. Wm. Smith. Woodcuts. Post 8vo. 7s. 6d.

GIFFARD'S (EDWARD) Deeds of Naval Daring; or, Anecdotes of the British Navy. Fcap. 8vo. 3s. 6d.

GLADSTONE'S (W. E.) Financial Statements of 1853, 1860, 63–65. 8vo. 12s.

GLEIG'S (G. R.) Campaigns of the British Army at Washington and New Orleans. Post 8vo. 2s.

—— Story of the Battle of Waterloo. Post 8vo. 3s. 6d.

—— Narrative of Sale's Brigade in Affghanistan. Post 8vo. 2s.

—— Life of Lord Clive. Post 8vo. 3s. 6d.

———————— Sir Thomas Munro. Post 8vo. 3s. 6d.

GOLDSMITH'S (OLIVER) Works. Edited with Notes by PETER CUNNINGHAM. Vignettes. 4 Vols. 8vo. 30s.

GORDON'S (SIR ALEX.) Sketches of German Life, and Scenes from the War of Liberation. Post 8vo. 3s. 6d.

———— (LADY DUFF) Amber-Witch: A Trial for Witchcraft. Post 8vo. 2s.

———— French in Algiers. 1. The Soldier of the Foreign Legion. 2. The Prisoners of Abd-el-Kadir. Post 8vo. 2s.

GRAMMARS. See CURTIUS; HALL; HUTTON; KING EDWARD; MATTHIÆ; MAETZNER; SMITH.

GREECE. See GROTE—SMITH—Student.

GREY'S (EARL) Correspondence with King William IVth and Sir Herbert Taylor, from 1830 to 1832. 2 Vols. 8vo. 30s.

———— Parliamentary Government and Reform; with Suggestions for the Improvement of our Representative System. Second Edition. 8vo. 9s.

GRUNER'S (LEWIS) Terra-Cotta Architecture of North Italy, from careful Drawings and Restorations. With Illustrations, engraved and printed in Colours. Small folio. 5l. 5s.

GUIZOT'S (M.) Meditations on Christianity, and on the Religious Questions of the Day. Part I. The Essence. Part II. Present State. Part III. Relation to Society and Opinion. 3 Vols. Post 8vo. 30s.

GROTE'S (GEORGE) History of Greece. From the Earliest Times to the close of the generation contemporary with the death of Alexander the Great. Library Edition. Portrait, Maps, and Plans. 10 Vols. 8vo. 120s. Cabinet Edition. Portrait and Plans. 12 Vols. Post 8vo. 6s. each.

———— PLATO, and other Companions of Socrates. 3 Vols. 8vo. 45s.

———— ARISTOTLE. 2 Vols. 8vo. 32s.

———— Minor Works. With Critical Remarks on his Intellectual Character, Writings, and Speeches. By ALEX. BAIN. LL.D. Portrait. 8vo. 14s.

———— Personal Life. Compiled from Family Documents, Private Memoranda, and Original Letters to and from Various Friends. By Mrs. Grote. Portrait. 8vo. 12s.

———— (MRS.) Memoir of Ary Scheffer. Portrait. 8vo. 8s. 6d.

HALL'S (T. D.) School Manual of English Grammar. With Copious Exercises. 12mo. 3s. 6d.

———— Primary English Grammar for Elementary Schools. 16mo. 1s.

———— Child's First Latin Book, including a Systematic Treatment of the New Pronunciation, and a full Praxis of Nouns, Adjectives, and Pronouns. 16mo. 1s. 6d.

LIST OF WORKS

HALLAM'S (HENRY) Constitutional History of England, from the Accession of Henry the Seventh to the Death of George the Second. *Library Edition.* 3 Vols. 8vo. 30s. *Cabinet Edition,* 3 Vols. Post 8vo. 12s.
—— Student's Edition of the above work. Edited by WM. SMITH, D.C.L. Post 8vo. 7s. 6d.
—— History of Europe during the Middle Ages. *Library Edition.* 3 Vols. 8vo. 30s. *Cabinet Edition,* 3 Vols. Post 8vo. 12s.
—— Student's Edition of the above work. Edited by WM. SMITH, D.C.L. Post 8vo. 7s. 6d.
—— Literary History of Europe, during the 15th, 16th and 17th Centuries. *Library Edition.* 3 Vols. 8vo. 36s. *Cabinet Edition.* 4 Vols. Post 8vo. 16s.
—— (ARTHUR) Literary Remains; in Verse and Prose. Portrait. Fcap. 8vo. 3s. 6d.

HAMILTON'S (GEN. SIR F. W.) History of the Grenadier Guards. From Original Documents in the Rolls' Records, War Office, Regimental Records, &c. With Illustrations. 3 Vols. 8vo.

HANNAH'S (REV. DR.) Divine and Human Elements in Holy Scripture. 8vo. 10s. 6d.

HART'S ARMY LIST. (*Published Quarterly and Annually.*)

HAY'S (SIR J. H. DRUMMOND) Western Barbary, its Wild Tribes and Savage Animals. Post 8vo. 2s.

HEAD'S (SIR FRANCIS) Royal Engineer. Illustrations. 8vo. 12s.
—— Life of Sir John Burgoyne. Post 8vo. 1s.
—— Rapid Journeys across the Pampas. Post 8vo. 2s.
—— Bubbles from the Brunnen of Nassau. Illustrations. Post 8vo. 7s. 6d.
—— Emigrant. Fcap. 8vo. 2s. 6d.
—— Stokers and Pokers; or, the London and North Western Railway. Post 8vo. 2s.
—— (SIR EDMUND) Shall and Will; or, Future Auxiliary Verbs. Fcap. 8vo. 4s.

HEBER'S (BISHOP) Journals in India. 2 Vols. Post 8vo. 7s.
—— Poetical Works. Portrait. Fcap. 8vo. 3s. 6d.
—— Hymns adapted to the Church Service. 16mo. 1s. 6d.

HERODOTUS. A New English Version. Edited, with Notes and Essays, historical, ethnographical, and geographical, by CANON RAWLINSON, assisted by SIR HENRY RAWLINSON and SIR J. G. WILKINSON. *Second Edition.* Maps and Woodcuts. 4 Vols. 8vo. 48s.

HATHERLEY'S (LORD) Continuity of Scripture, as Declared by the Testimony of our Lord and of the Evangelists and Apostles. *Fourth Edition.* 6vo. 6s. *Popular Edition.* Post 8vo. 2s. 6d.

HESSEY (REV. DR.). Sunday—Its Origin, History, and Present Obligations. Post 8vo. 9s.

HOLLWAY'S (J. G.) Month in Norway. Fcap. 8vo. 2s.

HONEY BEE. By REV. THOMAS JAMES. Fcap. 8vo. 1s.

HOOK'S (DEAN) Church Dictionary. *Tenth Edition.* 8vo. 16s.
—— (THEODORE) Life. By J. G. LOCKHART. Fcap. 8vo. 1s.

HOPE'S (T. C.) ARCHITECTURE OF AHMEDABAD, with Historical Sketch and Architectural Notes. With Maps, Photographs, and Woodcuts. 4to. 5l. 5s.

FOREIGN HANDBOOKS.

HAND-BOOK—TRAVEL-TALK. English, French, German, and Italian. 18mo. 3s. 6d.

———— HOLLAND,—BELGIUM, and the Rhine to Mayence. Map and Plans. Post 8vo. 6s

———— NORTH GERMANY,—PRUSSIA, SAXONY, HANOVER, and the Rhine from Mayence to Switzerland. Map and Plans. Post 8vo. 6s.

———— SOUTH GERMANY, Bavaria, Austria, Styria, Salzburg, the Austrian and Bavarian Alps, the Tyrol, Hungary, and the Danube, from Ulm to the Black Sea. Map. Post 8vo. 10s.

———— KNAPSACK GUIDE TO THE TYROL. 16mo. 6s.

———— PAINTING. German, Flemish, and Dutch Schools. Illustrations. 2 Vols. Post 8vo. 24s.

———— LIVES OF EARLY FLEMISH PAINTERS. By CROWE and CAVALCASELLE. Illustrations. Post 8vo. 10s. 6d.

———— SWITZERLAND, Alps of Savoy, and Piedmont. Maps. Post 8vo. 10s.

———— FRANCE, Normandy, Brittany, the French Alps, the Rivers Loire, Seine, Rhone, and Garonne, Dauphiné, Provence, and the Pyrenees. Maps. 2 Parts. Post 8vo. 12s.

———— CORSICA and SARDINIA. Maps. Post 8vo. 4s.

———— ALGERIA. Map. Post 8vo. 6s.

———— PARIS, and its Environs. Map. 16mo. 3s. 6d.
„ MURRAY'S PLAN OF PARIS, mounted on canvas. 3s. 6d.

———— SPAIN, Madrid, The Castiles, The Basque Provinces, Leon, The Asturias, Galicia, Estremadura, Andalusia, Ronda, Granada, Murcia, Valencia, Catalonia, Aragon, Navarre, The Balearic Islands, &c. &c. Maps. 2 Vols. Post 8vo. 24s.

———— PORTUGAL, LISBON, Porto, Cintra, Mafra, &c. Map. Post 8vo. 9s.

———— NORTH ITALY, Piedmont, Liguria, Venetia, Lombardy, Parma, Modena, and Romagna. Map. Post 8vo.

———— CENTRAL ITALY, Lucca, Tuscany, Florence, The Marches, Umbria, and the Patrimony of St. Peter's. Map. Post 8vo.

———— ROME AND ITS ENVIRONS. Map. Post 8vo. 10s.

———— SOUTH ITALY, Two Sicilies, Naples, Pompeii, Herculaneum, and Vesuvius. Map. Post 8vo. 10s.

———— KNAPSACK GUIDE TO ITALY. 16mo. 6s.

———— SICILY, Palermo, Messina, Catania, Syracuse, Etna, and the Ruins of the Greek Temples. Map. Post 8vo. 12s.

———— PAINTING. The Italian Schools. Illustrations. 2 Vols. Post 8vo.

———— LIVES OF ITALIAN PAINTERS, FROM CIMABUE to BASSANO. By Mrs. JAMESON. Portraits. Post 8vo. 12s.

———— RUSSIA, ST. PETERSBURGH, MOSCOW, POLAND, and FINLAND. Maps. Post 8vo. 15s.

———— DENMARK, SWEDEN, and NORWAY. Maps. Post 8vo. 15s.

———— KNAPSACK GUIDE TO NORWAY. Map. 6s.

LIST OF WORKS

HAND-BOOK—GREECE, the Ionian Islands, Continental Greece, Athens, the Peloponnesus, the Islands of the Ægean Sea, Albania, Thessaly, and Macedonia. Maps. Post 8vo. 15s.
—————— TURKEY IN ASIA—Constantinople, the Bosphorus, Dardanelles, Brousa, Plain of Troy, Crete, Cyprus, Smyrna, Ephesus, the Seven Churches, Coasts of the Black Sea, Armenia, Mesopotamia, &c. Maps. Post 8vo. 15s.
—————— EGYPT, including Descriptions of the Course of the Nile through Egypt and Nubia, Alexandria, Cairo, and Thebes, the Suez Canal, the Pyramids, the Peninsula of Sinai, the Oases, the Fyoom, &c. Map. Post 8vo. 15s
—————— HOLY LAND—Syria Palestine, Peninsula of Sinai, Edom, Syrian Desert, &c. Maps. 2 vols. Post 8vo. 24s.
—————— INDIA—Bombay and Madras. Map. 2 Vols. Post 8vo. 12s. each.

ENGLISH HANDBOOKS.

HAND-BOOK—MODERN LONDON. Map. 16mo. 3s. 6d.
—————— ESSEX, CAMBRIDGE, SUFFOLK, AND NORFOLK. Chelmsford, Colchester, Maldon, Cambridge, Ely, Newmarket, Bury, Ipswich, Woodbridge, Felixstowe, Lowestoft, Norwich, Yarmouth, Cromer, &c. Map and Plans. Post 8vo. 12s.
—————— CATHEDRALS of Oxford, Peterborough, Norwich, Ely, and Lincoln. With 90 Illustrations. Crown 8vo. 18s.
—————— KENT AND SUSSEX, Canterbury, Dover, Ramsgate, Sheerness, Rochester, Chatham, Woolwich, Brighton, Chichester, Worthing, Hastings, Lewes, Arundel, &c. Map. Post 8vo. 10s.
—————— SURREY AND HANTS, Kingston, Croydon, Reigate, Guildford, Dorking, Boxhill, Winchester, Southampton, New Forest, Portsmouth, and Isle of Wight. Maps. Post 8vo. 10s.
—————— BERKS, BUCKS, AND OXON, Windsor, Eton, Reading, Aylesbury, Uxbridge, Wycombe, Henley, the City and University of Oxford, Blenheim, and the Descent of the Thames. Map. Post 8vo. 7s. 6d.
—————— WILTS, DORSET, AND SOMERSET, Salisbury, Chippenham, Weymouth, Sherborne, Wells, Bath, Bristol, Taunton, &c. Map. Post 8vo. 10s.
—————— DEVON AND CORNWALL, Exeter, Ilfracombe, Linton, Sidmouth, Dawlish, Teignmouth, Plymouth, Devonport, Torquay, Launceston, Truro, Penzance, Falmouth, the Lizard, Land's End, &c. Maps. Post 8vo. 12s.
—————— CATHEDRALS of Winchester, Salisbury, Exeter, Wells, Chichester, Rochester, Canterbury. With 110 Illustrations. 2 Vols. Crown 8vo. 24s.
—————— GLOUCESTER, HEREFORD, and WORCESTER, Cirencester, Cheltenham, Stroud, Tewkesbury, Leominster, Ross, Malvern, Kidderminster, Dudley, Bromsgrove, Evesham. Map. Post 8vo. 9s.
—————— CATHEDRALS of Bristol, Gloucester, Hereford, Worcester, and Lichfield. With 50 Illustrations. Crown 8vo. 16s.
—————— NORTH WALES, Bangor, Carnarvon, Beaumaris, Snowdon, Llanberis, Dolgelly, Cader Idris, Conway, &c. Map. Post 8vo.
—————— SOUTH WALES, Monmouth, Llandaff, Merthyr, Vale of Neath, Pembroke, Carmarthen, Tenby, Swansea, and The Wye, &c. Map. Post 8vo. 7s.

HAND-BOOK—CATHEDRALS OF BANGOR, ST. ASAPH,
Llandaff, and St. David's. With Illustrations. Post 8vo. 15s.

—————— DERBY, NOTTS, LEICESTER, STAFFORD,
Matlock, Bakewell, Chatsworth, The Peak, Buxton, Hardwick, Dove
Dale, Ashborne, Southwell, Mansfield, Retford, Burton, Belvoir, Melton
Mowbray, Wolverhampton, Lichfield, Walsall, Tamworth. Map.
Post 8vo.

—————— SHROPSHIRE, CHESHIRE AND LANCASHIRE
—Shrewsbury, Ludlow, Bridgnorth, Oswestry, Chester, Crewe, Alderley,
Stockport, Birkenhead, Warrington, Bury, Manchester, Liverpool,
Burnley, Clitheroe, Bolton, Blackburn, Wigan, Preston, Rochdale,
Lancaster. Southport, Blackpool, &c. Map. Post 8vo. 10s.

—————— YORKSHIRE, Doncaster, Hull, Selby, Beverley,
Scarborough, Whitby, Harrogate, Ripon, Leeds, Wakefield, Bradford,
Halifax, Huddersfield, Sheffield. Map and Plans. Post 8vo.

—————— CATHEDRALS of York, Ripon, Durham, Carlisle,
Chester, and Manchester. With 60 Illustrations. 2 Vols. Crown 8vo.
21s.

—————— DURHAM AND NORTHUMBERLAND, New-
castle, Darlington, Gateshead, Bishop Auckland, Stockton, Hartlepool,
Sunderland, Shields, Berwick-on-Tweed, Morpeth, Tynemouth, Cold-
stream, Alnwick, &c. Map. Post 8vo. 9s.

—————— WESTMORLAND AND CUMBERLAND—Lan-
caster, Furness Abbey, Ambleside, Kendal, Windermere, Coniston,
Keswick, Grasmere, Ulswater, Carlisle, Cockermouth, Penrith, Appleby.
Map. Post 8vo. 6s.

*** MURRAY'S MAP OF THE LAKE DISTRICT, on canvas. 3s. 6d.

—————— SCOTLAND, Edinburgh, Melrose, Kelso, Glasgow,
Dumfries, Ayr, Stirling, Arran, The Clyde, Oban, Inverary, Loch
Lomond, Loch Katrine and Trossachs, Caledonian Canal, Inverness,
Perth, Dundee, Aberdeen, Braemar, Skye, Caithness, Ross, Suther-
land, &c. Maps and Plans. Post 8vo. 9s.

—————— IRELAND, Dublin, Belfast, Donegal, Galway,
Wexford, Cork, Limerick, Waterford, Killarney, Munster, &c. Maps.
Post 8vo. 12s.

—————— FAMILIAR QUOTATIONS. From English
Authors. Third Edition. Fcap. 8vo. 5s.

HORACE; a New Edition of the Text. Edited by DEAN MILMAN.
With 100 Woodcuts. Crown 8vo. 7s. 6d.

—————— Life of. By DEAN MILMAN. Illustrations. 8vo. 9s.

HOUGHTON'S (LORD) Monographs, Personal and Social. With
Portraits. Crown 8vo. 10s. 6d.

HUME'S (The Student's) History of England, from the Invasion of Julius Cæsar to the Revolution of 1688. Corrected and continued to 1868. Woodcuts. Post 8vo. 7s. 6d.

HUTCHINSON (GEN.), on the most expeditious, certain, and
easy Method of Dog-Breaking. Fifth Edition. With 40 Illustrations.
Crown 8vo. 9s.

HUTTON'S (H. E.) Principia Græca; an Introduction to the Study
of Greek. Comprehending Grammar, Delectus, and Exercise-book,
with Vocabularies. Sixth Edition. 12mo. 3s. 6d.

IRBY AND MANGLES' Travels in Egypt, Nubia, Syria, and
the Holy Land. Post 8vo. 2s.

JAMES' (REV. THOMAS) Fables of Æsop. A New Translation, with
Historical Preface. With 100 Woodcuts by TENNIEL and WOLF.
Sixty-fourth Thousand. Post 8vo. 2s. 6d.

c

18   LIST OF WORKS

HOME AND COLONIAL LIBRARY. A Series of Works adapted for all circles and classes of Readers, having been selected for their acknowledged interest, and ability of the Authors. Post 8vo. Published at 2s. and 3s. 6d. each, and arranged under two distinctive heads as follows:—

CLASS A.
HISTORY, BIOGRAPHY, AND HISTORIC TALES.

1. SIEGE OF GIBRALTAR. By JOHN DRINKWATER. 2s.
2. THE AMBER-WITCH. By LADY DUFF GORDON. 2s.
3. CROMWELL AND BUNYAN. By ROBERT SOUTHEY. 2s.
4. LIFE OF SIR FRANCIS DRAKE. By JOHN BARROW. 2s.
5. CAMPAIGNS AT WASHINGTON. By REV. G. R. GLEIG. 2s.
6. THE FRENCH IN ALGIERS. By LADY DUFF GORDON. 2s.
7. THE FALL OF THE JESUITS. 2s.
8. LIVONIAN TALES. 2s.
9. LIFE OF CONDÉ. By LORD MAHON. 3s. 6d.
10. SALE'S BRIGADE. By REV. G. R. GLEIG. 2s.
11. THE SIEGES OF VIENNA. By LORD ELLESMERE. 2s.
12. THE WAYSIDE CROSS. By CAPT. MILMAN. 2s.
13. SKETCHES OF GERMAN LIFE. By SIR A. GORDON. 3s. 6d.
14. THE BATTLE OF WATERLOO. By REV. G. R. GLEIG. 3s. 6d.
15. AUTOBIOGRAPHY OF STEFFENS. 2s.
16. THE BRITISH POETS. By THOMAS CAMPBELL. 3s. 6d.
17. HISTORICAL ESSAYS. By LORD MAHON. 3s. 6d.
18. LIFE OF LORD CLIVE. By REV. G. R. GLEIG. 3s. 6d.
19. NORTH - WESTERN RAILWAY. By SIR F. B. HEAD. 2s.
20. LIFE OF MUNRO. By REV. G. R. GLEIG. 3s. 6d.

CLASS B.
VOYAGES, TRAVELS, AND ADVENTURES.

1. BIBLE IN SPAIN. By GEORGE BORROW. 3s. 6d.
2. GYPSIES OF SPAIN. By GEORGE BORROW. 3s. 6d.
3 & 4. JOURNALS IN INDIA. By BISHOP HEBER. 2 Vols. 7s.
5. TRAVELS IN THE HOLY LAND. By IRBY and MANGLES. 2s.
6. MOROCCO AND THE MOORS. By J. DRUMMOND HAY. 2s.
7. LETTERS FROM THE BALTIC. By a LADY. 2s.
8. NEW SOUTH WALES. By MRS. MEREDITH. 2s.
9. THE WEST INDIES. By M. G. LEWIS. 2s.
10. SKETCHES OF PERSIA. By SIR JOHN MALCOLM. 3s. 6d.
11. MEMOIRS OF FATHER RIPA. 2s.
12, 13. TYPEE AND OMOO. By HERMANN MELVILLE. 2 Vols. 7s.
14. MISSIONARY LIFE IN CANADA. By REV. J. ABBOTT. 2s.
15. LETTERS FROM MADRAS. By a LADY. 2s.
16. HIGHLAND SPORTS. By CHARLES ST. JOHN. 3s. 6d.
17. PAMPAS JOURNEYS. By SIR F. B. HEAD. 2s.
18. GATHERINGS FROM SPAIN. By RICHARD FORD. 3s. 6d.
19. THE RIVER AMAZON. By W. H. EDWARDS. 2s.
20. MANNERS & CUSTOMS OF INDIA. By REV. C. ACLAND. 2s.
21. ADVENTURES IN MEXICO. By G. F. RUXTON. 3s. 6d.
22. PORTUGAL AND GALLICIA. By LORD CARNARVON. 3s. 6d.
23. BUSH LIFE IN AUSTRALIA. By REV. H. W. HAYGARTH. 2s.
24. THE LIBYAN DESERT. By BAYLE ST. JOHN. 2s.
25. SIERRA LEONE. By A LADY. 3s. 6d.

⁎ Each work may be had separately.

PUBLISHED BY MR. MURRAY. 19

JAMESON'S (Mrs.) Lives of the Early Italian Painters—
and the Progress of Painting in Italy—Cimabue to Bassano. *New
Edition.* With 50 Portraits. Post 8vo. 12s.

JENNINGS' (L. J.) Eighty Years of Republican Government in
the United States. Post 8vo. 10s. 6d.

JERVIS'S (Rev. W. H.) Gallican Church, from the Concordat of Bologna, 1516, to the Revolution. With an Introduction.
Portraits. 2 Vols. 8vo. 28s.

JESSE'S (Edward) Gleanings in Natural History. Fcp. 8vo. 3s. 6d.

JOHNS' (Rev. B. G.) Blind People; their Works and Ways. With
Sketches of the Lives of some famous Blind Men. With Illustrations.
Post 8vo. 7s. 6d.

JOHNSON'S (Dr. Samuel) Life. By James Boswell. Including
the Tour to the Hebrides. Edited by Mr. Croker. *New Library
Edition.* Edited by Alexander Napier, M.A. Portraits. 4 Vols. 8vo.
[*In Preparation.*

——— Lives of the most eminent English Poets, with
Critical Observations on their Works. Edited with Notes, Corrective
and Explanatory, by Peter Cunningham. 3 vols. 8vo. 22s. 6d.

JUNIUS' Handwriting Professionally investigated. By Mr. Chabot,
Expert. With Preface and Collateral Evidence, by the Hon. Edward
Twisleton. With Facsimiles, Woodcuts, &c. 4to. £3 3s.

KEN'S (Bishop) Life. By a Layman. Portrait. 2 Vols. 8vo. 18s.

——— Exposition of the Apostles' Creed. 16mo. 1s. 6d.

KERR'S (Robert) GENTLEMAN'S HOUSE; or, How to Plan
English Residences, from the Parsonage to the Palace. *Third
Edition.* With Views and Plans. 8vo. 24s.

——— Small Country House. A Brief Practical Discourse on
the Planning of a Residence from 2000l. to 5000l. With Supplementary Estimates to 7000l. Post 8vo. 3s.

——— Ancient Lights; a Book for Architects, Surveyors,
Lawyers, and Landlords. 8vo. 5s. 6d.

——— (R. Malcolm) Student's Blackstone. A Systematic
Abridgment of the entire Commentaries, adapted to the present state
of the law. Post 8vo. 7s. 6d.

KING EDWARD VIth's Latin Grammar; or, an Introduction
to the Latin Tongue. *Seventeenth Edition.* 12mo. 3s. 6d.

——————————— First Latin Book; or, the Accidence,
Syntax, and Prosody, with an English Translation. *Fifth Edition.* 12mo.
2s. 6d.

KING GEORGE IIIrd's CORRESPONDENCE WITH LORD
NORTH, 1769-82. Edited, with Notes and Introduction, by W. Bodham
Donne. 2 vols. 8vo. 32s.

KIRK'S (J. Foster) History of Charles the Bold, Duke of Burgundy. Portrait. 3 Vols. 8vo. 45s.

KIRKES' Handbook of Physiology. Edited by W. Morrant
Baker, F.R.C.S. *Eighth Edit.* With 240 Illustrations. Post 8vo. 12s. 6d.

KUGLER'S Handbook to the Italian Schools of Painting. Edited,
with Notes, by Sir Charles Eastlake. Woodcuts. 2 Vols. Post 8vo.

——— German, Dutch, and Flemish Schools of Painting.
Edited, with Notes, by J. A. Crowe. Woodcuts. 2 Vols. Post 8vo. 24s.

LANE'S (E. W.) Account of the Manners and Customs of Modern
Egyptians. *New Edition.* With Illustrations. 2 Vols. Post 8vo. 12s.

LAWRENCE'S (Sir Geo.) Reminiscences of Forty-three Years'
Service in India; including Captivities in Cabul among the Affghans
and among the Sikhs; and a Narrative of the Mutiny in Rajputana.
Edited by W. Edwards, H.M.C.B.S. Crown 8vo.

c 2

LAYARD'S (A. H.) Nineveh and its Remains. Being a Narrative of Researches and Discoveries amidst the Ruins of Assyria. With an Account of the Chaldean Christians of Kurdistan; the Yezedis, or Devil-worshippers; and an Enquiry into the Manners and Arts of the Ancient Assyrians. *Sixth Edition.* Plates and Woodcuts. 2 Vols. 8vo. 36s.

*** A POPULAR EDITION of the above work. With Illustrations. Post 8vo. 7s. 6d.

———— **Nineveh and Babylon**; being the Narrative of Discoveries in the Ruins, with Travels in Armenia, Kurdistan and the Desert, during a Second Expedition to Assyria. With Map and Plates. 8vo. 21s.

*** A POPULAR EDITION of the above work. With Illustrations. Post 8vo. 7s. 6d.

LEATHES' (STANLEY) Practical Hebrew Grammar. With the Hebrew Text of Genesis i.—vi., and Psalms i.—vi. Grammatical Analysis and Vocabulary. Post 8vo. 7s. 6d.

LENNEP'S (REV. H. J. VAN) Missionary Travels in Asia Minor. With Illustrations of Biblical History and Archæology. With Map and Woodcuts. 2 Vols. Post 8vo. 24s.

LESLIE'S (C. R.) Handbook for Young Painters. With Illustrations. Post 8vo. 7s. 6d.

———— **Life and Works of Sir Joshua Reynolds.** Portraits and Illustrations. 2 Vols. 8vo. 42s.

LETTERS FROM THE BALTIC. By a LADY. Post 8vo. 2s.

———— **MADRAS.** By a LADY. Post 8vo. 2s.

———— **SIERRA LEONE.** By a LADY. Post 8vo. 3s. 6d.

LEVI'S (LEONE) History of British Commerce; and of the Economic Progress of the Nation, from 1763 to 1870. 8vo. 16s.

LEWIS'S (M. G.) Journal of a Residence among the Negroes in the West Indies. Post 8vo. 2s.

LIDDELL'S (DEAN) Student's History of Rome, from the earliest Times to the establishment of the Empire. With Woodcuts. Post 8vo. 7s. 6d.

LINDSAY'S (LORD) Lives of the Lindsays; Memoir of the Houses of Crawfurd and Balcarres. With Extracts from Official Papers and Personal Narratives. 3 Vols. 8vo. 24s.

———— **Etruscan Inscriptions.** Analysed, Translated, and Commented upon. 8vo. 12s.

LLOYD'S (W. WATKISS) History of Sicily to the Athenian War; with Elucidations of the Sicilian Odes of Pindar. With Map. 8vo. 14s.

LISPINGS from LOW LATITUDES; or, the Journal of the Hon. Impulsia Gushington. Edited by LORD DUFFERIN. With 24 Plates. 4to. 21s.

LITTLE ARTHUR'S HISTORY OF ENGLAND. By LADY CALLCOTT. *New Edition, continued to* 1872. With Woodcuts. Fcap. 8vo. 2s. 6d.

LIVINGSTONE'S (DR.) Popular Account of Missionary Travels and Researches in South Africa. Illustrations. Post 8vo. 6s.

———— **Narrative of an Expedition to the Zambezi and its Tributaries,** with the Discovery of the Lakes Shirwa and Nyassa. Map and Illustrations. 8vo. 21s.

LIVONIAN TALES. By the Author of "Letters from the Baltic." Post 8vo. 2s.

LOCH'S (H. B.) Personal Narrative of Events during Lord Elgin's Second Embassy to China. *Second Edition.* With Illustrations. Post 8vo. 9s.

LOCKHART'S (J. G.) Ancient Spanish Ballads. Historical and Romantic. Translated, with Notes. *New Edition*. With Portrait and Illustrations. Crown 8vo. 5s.
—————— Life of Theodore Hook. Fcap. 8vo. 1s.
LONSDALE'S (Bishop) Life. With Selections from his Writings. By E. B. Denison. With Portrait. Crown 8vo. 10s. 6d.
LOUDON'S (Mrs.) Gardening for Ladies. With Directions and Calendar of Operations for Every Month. *Eighth Edition.* Woodcuts. Fcap. 8vo. 3s. 6d.
LUCKNOW: A Lady's Diary of the Siege. Fcap. 8vo. 4s. 6d.
LYELL'S (Sir Charles) Principles of Geology; or, the Modern Changes of the Earth and its Inhabitants considered as illustrative of Geology. *Eleventh Edition.* With Illustrations. 2 Vols. 8vo. 32s.
—————— Student's Elements of Geology. *Second Edition.* With Table of British Fossils and 600 Illustrations. Post 8vo. 9s.
—————— Geological Evidences of the Antiquity of Man. including an Outline of Glacial Post-Tertiary Geology, and Remarks on the Origin of Species. *Fourth Edition.* Illustrations. 8vo. 14s.
—————— (K. M.) Geographical Handbook of Ferns. With Tables to show their Distribution. Post 8vo. 7s. 6d.
LYTTELTON'S (Lord) Ephemera. 2 Vols. Post 8vo. 19s. 6d.
LYTTON'S (Lord) Poems. Post 8vo. 10s. 6d.
—————— Lost Tales of Miletus. Post 8vo. 7s. 6d.
—————— Memoir of Julian Fane. With Portrait. Post 8vo. 5s.
McCLINTOCK'S (Sir L.) Narrative of the Discovery of the Fate of Sir John Franklin and his Companions in the Arctic Seas. *Third Edition.* With Illustrations. Post 8vo. 7s. 6d.
MACDOUGALL'S (Col.) Modern Warfare as Influenced by Modern Artillery. With Plans. Post 8vo. 12s.
MACGREGOR (J.), Rob Roy on the Jordan, Nile, Red Sea, Gennesareth, &c. A Canoe Cruise in Palestine and Egypt and the Waters of Damascus. With Map, and 70 Illustrations. Crown 8vo. 12s.
MACPHERSON'S (Major) Services in India, while Political Agent at Gwalior during the Mutiny. Illustrations. 8vo. 12s.
MAETZNER'S ENGLISH GRAMMAR. A Methodical, Analytical, and Historical Treatise on the Orthography, Prosody, Inflections, and Syntax of the English Tongue. Translated from the German. By Clair J. Grece, LL.D. 3 Vols. 8vo. 36s.
MAHON (Lord), see Stanhope.
MAINE'S (Sir H. Sumner) Ancient Law: its Connection with the Early History of Society, and its Relation to Modern Ideas. *Fifth Edition.* 8vo. 12s.
—————— Village Communities in the East and West. *Second Edition.* 8vo. 9s.
MALCOLM'S (Sir John) Sketches of Persia. Post 8vo. 3s. 6d.
MANSEL'S (Dean) Limits of Religious Thought Examined. *Fifth Edition.* Post 8vo. 8s. 6d.
—————— Letters, Lectures, and Papers, including the Phrontisterion, or Oxford in the XIXth Century. Edited by H. W. Chandler, M.A. 8vo. 12s.
MANTELL'S (Gideon A.) Thoughts on Animalcules; or, the Invisible World, as revealed by the Microscope. Plates. 16mo. 6s.
MANUAL OF SCIENTIFIC ENQUIRY. For the Use of Travellers. Edited by Sir J. F. Herschel & Rev. R. Main. Post 8vo. 3s. 6d. (*Published by order of the Lords of the Admiralty.*)

MARCO POLO'S TRAVELS. With Copious Illustrative Notes. By Col. Henry Yule. Maps and Illustrations. 2 Vols. Medium 8vo. 42s.

MARKHAM'S (Mrs.) History of England. From the First Invasion by the Romans to 1867. Woodcuts. 12mo. 3s. 6d.

————— History of France. From the Conquest by the Gauls to 1861. Woodcuts. 12mo. 3s. 6d.

————— History of Germany. From the Invasion by Marius to 1867. Woodcuts. 12mo. 3s. 6d.

————— (Clements R.) Travels in Peru and India. Maps and Illustrations. 8vo. 16s.

MARRYAT'S (Joseph) History of Modern and Mediæval Pottery and Porcelain. With a Description of the Manufacture. *Third Edition*. Plates and Woodcuts. 8vo. 42s.

MARSH'S (G. P.) Student's Manual of the English Language. Edited by Dr. Wm. Smith. Post 8vo. 7s. 6d.

MATTHIÆ'S GREEK GRAMMAR. Abridged by Blomfield, and *Revised* by E. S. Crooke. 12mo. 4s.

MAUREL'S Character, Actions, and Writings of Wellington. Fcap. 8vo. 1s. 6d.

MAYNE'S (Capt.) Four Years in British Columbia and Vancouver Island. Illustrations. 8vo. 16s.

MEADE'S (Hon. Herbert) Ride through the Disturbed Districts of New Zealand, with a Cruise among the South Sea Islands. With Illustrations. Medium 8vo. 12s.

MELVILLE'S (Hermann) Marquesas and South Sea Islands. 2 Vols. Post 8vo. 7s.

MEREDITH'S (Mrs. Charles) Notes and Sketches of New South Wales. Post 8vo. 2s.

MESSIAH (THE): The Life, Travels, Death, Resurrection, and Ascension of our Blessed Lord. By A Layman. Map. 8vo. 18s.

MILLINGTON'S (Rev. T. S.) Signs and Wonders in the Land of Ham, or the Ten Plagues of Egypt, with Ancient and Modern Illustrations. Woodcuts. Post 8vo. 7s. 6d.

MILLS' (Rev. John) Three Months' Residence at Nablus, with an Account of the Modern Samaritans. Illustrations. Post 8vo. 10s. 6d.

MILMAN'S (Dean) History of the Jews, from the earliest Period down to Modern Times. *Fourth Edition*. 3 Vols. Post 8vo. 18s.

————— Early Christianity, from the Birth of Christ to the Abolition of Paganism in the Roman Empire. *Fourth Edition*. 3 Vols. Post 8vo. 18s.

————— Latin Christianity, including that of the Popes to the Pontificate of Nicholas V. *Fourth Edition*. 9 Vols. Post 8vo. 54s.

————— Annals of St. Paul's Cathedral, from the Romans to the funeral of Wellington. *Second Edition*. Portrait and Illustrations. 8vo. 18s.

————— Character and Conduct of the Apostles considered as an Evidence of Christianity. 8vo. 10s. 6d.

————— Quinti Horatii Flacci Opera. With 100 Woodcuts. Small 8vo. 7s. 6d.

————— Life of Quintus Horatius Flaccus. With Illustrations. 8vo. 9s.

————— Poetical Works. The Fall of Jerusalem—Martyr of Antioch—Balshazzar—Tamor—Anne Boleyn—Fazio, &c. With Portrait and Illustrations. 3 Vols. Fcap. 8vo. 18s.

————— Fall of Jerusalem. Fcap. 8vo. 1s.

————— (Capt. E. A.) Wayside Cross. Post 8vo. 2s.

MICHIE'S (ALEXANDER) Siberian Overland Route from Peking to Petersburg. Maps and Illustrations. 8vo. 16s.

MODERN DOMESTIC COOKERY. Founded on Principles of Economy and Practical Knowledge. *New Edition.* Woodcuts. Fcap. 8vo. 5s.

MONGREDIEN'S (AUGUSTUS) Trees and Shrubs for English Plantation. A Selection and Description of the most Ornamental which will flourish in the open air in our climate. With Classified Lists. With 30 Illustrations. 8vo. 16s.

MOORE & JACKMAN on the Clematis as a Garden Flower. Descriptions of the Hardy Species and Varieties, with Directions for their Cultivation. 8vo. 10s. 6d.

MOORE'S (THOMAS) Life and Letters of Lord Byron. *Cabinet Edition.* With Plates. 6 Vols. Fcap. 8vo. 18s.; *Popular Edition,* with Portraits. Royal 8vo. 9s.

MOSSMAN'S (SAMUEL) New Japan; the Land of the Rising Sun; its Annals and Progress during the past Twenty Years, recording the remarkable Progress of the Japanese in Western Civilisation. With Map. 8vo. 15s.

MOTLEY'S (J. L.) History of the United Netherlands: from the Death of William the Silent to the Twelve Years' Truce, 1609. *Library Edition.* Portraits. 4 Vols. 8vo. 60s. *Cabinet Edition.* 4 Vols. Post 8vo. 6s. each.

———— Life and Death of John of Barneveld, Advocate of Holland. With a View of the Primary Causes and Movements of the Thirty Years' War. Illustrations. 2 Vols. 8vo. 28s.

MOUHOT'S (HENRI) Siam, Cambojia, and Lao; a Narrative of Travels and Discoveries. Illustrations. 2 vols. 8vo.

MOZLEY'S (CANON) Treatise on Predestination. 8vo. 14s.

———— Primitive Doctrine of Baptismal Regeneration. 8vo. 7s. 6d.

MUNDY'S (GENERAL) Pen and Pencil Sketches in India. *Third Edition.* Plates. Post 8vo. 7s. 6d.

MUNRO'S (GENERAL) Life and Letters. By REV. G. R. GLEIG. Post 8vo. 3s. 6d.

MURCHISON'S (SIR RODERICK) Russia in Europe and the Ural Mountains. With Coloured Maps, &c. 2 Vols. 4to. 5l. 5s.

———— Siluria; or, a History of the Oldest Rocks containing Organic Remains. *Fifth Edition.* Map and Plates. 8vo. 18s.

———— Memoirs. With Notices of his Contemporaries, and Rise and Progress of Palæozoic Geology. By ARCHIBALD GEIKIE. Portraits. 2 Vols. 8vo. (*In the Press.*)

MURRAY'S RAILWAY READING. Containing:—

WELLINGTON. By LORD ELLESMERE. 6d.
NIMROD ON THE CHASE, 1s.
MUSIC AND DRESS, 1s.
MILMAN'S FALL OF JERUSALEM. 1s.
MAHON'S "FORTY-FIVE." 3s.
LIFE OF THEODORE HOOK. 1s.
DEEDS OF NAVAL DARING. 3s. 6d.
THE HONEY BEE. 1s.
ÆSOP'S FABLES. 2s. 6d.
NIMROD ON THE TURF. 1s. 6d.
ART OF DINING. 1s. 6d.
MAHON'S JOAN OF ARC. 1s.
HEAD'S EMIGRANT. 2s. 6d.
NIMROD ON THE ROAD. 1s.
CROKER ON THE GUILLOTINE. 1s.
HOLLWAY'S NORWAY. 2s.
MAUREL'S WELLINGTON. 1s. 6d.
CAMPBELL'S LIFE OF BACON. 2s. 6d.
THE FLOWER GARDEN. 1s.
TAYLOR'S NOTES FROM LIFE. 2s.
REJECTED ADDRESSES. 1s.
PENN'S HINTS ON ANGLING. 1s.

MUSTERS' (CAPT.) At Home with the Patagonians; a Year's Wanderings over Untrodden Ground from the Straits of Magellan to the Rio Negro. *2nd Edition.* Illustrations. Post 8vo. 7s. 6d.

NAPIER'S (SIR CHAS.) Life, Journals, and Letters. By SIR W. NAPIER. *Second Edition.* Portraits. 4 Vols. Post 8vo. 48s.

———— (SIR WM.) Life and Letters. Edited by RT. HON. H. A. BRUCE. Portraits. 2 Vols. Crown 8vo. 28s.

———— English Battles and Sieges of the Peninsular War. *Fourth Edition.* Portrait. Post 8vo. 9s.

NAPOLEON AT FONTAINEBLEAU AND ELBA. A Journal of Occurrences and Notes of Conversations. By SIR NEIL CAMPBELL, C.B. With a Memoir. By REV. A. N. C. MACLACHLAN, M.A. Portrait. 8vo. 15s.

NASMYTH (JAS.) AND CARPENTER (JAS.) The Moon. Considered as a Planet, a World, and a Satellite. With Illustrations from Drawings made with the aid of Powerful Telescopes, Woodcuts, &c. 4to. 30s

NAUTICAL ALMANAC (THE). (*By Authority.*) 2s. 6d.

NAVY LIST. (Monthly and Quarterly.) Post 8vo.

NEW TESTAMENT. With Short Explanatory Commentary. By ARCHDEACON CHURTON, M.A., and ARCHDEACON BASIL JONES, M.A. With 110 authentic Views, &c. 2 Vols. Crown 8vo. 21s. *bound.*

NEWTH'S (SAMUEL) First Book of Natural Philosophy; an Introduction to the Study of Statics, Dynamics, Hydrostatics, Optics, and Acoustics, with numerous Examples. Small 8vo. 3s. 6d.

—————— Elements of Mechanics, including Hydrostatics, with numerous Examples. *Fifth Edition.* Small 8vo. 8s. 6d. Cloth.

—————— Mathematical Examinations. A Graduated Series of Elementary Examples in Arithmetic, Algebra, Logarithms, Trigonometry, and Mechanics. *Third Edition.* Small 8vo. 8s. 6d. each.

NICHOLLS' (SIR GEORGE) History of the English, Irish and Scotch Poor Laws. 4 Vols. 8vo.

NICOLAS' (SIR HARRIS) Historic Peerage of England. Exhibiting the Origin, Descent, and Present State of every Title of Peerage which has existed in this Country since the Conquest. By WILLIAM COURTHOPE. 8vo. 30s.

NIMROD, On the Chace—Turf—and Road. With Portrait and Plates. Crown 8vo. 5s. Or with Coloured Plates, 7s. 6d.

OLD LONDON; Papers read at the Archæological Institute. By various Authors. 8vo. 12s.

ORMATHWAITE'S (LORD) Astronomy and Geology—Darwin and Buckle—Progress and Civilisation. Crown 8vo. 6s.

OWEN'S (LIEUT.-COL.) Principles and Practice of Modern Artillery, including Artillery Material, Gunnery, and Organisation and Use of Artillery in Warfare. *Second Edition.* With Illustrations. 8vo. 15s.

OXENHAM'S (REV. W.) English Notes for Latin Elegiacs; designed for early Proficients in the Art of Latin Versification, with Prefatory Rules of Composition in Elegiac Metre. *Fifth Edition.* 12mo. 3s. 6d.

PALGRAVE'S (R. H. I.) Local Taxation of Great Britain and Ireland. 8vo. 5s.

—————— NOTES ON BANKING IN GREAT BRITAIN AND IRELAND, SWEDEN, DENMARK, AND HAMBURG, with some Remarks on the amount of Bills in circulation, both Inland and Foreign. 8vo. 6s.

PALLISER'S (MRS.) Brittany and its Byeways, its Inhabitants, and Antiquities. With Illustrations. Post 8vo. 12s.

—————— Mottoes for Monuments, or Epitaphs selected for General Use and Study. With Illustrations. Crown 8vo. 7s. 6d.

PARIS' (DR.) Philosophy in Sport made Science in Earnest; or, the First Principles of Natural Philosophy inculcated by aid of the Toys and Sports of Youth. *Ninth Edition.* Woodcuts. Post 8vo. 7s. 6d.

PARKMAN'S (FRANCIS) Discovery of the Great West; or, the Valleys of the Mississippi and the Lakes of North America. An Historical Narrative. Map. 8vo. 10s. 6d.

PARKYNS' (MANSFIELD) Three Years' Residence in Abyssinia: with Travels in that Country. *Second Edition*, with Illustrations. Post 8vo. 7s. 6d.

PEEK'S PRIZE ESSAYS. The Maintenance of the Church of England as an Established Church. By REV. CHARLES HOLE—REV. R. WATSON DIXON—and REV. JULIUS LLOYD. 8vo. 10s. 6d.

PEEL'S (SIR ROBERT) Memoirs. Edited by EARL STANHOPE and Mr. CARDWELL. 2 Vols. Post 8vo. 7s. 6d. each.

PENN'S (RICHARD) Maxims and Hints for an Angler and Chess-player. Woodcuts. Fcap. 8vo. 1s.

PERCY'S (JOHN, M.D.) Metallurgy. Vol. I. Fuel, Coal, Fire-Clays, Copper, Zinc, Brass, &c. *Second Edition*. With Illustrations. 8vo.

——— Vol. II. Iron and Steel. *New Edition*. With Illustrations. 8vo. (*In Preparation*.)

——— Vol. III. Lead, including Desilverization and Cupellation. With Illustrations. 8vo. 30s.

——— Vols. IV. and V. Gold, Silver, and Mercury, Platinum, Tin, Nickel, Cobalt, Antimony, Bismuth, Arsenic, and other Metals. With Illustrations. 8vo. (*In Preparation*.)

PHILLIPS' (JOHN) Memoirs of William Smith. 8vo. 7s. 6d.

——— Geology of Yorkshire, The Coast, and Limestone District. Plates. 4to.

——— Rivers, Mountains, and Sea Coast of Yorkshire. With Essays on the Climate, Scenery, and Ancient Inhabitants. *Second Edition*, Plates. 8vo. 15s.

——— (SAMUEL) Literary Essays from "The Times." With Portrait. 2 Vols. Fcap. 8vo. 7s.

PHILPOTTS' (BISHOP) Letters to the late Charles Butler, on his "Book of the Roman Catholic Church." *New Edition*. Post 8vo. 6s.

PICK'S (DR.) Popular Etymological Dictionary of the French Language. 8vo. 7s. 6d.

POPE'S (ALEXANDER) Works. With Introductions and Notes, by REV. WHITWELL ELWIN. Vols. I., II., VI., VII., VIII. With Portraits. 8vo. 10s. 6d. each.

PORTER'S (REV. J. L.) Damascus, Palmyra, and Lebanon. With Travels among the Giant Cities of Bashan and the Hauran. *New Edition*. Map and Woodcuts. Post 8vo. 7s. 6d.

——— Life and Times of Henry Cooke, D.D., of Belfast. Portrait. 8vo. 14s.

PRAYER-BOOK (ILLUSTRATED), with Borders, Initials, Vignettes, &c. Edited, with Notes, by REV. THOS. JAMES. Medium 8vo. 18s. *cloth*; 31s. 6d. *calf*; 36s. *morocco*.

PRINCESS CHARLOTTE OF WALES. A Brief Memoir. With Selections from her Correspondence and other unpublished Papers. By LADY ROSE WEIGALL. With Portrait. 8vo. 8s. 6d.

PUSS IN BOOTS. With 12 Illustrations. By OTTO SPECKTER. 16mo. 1s. 6d. Or coloured, 2s. 6d.

PRINCIPLES AT STAKE. Essays on Church Questions of the Day. 8vo. 12s. Contents:—

Ritualism and Uniformity.—Benjamin Shaw.	Scripture and Ritual.—Canon Bernard.
The Episcopate.—Bishop of Bath and Wells.	Church in South Africa.—Arthur Mills.
The Priesthood.—Dean of Canterbury.	Schismatical Tendency of Ritualism.—Rev. Dr. Salmon.
National Education.—Rev. Alexander R. Grant.	Revisions of the Liturgy.—Rev. W. G. Humphry.
Doctrine of the Eucharist.—Rev. G. H. Sumner.	Parties and Party Spirit.—Dean of Chester.

PRIVY COUNCIL JUDGMENTS in Ecclesiastical Cases relating to Doctrine and Discipline. With Historical Introduction, by G. C. BRODRICK and W. H. FREMANTLE. 8vo. 10s. 6d.

QUARTERLY REVIEW (THE). 8vo. 6s.

RAMBLES in the Syrian Deserts. Post 8vo. 10s. 6d.

RANKE'S (LEOPOLD) History of the Popes of Rome during the 16th and 17th Centuries. Translated from the German by SARAH AUSTIN. Third Edition. 3 Vols. 8vo. 30s.

RASSAM'S (HORMUZD) Narrative of the British Mission to Abyssinia. With Notices of the Countries Traversed from Massowah to Magdala. Illustrations. 2 Vols. 8vo. 28s.

RAWLINSON'S (CANON) Herodotus. A New English Version. Edited with Notes and Essays. Second Edition. Maps and Woodcuts. 4 Vols. 8vo. 48s.

—————— Five Great Monarchies of Chaldæa, Assyria, Media, Babylonia, and Persia. Third Edition. With Maps and Illustrations. 3 Vols. 8vo. 42s.

REED'S (E. J.) Shipbuilding in Iron and Steel; a Practical Treatise, giving full details of Construction, Processes of Manufacture, and Building Arrangements. With 5 Plans and 250 Woodcuts. 8vo. 30s.

—————— Iron-Clad Ships; their Qualities, Performances, and Cost. With Chapters on Turret Ships, Iron-Clad Rams, &c. With Illustrations. 8vo. 12s.

REJECTED ADDRESSES (THE). By JAMES AND HORACE SMITH. New Edition. Woodcuts. Post 8vo. 3s. 6d.; or Popular Edition, Fcap. 8vo. 1s.

RENNIE'S (D. F.) British Arms in Peking, 1860. Post 8vo. 12s.

—————— Narrative of the British Embassy in China. Illustrations. 2 Vols. Post 8vo. 24s.

—————— Story of Bhotan and the Dooar War. Map and Woodcut. Post 8vo. 12s.

RESIDENCE IN BULGARIA; or, Notes on the Resources and Administration of Turkey, &c. By S. G. B. ST. CLAIR and CHARLES A. BROPHY. 8vo. 12s.

REYNOLDS' (SIR JOSHUA) Life and Times. By C. R. LESLIE, R.A. and TOM TAYLOR. Portraits. 2 Vols. 8vo.

RICARDO'S (DAVID) Political Works. With a Notice of his Life and Writings. By J. R. M'CULLOCH. New Edition. 8vo. 16s.

RIPA'S (FATHER) Thirteen Years' Residence at the Court of Peking. Post 8vo. 2s.

ROBERTSON'S (CANON) History of the Christian Church, from the Apostolic Age to the Reformation, 1517. Library Edition. 4 Vols. 8vo. Cabinet Edition. 8 Vols. Post 8vo. 6s. each.

—————— How shall we Conform to the Liturgy. 12mo. 9s.

ROME. See LIDDELL and SMITH.

ROWLAND'S (DAVID) Manual of the English Constitution. Its Rise, Growth, and Present State. Post 8vo. 10s. 6d.

—————— Laws of Nature the Foundation of Morals. Post 8vo. 6s.

ROBSON'S (E. R.) SCHOOL ARCHITECTURE. Being Practical Remarks on the Planning, Designing, Building, and Furnishing of School-houses. With 300 Illustrations of School-buildings in all Parts of the World, drawn to scale. Medium 8vo.

RUNDELL'S (MRS.) Modern Domestic Cookery. Fcap. 8vo. 5s.

RUXTON'S (GEORGE F.) Travels in Mexico; with Adventures among the Wild Tribes and Animals of the Prairies and Rocky Mountains. Post 8vo. 3s. 6d.

ROBINSON'S (Rev. Dr.) Biblical Researches in Palestine and the Adjacent Regions, 1838—52. *Third Edition.* Maps. 3 Vols. 8vo. 42s.

——— Physical Geography of the Holy Land. Post 8vo. 10s. 6d.

——— (Wm.) Alpine Flowers for English Gardens. With 70 Illustrations. Crown 8vo.

——— Wild Garden; or, our Groves and Shrubberies made beautiful by the Naturalization of Hardy Exotic Plants. With Frontispiece. Small 8vo. 6s.

——— Sub-Tropical Garden ; or, Beauty of Form in the Flower Garden. With Illustrations. Small 8vo. 7s. 6d.

SALE'S (Sir Robert) Brigade in Affghanistan. With an Account of the Defence of Jellalabad. By Rev. G. R. Gleig. Post 8vo. 2s.

SCOTT'S (Sir G. G.) Secular and Domestic Architecture, Present and Future. 8vo. 9s.

——— Rise and Development of Mediæval Architecture. 8vo. (*Nearly Ready.*)

——— (Dean) University Sermons. Post 8vo. 8s. 6d.

SHADOWS OF A SICK ROOM. 16mo. 2s. 6d.

SCROPE'S (G. P.) Geology and Extinct Volcanoes of Central France. Illustrations. Medium 8vo. 30s.

SHAW'S (T. B.) Manual of English Literature. Post 8vo. 7s. 6d.

——— Specimens of English Literature. Selected from the Chief Writers. Post 8vo. 7s. 6d.

——— (Robert) Visit to High Tartary, Yarkand, and Kashgar (formerly Chinese Tartary), and Return Journey over the Karakorum Pass. With Map and Illustrations. 8vo. 16s.

SMILES' (Samuel) Lives of British Engineers; from the Earliest Period. With 9 Portraits and 400 Illustrations. 4 Vols. 8vo. 21s. each.

——— Lives of George and Robert Stephenson. With Portraits and Illustrations. Medium 8vo. 21s. *Popular Edition*, with Woodcuts. Post 8vo. 6s.

——— Lives of Boulton and Watt. With Portraits and Illustrations. Medium 8vo. 21s.

——— Self-Help. With Illustrations of Conduct and Perseverance. Post 8vo. 6s Or in French, 5s.

——— Character. A Companion Volume to "Self-Help." Post 8vo. 6s.

——— Industrial Biography : Iron-Workers and Tool-Makers. Post 8vo. 6s.

——— Lives of Brindley and the Early Engineers. With Portrait and 50 Woodcuts. Post 8vo. 6s.

——— Life of Thomas Telford. With a History of Roads and Travelling in England. Woodcuts. Post 8vo. 6s.

——— Boy's Voyage round the World; including a Residence in Victoria, and a Journey by Rail across North America. With Illustrations. Post 8vo. 6s.

SHIRLEY'S (Evelyn P.) Deer and Deer Parks; or some Account of English Parks, with Notes on the Management of Deer. Illustrations. 4to. 21s.

SIERRA LEONE; Described in Letters to Friends at Home. By A Lady. Post 8vo. 3s. 6d.

SMITH'S (Dr. Wm.) Dictionary of the Bible; its Antiquities, Biography, Geography, and Natural History. Illustrations. 3 Vols. 8vo. 105s.

────── Concise Bible Dictionary. With 300 Illustrations. Medium 8vo. 21s.

────── Smaller Bible Dictionary. With Illustrations. Post 8vo. 7s. 6d.

────── Historical Atlas of Ancient Geography—Biblical and Classical. (5 Parts.) Folio. 21s. each.

────── Greek and Roman Antiquities. With 500 Illustrations. Medium 8vo. 28s.

────── Biography and Mythology. With 600 Illustrations. 3 Vols. Medium 8vo. 4l. 4s.

────── Geography. 2 Vols. With 500 Illustrations. Medium 8vo. 56s.

────── Classical Dictionary of Mythology, Biography, and Geography. 1 Vol. With 750 Woodcuts. 8vo. 18s.

────── Smaller Classical Dictionary. With 200 Woodcuts. Crown 8vo. 7s. 6d.

────── Greek and Roman Antiquities. With 200 Woodcuts. Crown 8vo. 7s. 6d.

────── Latin-English Dictionary. With Tables of the Roman Calendar, Measures, Weights, and Money. Medium 8vo. 21s.

────── Smaller Latin-English Dictionary. 12mo. 7s. 6d.

────── English-Latin Dictionary. Medium 8vo. 21s.

────── Smaller English-Latin Dictionary. 12mo. 7s. 6d.

────── School Manual of English Grammar, with Copious Exercises. Post 8vo. 3s. 6d.

────── Primary English Grammar, for Elementary Schools. 16mo. 1s.

────── History of Britain, for Elementary Schools. 12mo. 2s. 6d.

────── French Principia. Part I. A First French Course for Schools, containing Grammar, Delectus, Exercises, and Vocabularies. 12mo. 3s. 6d.

────── Principia Latina—Part I. A Grammar, Delectus, and Exercise Book, with Vocabularies. With the Accidence arranged for the "Public School Primer." 12mo. 3s. 6d.

────── Part II. A Reading-book of Mythology, Geography, Roman Antiquities, and History. With Notes and Dictionary. 12mo. 3s. 6d.

────── Part III. A Latin Poetry Book. Hexameters and Pentameters; Eclog. Ovidianæ; Latin Prosody. 12mo. 3s. 6d.

────── Part IV. Latin Prose Composition. Rules of Syntax, with Examples, Explanations of Synonyms, and Exercises on the Syntax. 12mo. 3s. 6d.

────── Part V. Short Tales and Anecdotes for Translation into Latin. 12mo. 3s.

────── Latin-English Vocabulary and First Latin-English Dictionary for Phædrus, Cornelius Nepos, and Cæsar. 12mo. 3s. 6d.

────── Student's Latin Grammar. Post 8vo. 6s.

────── Smaller Latin Grammar. Abridged from the above. 12mo. 3s. 6d.

────── Tacitus, Germania, Agricola, and First Book of the Annals. With English Notes. 378 pp. 12mo. 3s. 6d.

SMITH'S (Dr. Wm.) Initia Græca, Part I. An Introduction to Greek; comprehending Grammar, Delectus, and Exercise-book. With Vocabularies. 12mo. 3s. 6d.
—— Initia Græca, Part II. A Reading Book. Containing Short Tales, Anecdotes, Fables, Mythology, and Grecian History. 12mo. 3s. 6d.
—— Initia Græca, Part III. Greek Prose Composition. Containing the Rules of Syntax, with copious Examples and Exercises. 12mo. 3s. 6d.
—— Student's Greek Grammar. By Professor Curtius. Post 8vo. 6s.
—— Smaller Greek Grammar. Abridged from the above. 12mo. 3s. 6d.
—— Greek Accidence. Extracted from the above work. 12mo. 2s. 6d.
—— Plato. The Apology of Socrates, the Crito, and Part of the Phædo; with Notes in English from Stallbaum and Schleiermacher's Introductions. 242 pp. 12mo. 3s. 6d.
—— Smaller History of England. Woodcuts. 16mo. 3s. 6d.
—————— Greece. Woodcuts. 16mo. 3s. 6d.
—————— Rome. Woodcuts. 16mo. 3s. 6d.
—— Scripture History. Woodcuts. 16mo. 3s. 6d.
—— English Literature. 16mo. 3s. 6d.
—— Specimens of English Literature. 16mo. 3s. 6d.
—— Ancient History. Woodcuts. 16mo. 3s. 6d.
—————— Geography. Woodcuts. 16mo. 3s. 6d.
—— Classical Mythology. With Translations from the Poets. Woodcuts. 16mo. 3s. 6d.
—— (Philip) History of the Ancient World, from the Creation to the Fall of the Roman Empire, A.D. 455. *Fourth Edition.* 3 Vols. 8vo. 31s. 6d.
—— (Rev. A. C.) Nile and its Banks. Woodcuts. 2 Vols. Post 8vo. 18s.

SIMMONS' (Capt.) Constitution and Practice of Courts-Martial; with a Summary of the Law of Evidence, and some Notice of the Criminal Law of England with reference to the Trial of Civil Offences. *Sixth Edition.* 8vo. 15s.

STANLEY'S (Dean) Sinai and Palestine. 20*th Edit.* Map. 8vo. 14s.
—— Bible in the Holy Land; Extracted from the above Work. *Second Edition.* Woodcuts. Fcap. 8vo. 2s. 6d.
—— St. Paul's Epistles to the Corinthians. With Dissertations and Notes. *Fourth Edition.* 8vo. 18s.
—— Eastern Church. *Fourth Edition.* Plans. 8vo. 12s.
—— Jewish Church. *Fifth Edition.* 2 Vols. 8vo. 24s.
—— Church of Scotland. 8vo. 7s. 6d.
—— Historical Memorials of Canterbury Cathedral. *Fifth Edition.* Woodcuts. Post 8vo. 7s. 6d.
—————— Westminster Abbey. *Third Edition.* With Illustrations. 8vo. 21s.
—— Sermons during a Tour in the East. 8vo. 9s.
—— on Evangelical and Apostolical Teaching. Post 8vo. 7s. 6d.
—— Addresses and Charges of Bishop Stanley. With Memoir. 8vo. 10s. 6d.

STUDENT'S HUME'S History of England from the Invasion of Julius Cæsar to the Revolution in 1688. Continued down to 1868. Woodcuts. Post 8vo. 7s. 6d.
*** Questions on the above Work, 12mo. 2s.
———— HALLAM'S HISTORY OF EUROPE during the Middle Ages. Post 8vo. 7s. 6d.
———— HISTORY OF ENGLAND; from the Accession of Henry VII. to the Death of George II. Post 8vo. 7s. 6d.
———— HISTORY OF FRANCE; from the Earliest Times to the Establishment of the Second Empire, 1852. By REV. H. W. JERVIS. Woodcuts. Post 8vo. 7s. 6d.
———— HISTORY OF ROME; from the Earliest Times to the Establishment of the Empire. By DEAN LIDDELL. Woodcuts. Crown 8vo. 7s. 6d.
———— GIBBON'S Decline and Fall of the Roman Empire. Woodcuts. Post 8vo. 7s. 6d.
———— HISTORY OF GREECE; from the Earliest Times to the Roman Conquest. By WM. SMITH, D.C.L. Woodcuts. Crown 8vo. 7s. 6d.
*** Questions on the above Work, 12mo. 2s.
———— ANCIENT HISTORY OF THE EAST; Egypt, Assyria, Babylonia, Media, Persia, Asia Minor, and Phœnicia. By PHILIP SMITH. Woodcuts. Post 8vo. 7s. 6d.
———— OLD TESTAMENT HISTORY; from the Creation to the Return of the Jews from Captivity. Maps and Woodcuts. Post 8vo. 7s. 6d.
———— NEW TESTAMENT HISTORY. With an Introduction connecting the History of the Old and New Testaments. Maps and Woodcuts. Post 8vo. 7s. 6d.
———— ECCLESIASTICAL HISTORY. Post 8vo.
———— ANCIENT GEOGRAPHY. By REV. W. L. BEVAN. Woodcuts. Post 8vo. 7s. 6d.
———— MODERN GEOGRAPHY; Mathematical, Physical, and Descriptive. By REV. W. L. BEVAN. Woodcuts. Post 8vo. 7s. 6d.
———— ENGLISH LANGUAGE. By GEO. P. MARSH. Post 8vo. 7s. 6d.
———————— LITERATURE. By T. B. SHAW, M.A. Post 8vo. 7s. 6d.
———— SPECIMENS of English Literature from the Chief Writers. By T. B. SHAW, Post 8vo. 7s. 6d.
———— MORAL PHILOSOPHY. By WILLIAM FLEMING, D.D. Post 8vo. 7s. 6d.
———— BLACKSTONE'S Commentaries on the Laws of England. By R. MALCOLM KERR, LL.D. Post 8vo. 7s. 6d.

SPALDING'S (CAPTAIN) Tale of Frithiof. Translated from the Swedish of ESIAS TEGNER. Post 8vo. 7s. 6d.

STEPHEN'S (REV. W. R.) Life and Times of St. Chrysostom. With Portrait. 8vo. 15s.

ST. CLAIR and BROPHY'S BULGARIA; the Resources and Administration of Turkey. 8vo. 12s.

ST. JOHN'S (CHARLES) Wild Sports and Natural History of the Highlands. Post 8vo. 3s. 6d.
———————— (BAYLE) Adventures in the Libyan Desert. Post 8vo. 2s.

STORIES FOR DARLINGS. With Illustrations. 16mo. 5s.

STOTHARD'S (THOS.) Life. With Personal Reminiscences. By Mrs. BRAY. With Portrait and 60 Woodcuts. 4to. 21s.

STREET'S (G. E.) Gothic Architecture in Spain. From Personal Observations made during several Journeys. *Second Edition.* With Illustrations. Royal 8vo. 30s.
────── Brick and Marble in the Middle Ages. With Notes of Tours in the North of Italy. *Second Edition.* With 60 Illustrations. Royal 8vo.
STANHOPE'S (EARL) History of England during the Reign of Queen Anne, 1701—13. *Library Edition.* 8vo. 16s. *Cabinet Edition.* With Portrait, 2 Vols. Post 8vo. 10s.
────── from the Peace of Utrecht to the Peace of Versailles, 1713-83. *Library Edition.* 7 vols. 8vo. 93s. *Cabinet Edition,* 7 vols. Post 8vo. 5s. each.
────── British India, from its Origin to 1783. 8vo. 3s. 6d.
────── History of "Forty-Five." Post 8vo. 3s.
────── Spain under Charles the Second. Post 8vo. 6s. 6d.
────── Historical and Critical Essays. Post 8vo. 3s. 6d.
────── Life of Belisarius. Post 8vo. 10s. 6d.
────── Condé. Post 8vo. 3s. 6d.
────── William Pitt. Portraits. 4 Vols. 8vo. 24s.
────── Miscellanies. 2 Vols. Post 8vo. 13s.
────── Story of Joan of Arc. Fcap. 8vo. 1s.
────── Addresses Delivered on Various Occasions. 16mo. 1s.
STYFFE'S (KNUTT) Strength of Iron and Steel. Plates. 8vo. 12s.
SOMERVILLE'S (MARY) Physical Geography. *Sixth Edition,* Portrait. Post 8vo. 9s.
────── Connexion of the Physical Sciences. *Ninth Edition.* Portrait. Post 8vo. 9s.
────── Molecular and Microscopic Science. Illustrations. 2 Vols. Post 8vo. 21s.
────── Personal Recollections from Early Life to Old Age. With Selections from her Correspondence. Edited by HER DAUGHTER. *Fourth Edition.* Portrait. Crown 8vo. 12s.
SOUTH'S (JOHN F.) Household Surgery; or, Hints on Emergencies. Woodcuts. Fcp. 8vo.
SOUTHEY'S (ROBERT) Book of the Church. Post 8vo. 7s. 6d.
────── Lives of Bunyan and Cromwell. Post 8vo. 2s.
SYBEL'S (VON) History of Europe during the French Revolution; 1789—1795. 4 Vols. 8vo. 48s.
SYMONDS' (REV. W.) Records of the Rocks; or Notes on the Geology, Natural History, and Antiquities of North and South Wales, Siluria, Devon, and Cornwall. With Illustrations. Crown 8vo. 12s.
TAYLOR'S (SIR HENRY) Notes from Life. Fcap. 8vo. 2s.
THOMS' (W. J.) Longevity of Man; its Facts and its Fiction. Including Observations on the more Remarkable Instances. Illustrated by examples. Post 8vo. 10s. 6d.
THOMSON'S (ARCHBISHOP) Lincoln's Inn Sermons. 8vo. 10s. 6d.
────── Life in the Light of God's Word. Post 8vo. 5s.
TOCQUEVILLE'S State of Society in France before the Revolution, 1789, and on the Causes which led to that Event. Translated by HENRY REEVE. *2nd Edition.* 8vo. 12s.
TOZER'S (REV. H. F.) Highlands of Turkey, with Visits to Mounts Ida, Athos, Olympus, and Pelion. Illustrations. 2 Vols. Crown 8vo. 24s.
────── Lectures on the Geography of Greece. With Map. Post 8vo. 9s.

TRISTRAM'S (Canon) Great Sahara. Illustrations. Crown 8vo. 15s.
—————— Land of Moab; Travels and Discoveries on the East Side of the Dead Sea and the Jordan. *Second Edition.* Illustrations. Crown 8vo. 15s.

TWISLETON (Edward). The Tongue not Essential to Speech, with Illustrations of the Power of Speech in the case of the African Confessors. Post 8vo. 6s.

TWISS' (Horace) Life of Lord Eldon. 2 Vols. Post 8vo. 21s.

TYLOR'S (E. B.) Early History of Mankind, and Development of Civilization. *Second Edition.* 8vo. 12s.
—————— Primitive Culture; the Development of Mythology, Philosophy, Religion, Art, and Custom. *Second Edition.* 2 Vols. 8vo. 24s.

VAMBERY'S (Arminius) Travels from Teheran across the Turkoman Desert on the Eastern Shore of the Caspian. Illustrations. 8vo. 21s.

VAN LENNEP'S (Henry J.) Travels in Asia Minor. With Illustrations of Biblical Literature, and Archæology. With Woodcuts. 2 Vols. Post 8vo. 24s.

WELLINGTON'S Despatches during his Campaigns in India, Denmark, Portugal, Spain, the Low Countries, and France. [Edited by Colonel Gurwood. 8 Vols. 8vo. 20s. each.
—————— Supplementary Despatches, relating to India, Ireland, Denmark, Spanish America, Spain, Portugal, France, Congress of Vienna, Waterloo and Paris. Edited by his Son. 14 Vols. 8vo. 20s. each. *₊* *An Index.* 8vo. 20s.
—————— Civil and Political Correspondence. Edited by his Son. Vols. I. to V. 8vo. 20s. each.
—————— Despatches (Selections from). 8vo. 18s.
—————— Speeches in Parliament. 2 Vols. 8vo. 42s.

WHEELER'S (G.) Choice of a Dwelling; a Practical Handbook of Useful Information on all Points connected with Building a House. *Third Edition.* Plans. Post 8vo. 7s. 6d.

WHITE'S (Henry) Massacre of St. Bartholomew. Based on Documents in the Archives of France. 8vo. 16s.

WHYMPER'S (Edward) Scrambles among the Alps. With the First Ascent of the Matterhorn, and Notes on Glacial Phenomena. *Second Edition.* With 100 Illustrations. 8vo. 21s.
—————— (Frederick) Travels and Adventures in Alaska and on the River Yukon. With Illustrations. 8vo. 16s.

WILBERFORCE'S (Bishop) Essays on Various Subjects. 2 vols. 8vo.
—————— Life of William Wilberforce. Portrait. Crown 8vo. 6s.

WILKINSON'S (Sir J. G.) Popular Account of the Ancient Egyptians. With 500 Woodcuts. 2 Vols. Post 8vo. 12s.

WOOD'S (Captain) Source of the Oxus. With the Geography of the Valley of the Oxus. By Col. Yule. With Map. 8vo. 12s.

WORDS OF HUMAN WISDOM. Collected and Arranged by E. S. With a Preface by Canon Liddon, D.D. Fcp. 8vo. 3s. 6d.

WORDSWORTH'S (Bishop) Athens and Attica. Plates. Post 8vo. 5s.
—————— Pictorial, Descriptive, and Historical Account of Greece. *New Edition.* With 600 Woodcuts. Royal 8vo. 21s.

YULE'S (Colonel) Book of Marco Polo. Illustrated by the Light of Oriental Writers and Modern Travels. With Maps and 80 Plates. 2 Vols. Medium 8vo. 42s.

ZINCKE'S (Rev. F. B.) Winter in the United States. Post 8vo. 10s. 6d.

BRADBURY, AGNEW, & CO., PRINTERS, WHITEFRIARS.

www.ingramcontent.com/pod-product-compliance
Lightning Source LLC
Chambersburg PA
CBHW030819230426
43667CB00008B/1294